The 20 Hottest Investments for the 21st Century

ANDREW LECKEY

CB

CONTEMPORARY
BOOKS

A TRIBUNE NEW MEDIA COMPANY

Library of Congress Cataloging-in-Publication Data

Leckey, Andrew.
    The 20 hottest investments for the 21st century / Andrew
Leckey.
        p.   cm.
    ISBN 0-8092-3558-7 (cloth)
    ISBN 0-8092-3339-8 (paper)
    1. Investments—United States.   2. High technology
industries—United States—Finance.   I. Title.   II. Title:
Twenty hottest investments for the 21st century.
HG4910.L443   1994
332.6'78—dc20   94-34756
                                                                    CIP

To the memory of Alex Leckey

Copyright © 1995, 1994 by Andrew A. Leckey
All rights reserved
Published by Contemporary Books, Inc.
Two Prudential Plaza, Chicago, Illinois 60601-6790
Manufactured in the United States of America
International Standard Book Number: 0-8092-3558-7 (cloth)
                                                    0-8092-3339-8 (paper)
10   9   8   7   6   5   4   3   2   1

Contents

Acknowledgments —————————————————— v

Introduction: Millennium Investing —————— 1

1   Silicon Graphics—————————————————— 13

2   International Investing ——————————— 26

3   Bell Sports————————————————————— 44

4   AT&T ——————————————————————————— 56

5   Booming Brokers ——————————————— 70

6   Long-Term Health Care——————————— 87

7   Motorola—————————————————————— 103

8   Variable Annuities —————————————— 117

9   Pfizer—————————————————————————— 129

10   Rebuilding America ——————————— 142

11   Toys "R" Us ——————————————————— 156

12   Biotech Breakthroughs ——————————— 168

13   Artificial Intelligence———————————— 184

14 Crime Prevention ————————————199
15 Hewlett-Packard ————————————213
16 Real Estate Investment Trusts————————226
17 Flexible Technology ———————————243
18 Value Funds————————————————258
19 Telecommunications Warriors———————276
20 Closed-End Funds ————————————290
   Afterword ——————————————————307
   Index ————————————————————310

Acknowledgments

This look into the investment future wouldn't have been possible without the help and advice of some outstanding individuals and organizations. Thanks to researcher Leslie Holland for her enthusiasm and diligence, which included the ambitious task of lining up my interviews with the top brass of companies and investments spotlighted here. The generous time given by chief executives, portfolio managers, and their staffs for interviews, background, and tours was also appreciated.

In addition, a number of distinguished professionals in investment and other fields brainstormed with me about the global future as I was undertaking this project. Special thanks to Edward Yardeni of C. J. Lawrence Inc.; Charles Clough of Merrill Lynch & Co.; John Rekenthaler, Jennifer Strickland, and Colin Matthews of Morningstar Inc.; Louis Navellier of the *MPT Review*; John Rogers Jr. of Ariel Capital Management; Barry Vinocur of *Realty Stock Review*; James

McCamant of *Medical Technology Stock Letter*; Arnold Kaufman of *Standard & Poor's Outlook*; Norman Fosback of the Institute for Econometric Research; Richard Hokenson of Donaldson, Lufkin & Jenrette; and Brad Edmondson of *American Demographics*. Also thanks to Rene Stender of Sun Valley Elementary School and her fourth-grade class.

Introduction:
Millennium Investing

For centuries, people have looked toward the 21st century as a time of awakening, change, and advancement. The benchmark of another thousand years, A.D. 2000 with all its nice round zeroes provided a focal point for the imagination. The curiosity has accelerated through constant musings about the future in the arts, literature, and journalism.

Surprisingly, the 21st century is likely to live up to much of its hype. Ushered in by the end of the Cold War and the worldwide rise of capitalism, it will mark a period of dramatic change in technology, global awareness, and demographics. Companies are hurriedly forming alliances, jumping into new markets, and restructuring their businesses as though they were racing against a preordained deadline.

Personal communication that draws together the telephone, computers, and video will be available anywhere on the planet. International investing will boom. An aging

American population will spend more of its dollars on health care and investments. Global potential will be a primary consideration in developing all new products. This nation's worrisome problems of infrastructure decline and crime will be put on the front burner. New forms of investment will rapidly rise in popularity.

The trends of the 21st century present opportunity—opportunity for companies that successfully capitalize on change and turn it into profit, leaving slower competitors in their dust. Opportunity for investors who buy the stocks and other instruments positioned to succeed in this new environment. How far into the 21st century these favored investments can navigate successfully is based on their managements' ability to keep up with ever-changing trends.

Crystal-ball gazing into this next millennium has always been imaginative, if not always entirely on the mark.

In the 1800s, magazine illustrations envisioned life in the year 2000 with steam power running everything and dark smoke billowing through the sky. Intricate aerial bridges were connected at the midpoint of skyscrapers to serve as walkways. Single-passenger, locomotive-powered aircraft lurched from building to building, flying around hot-air balloons and other unusual craft kept aloft by umbrellas. Rooftops provided convenient landing decks.

Inside the home, robotic machines with long steel arms would brush your hair, shave you with a straight razor, and do the dishes, according to accepted futurist theories of the time. Communications would also flourish, it was predicted. A 1906 *Punch* magazine illustration depicted a 21st-century man and woman seated on benches in separate parks, sending romantic messages through portable wireless telegraph boxes. Each wore a large, hat-mounted antenna, perhaps a precursor of "anywhere, anytime" communications.

The Fritz Lang film *Metropolis* in 1926 presented a futuristic world in which underground workers grimly operated mammoth machines to power the giant city above.

Charlie Chaplin's 1936 film *Modern Times* showed future humans lost in a dehumanizing world of giant cogs and gears. In 1968 Stanley Kubrick's *2001: A Space Odyssey* told a space-age tale in which a powerful supercomputer took over and attempted to eliminate its human operator.

However, most Americans in the 1960s probably envisioned the future to be more like the perky Hanna-Barbera cartoon series "The Jetsons." Rosie the Robot did most of the work, you could take one pill for a complete dinner, and a lot of time was spent flying around in mini-spacecraft.

Compare those visions about the 21st century to the following technology-rich predictions I recently received from nine-year-olds in a fourth-grade class in San Rafael, California. Remember, they're the ones who will inherit the next century:

"In the next 100 years, cars will be solar powered and safer because of automatic maps so you'll never get lost."

"Shoes will have small televisions on their tops. Jets will time travel. All video games will be 3-D."

"We will have virtual reality and headgear that can send telepathic messages."

"In the future, cars will float and video games will never end."

"Technology will be so powerful that robots will do everything for people."

We're still hoping that those robots will come through for us! Ironically, in most cases technology has simply made it possible for modern man and woman to accomplish much more and has not resulted in the two-day workweeks and lives of leisure once envisioned. Fewer employees have been accomplishing more work thanks to computers and other technology, which are the tools for downsizing and streamlining American industry to make it more competitive.

Some roles, however, may change a great deal. A recent issue of *The Futurist* magazine speculated that in the year 2010 farmers will primarily work indoors, analyzing soil con-

ditions, plant health, and moisture content using computers that transmit commands to field equipment. Police officers and detectives will have automatic access to database
information on criminals, and the squad car will become a
mobile crime lab. Utility workers will oversee completely automated operations, manipulating virtual reality equipment
to do maintenance work through robots. The physicians of
2010 will benefit from videoconferencing technologies to
receive the advice of experts who will observe from other
parts of the world the procedures being performed on
patients.

Picking out the hottest investments for the 21st century
requires more common sense than clairvoyance. Whether
the financial markets are up or down, boom or bust, the
investments presented in this book offer some of the best
opportunities.

While interviewing the chief executives or portfolio
managers of these investments, I encountered a real excitement about the coming century and a wealth of strategies for success. These are long-term selections with the
inventiveness and financial staying power to survive and
prosper. Because no vision of the future is ever perfect, they
also have the flexibility to change course effectively when
the marketplace dictates it. Some choices are considerably
more volatile than others and, depending on your personal
confidence level, might be best for just a portion of a diversified personal portfolio.

All are trailblazers worth monitoring as you map out
your investment course. They're in the right place at the
right time.

Trends are in place. Globally, the end of the Cold War
has led to a reallocation of resources toward economic
growth. The privatization of government industries around
the world totaled $50 billion annually during the past two
years and is expected to grow at an even faster pace in the
future. Worldwide markets are clearly ready to explode with

pent-up demand for the conveniences of modern life and a growing middle class capable of paying for them.

A reader of my syndicated investment column recently wrote to ask a question about an international mutual fund he'd just bought. It was performing splendidly, but the writer had some doubts about the bigger picture.

"This world just scares me," he wrote.

I guess it is a lot to worry about, but there's also a lot of good in it, too.

In telecommunications, the United States has more than 50 main telephone lines per 100 people, the former Soviet Union and Eastern Europe about 12 lines per 100 people, and Latin America fewer than 7 lines per 100 people. Yet India and China, with two billion citizens between them, have fewer than 1 main line per 100 people. Because they're so far behind, they're likely to adopt more advanced technologies such as cellular phones. Already the United States ranks fifth worldwide in terms of population penetration of cellular because other nations are quickly jumping ahead on the technology curve.

Change is under way in the United States as well. With daily newspapers filled with stories of communications mergers and alliances on the path to the digital future, there's a general agreement that this country's so-called information superhighway will be built by private industry with little government intervention, that many of the 60-year-old regulatory restrictions on telephone companies will be lifted, and that new regulatory policies will ensure that poor and rural America have access to this new technology. The administration envisions a high-speed computer network that would transmit video, voice, and information data over the same high-capacity fiber-optic lines. Vice President Al Gore has been a staunch supporter of the concept for years, saying it will "utterly change and enrich" the lives of Americans.

There are many different information delivery systems. It's possible to deliver video and other communications to homes and businesses over cable systems, conventional broadcast, videotape players, and telephone lines using digital signals and new compression technologies. Other systems include optical fiber, microwave radio signals, and direct broadcast satellite. The alliances and mergers, especially those between telephone companies and cable operators, are occurring because no one industry group seems to have all the pieces of the puzzle.

But don't start rearranging your living room entertainment center just yet. Whether the portable or home devices we'll use in the future will look more like televisions, personal computers, telephones, or some techno-hybrid remains to be seen. They could be wired or wireless. While companies can demonstrate their vision of how it will all shake out, no one can give a definitive answer. Don't lose much sleep worrying over what final shape the gadgets of the future will take. It's an evolving process. I recall watching a very early science fiction film in which the actors floated around in a shiny space machine, wearing nifty spacesuits and brandishing futuristic weapons. But when it was time to contact Earth, the captain pulled out an old-fashioned dial telephone and began dialing up his party just like in the good old days.

Whatever its form, rest assured that global "anywhere, anytime" communication will come into being. Strategic alliances will play a key role in development of multimedia. Such cooperative effort is unprecedented in periods other than wartime. But then again, perhaps this *is* war. The $33 billion merger between Bell Atlantic Corp. and Tele-Communications Inc. collapsed in early 1994 because of a cut in cable rates by the Federal Communications Commission, a culture clash between the telephone and cable mentalities involved, and the likelihood that the deal was simply too much, too soon. But its failure will not end future cooperative efforts and mergers. In fact, Bell Atlantic quickly awarded contracts to AT&T and others to help build an advanced video and data network. Tele-Communications initiated mergers with programming and cable companies.

Meanwhile, AT&T has put money into a dozen start-up companies producing innovative hardware and software for the new communications. It has also lined up top computer companies that have agreed to design products that can use its new video conferencing service for desktop computers. MCI Communications Corp., thanks to its new partnership with British Telecommunications, is launching jointly developed telephone products for use in sophisticated communications systems worldwide. Motorola Inc., a member of the multicompany venture to develop more powerful computer chips through an x-ray process, is also launching its 66-satellite Iridium communications network with corporate partners around the world.

Silicon Graphics Inc. and Hewlett-Packard Co. are participating in Time Warner Inc.'s interactive cable television venture. Sweden's L. M. Ericsson Telephone AB, developing products through ventures with companies such as General Electric Co., has snared 60 percent of the worldwide digital cellular market.

These represent just sidelights of the solid businesses and revenues of these companies. None of these competitors will be left out in the cold, no matter what form the new communications takes. They are either leading their field or have the financial strength to take some calculated risks and change course quickly. As Robert Allen, chairman of AT&T, told me: "Whatever the technology of the future, AT&T will be a worldwide, major part of it." Or as Gary Tooker, vice chairman and chief executive at Motorola, explained: "We're well positioned for the 21st century because our semiconductor and wireless businesses will provide consistent growth on a global basis."

There is room for error. Semiconductor giant Texas Instruments Inc. found its inventories filled with products consumers weren't buying, so it returned to the drawing board to come up with successful products geared directly to what the consumer wanted. It worked.

Worldwide markets are kid stuff. Companies such as Bell Sports Corp. in bicycle helmets and Toys "R" Us have products that sell exactly the same way in any locale. Their time-tested marketing can be easily transferred to other countries with only minor adjustments, and, in Bell's case, sales are being aided by more safety regulations requiring children to wear helmets while riding.

Fundamentals are changing. As emerging nations modernize and their financial markets grow, American investors have opportunities to snare some big returns as they diversify their holdings into foreign stocks. More than 20 countries have moved to market economies with open securities markets. There are 850 million people in developed countries, such as the United States and Japan, with open securities markets. In contrast, there are more than three billion people in countries that are developing or opening their markets. There is volatility in foreign markets, but a chance for excellent returns as well for patient investors.

Basic industries of many nations will grow dramatically, and the rush of money into international mutual funds attests to the fact that it's a convenient way to invest. Full-service broker Merrill Lynch & Co. expects that 20 percent of its client assets will be in international markets by the year 2000 and will continue to grow at a rapid pace as we enter the new century.

Other advances will make investing more accessible to more people, with investment firms such as discount broker Charles Schwab & Co. plowing more and more of their dollars into sophisticated computer systems to speed up trades. In a more futuristic vein, three stock mutual funds at Fidelity Investments are employing artificial intelligence in their stock selection, seeking to emulate the complex decision-making processes of the human brain.

There's a reason why brokers are optimistic these days.

A population eruption began in 1946 and lasted 18 years, creating a single generation so big that it includes one in three Americans. These baby boomers, who will start turning 65 in just 17 years, will have a significant effect on the first part of the 21st century. In the next two decades, these Americans will pursue the same goals their great-grandparents did, such as raising children and getting ahead. But they're doing so in much greater numbers. Their big mortgages and small savings accounts, with corporate downsizing and career uncertainty thrown into the mix, are cause for concern at retirement time. There is added worry about pension coverage and Social Security. All of this, along with improvements in the economy, will point to baby boomers getting serious about planning for retirement. It's hoped that the current minuscule baby boomer rate of savings can grow to as high as 10 percent of their earnings by the year 2000. That means continued fine opportunities for firms such as T. Rowe Price Associates in mutual funds, Charles Schwab, and Merrill Lynch.

It just might be time to try something new. Some instruments will gain favor among investors concerned about their retirement years. Some relatively new vehicles for those seeking tax deferrals include variable annuities, which provide not only a handy way to invest but surprisingly good returns through a choice of portfolios. Also expected to grow in popularity are closed-end funds, which afford an opportunity to invest at a discount in stocks that represent a specific country, region, or investment philosophy. Another rising choice, the real estate investment trust (REIT), lets an investor buy a stake in real estate projects, such as apartments and shopping malls, that the investor can sell at any time because it's traded on a stock exchange. Liquidity historically has not been a strong suit of real estate. Meanwhile, value mutual funds provide the opportunity to invest in the stock of companies that have stumbled in changing times but have a chance at a comeback.

The health care system still suffers from a bit of a temperature, but there are remedies. With costs exceeding $1 trillion in 1994, the industry and government are moving toward a form of managed care in which costs are more closely regulated by large entities, such as health maintenance organizations (HMOs). This new price consciousness will actually help some companies and their stocks. For example, long-term health care facilities will replace hospitals as economical places for short medical stays. Big pharmaceutical firms such as Pfizer will prosper by coming up with new drugs that keep patients out of the hospital. Similarly, biotechnology breakthroughs from firms such as Chiron Corp. will play a big role in curing and treating disease, saving money for the health care system and the consumer in the long run.

Some bumpy roads can be smoothed out a bit. As much as $3.3 trillion will be needed to rebuild America's crumbling roads, bridges, and waterways. If a combination of public and private funds can be mobilized to get the job done, heavy construction firms such as Kasler Holding Co. and Granite Construction Inc. will benefit.

Crime won't be taking a holiday. In this country it costs Americans more than $400 billion annually, a number that is expected to rise significantly as we enter the 21st century. The Clinton administration has targeted crime, along with health care, as one of its major concerns. The greater need for private security as local governments cut back services will be met by Borg-Warner Security Corp., while the problem of arson and the need to meet new building safety standards will be confronted by Central Sprinkler Corp.

Some questions to ask when considering investments likely to do well in the coming century include:

- Does the investment justify the hype being given by the salesperson pitching it? Just because a company sounds trendy doesn't mean its stock is going to be a winner.

Study the company and its products or services. Never invest in anything you don't understand. Obtain historical information on its revenues, earnings, and stock price.

- Does the investment have global potential for growth? A concept that works in America doesn't necessarily work overseas. See how much of a company's sales are abroad and then consider whether the product or services will be able to translate to new markets and provide significant long-term growth.

- Can this investment survive even if one of its main products or services doesn't pan out? If it's a "one-trick pony," it could be in deep trouble when the marketplace doesn't like that trick or a competitor hones in. Some diversity in product line and some underlying financial strength are always crucial.

- Is this likely to be a long-term holding, or can I hope to slip in and out to make a quick profit? Frequent trading in areas such as high tech or biotech can be tricky, and even many experts lose money with this strategy. Try to make selections you can live with a while. Buy and hold.

- Does my personal portfolio already feature the kind of diversity into which this choice will fit? Never put all your eggs in one basket, especially if your choice is an adventuresome one.

- Does the investment suit my confidence level? If you can't live with volatility and will be nervously watching every slight movement of your stock, perhaps you'd be better off with a more conservative choice.

- Will it be difficult to get my money back if I need it? Don't, for example, put money into a variable annuity if you're going to pull it out quickly, for you'll be hit with fees and taxes on early withdrawal. Don't put money into a volatile investment if you're going to need your principal back soon to fund an important event.

- Does the investment meet my needs? If income is your goal, don't go with a growth investment. If you don't want to pay a lot of taxes, don't go with an income investment. That seems obvious, but investors often get swept away with the popularity of an idea rather than think through what it means to their individual situation.

- Am I paying too much in fees? Get a clear rundown of how much the investment is costing you, from commissions to any annual fees or withdrawal penalties. Some choices can cost more than they're worth. Know in advance what you're paying.

In the following pages, the 20 hottest investments for the 21st century are scrutinized. Some are stocks of individual companies or groups of stocks that fit in a specific category. Other selections are mutual funds, closed-end funds, or variable annuities. I had considerable latitude in my selections but definitely wanted solid choices with long-term potential, not just a couple of guys working on an idea in a garage somewhere. In each chapter, the stories about the investments come first, including interviews with chief executives or portfolio managers. The financial section in each chapter has pertinent information about the investment, where to find it, and how it has performed in the past. Combined, these should give you excellent momentum in obtaining a stake in the future. Some choices are more volatile than those I typically spotlight in my syndicated column, but there's enough selection here for you to find something that fits your investment personality.

Here's wishing you long-term prosperity and a chance to personally experience a great portion of the exciting 21st century. Let the countdown to the millennium begin.

1

Silicon Graphics

As the herd of small Gallimimus dinosaurs stampeded across the grassy field in a flash, the human characters of the film *Jurassic Park* had scant time to take cover to avoid being trampled.

Those dinosaurs were the work of three-dimensional visualization computers from Silicon Graphics Inc.

Frozen by liquid nitrogen and shattered into a thousand pieces, the T-1000 android in *Terminator 2* wasn't conquered yet. The fragments quickly began to congeal into a shiny body of liquid chrome. Once again he was ready to walk through steel gates, his skin oozing between the bars.

Silicon Graphics strikes again.

In the film *Forrest Gump*, star Tom Hanks was electronically placed in a receiving line where he shook hands with President John F. Kennedy. Both film and star won Academy Awards.

These days, a picture is worth a thousand words—and

millions of dollars at the box office. But images similar to these could soon be in your living room through interactive digital cable television and virtual reality video games developed by Silicon Graphics.

The advanced 3-D computers of this 13-year-old Mountain View, California, company have been used for the special effects in several movies. Such work demands 100 million to 1 billion calculations per second and has made digital compositing a common process. This basically breaks a film image down into a complex numerical code that a computer can manipulate in nearly endless ways. To alter images, they are coded, fed into the computer, and then blended, or "morphed" (a shortening of the word *metamorphose*). Whether films or TV ads, everything and everyone seems to be morphing into something else lately.

Film publicity has helped turn Silicon Graphics into a hot company, and that high profile is leading to greater sales and solid investment potential for its stock. Thanks to its unique proprietary technology, it is an early beneficiary of the move toward an information superhighway.

Its superfast computers are also used by scientists doing AIDS research and drug design, by meteorologists analyzing weather patterns, by engineers designing NASA space vessels and automobiles, and by journalists presenting stories. As a television reporter, I saw the company's IRIS "paint boxes" revolutionize both the look and the making of the colorful graphics that appear on newscasts.

Silicon Graphics is one of America's fastest growing companies, with half its revenues coming from international sales. Its 30 percent growth rate draws raves from investment analysts, and President Bill Clinton and Vice President Al Gore made one of their first corporate visits to the company upon assuming office. In positioning itself for the 21st century, the Silicon Graphics philosophy is that companies will have to constantly reinvent both themselves and their products in order to remain competitive in the demanding international marketplace.

So Silicon Graphics is in the process of reinventing itself, expanding its reach beyond high-end computers for industry to enter the price-conscious mass consumer market.

For example, Silicon Graphics and AT&T have formed a joint venture to develop and sell computerized video jukeboxes for interactive information and entertainment in homes, schools, and businesses. Elsewhere, Nippon Telegraphic & Telephone Corp. will use Silicon Graphics multimedia technology in interactive video trials in Japan. In yet another breakthrough deal, Electronic Data Systems Corp. has agreed to sell Silicon Graphics' video and database servers to the commercial market for use in crunching sales data and handling billings.

The company's Silicon Studio/LA Training Center, providing a centralized Hollywood entertainment community forum, advanced supercomputers, and the latest in film and video techniques, was opened May 4, 1995, in Santa Monica, California. It offers training for creative workers, technicians, and executives. The company announced plans to open similar facilities in Berlin, London, and other cities throughout the world.

A full-service interactive digital cable television network in Orlando, Florida, using technology developed through an agreement between Silicon Graphics and Time Warner Cable, is the first stop on the way to the future. The test of this service, installed in 4,000 homes, began in the fourth quarter of 1994. Silicon Graphics' digital video servers will deliver multimedia through television-top devices. The servers provide the ability to store such information as hundreds of videos in digital format for instant delivery to TV screens. The technology is based on the company's supercomputer technologies, but with low cost a primary goal. The Orlando Full-Service Network will provide access to such services as video on demand, educational resources, interactive video games, and home shopping.

Such ambitious and sophisticated plans are not accomplished easily, however, and the launch of this advanced network was delayed from a start several months earlier in 1994 in part because Silicon Graphics needed more time to refine the operating software so that the viewer can navigate easily through all the new programming options. Fifty to 100 engineers have worked long and hard since May 1993 on the project. Silicon Graphics will also make the powerful microprocessor chips to be used in TV-top converters.

"By the year 2000, most homes will have the ability through TV to go to shopping malls, and a network will be in place for two-way home or office video, which can be used for everything from [electronic] mail to a walk-through of a proposed new building," said Edward McCracken, the Silicon Graphics chairman and chief executive, who joined the company in 1984 after spending 16 years with Hewlett-Packard. "I guess that's a way to finally wake up all the 'couch potatoes' sitting in front of the set, but it also means that no one will have to travel as much in the future."

A 3-D, 64-bit virtual reality Nintendo home video machine with a target price of $250, developed in an agreement between Silicon Graphics and Nintendo, is our second stop. Nintendo's Ultra64 is the first application of a new generation of video entertainment that enables players to step inside three-dimensional worlds. Unveiled in arcades in 1994, it will be available for home use by late 1995. Ultra64 will feature realistic graphics, high-fidelity audio, and record-setting speed. Under the long-term worldwide business relationship, Nintendo will pay Silicon Graphics royalties for use of the licensed 3-D technology, with the product and software made available from Nintendo.

This basically stuffs the computing power now found in Silicon Graphics' low-end $5,000 Indy workstation into a low-cost toy. The Indy, an engineering tool, can execute 85 million instructions per second.

"Ten years ago, only a $20 million supercomputer could have done a lot of these things," McCracken said proudly, adding that the ultra-expensive domain of those multimillion-dollar machines has been crumbling thanks to his company's efforts. "We've been trashing the supercomputer market with our new models that cost less than $1 million."

Thoughts of the compressing and decompressing of video images for the 21st-century information superhighway dance constantly in McCracken's mind. Special-purpose computers that can do the equivalent of hundreds of millions to perhaps even billions of calculations per second are necessary to make the superhighway a reality.

A look around the Silicon Graphics headquarters quickly lets you know that the company is as proud of its past as it is confident about its ever-changing future. My interview with its chief executive took place in the *Total Recall* conference room, which shouldn't be confused with the conference rooms upstairs bearing the titles *Terminator 2* or *Beauty and the Beast*.

For the moment, McCracken wasn't discussing those films or even *Jurassic Park*, the most popular film to feature the skills of animators and the company's machines, other than to point out that "the smaller running dinosaurs were more demanding to do than those [the Velociraptors] that were terrorizing the children in the kitchen."

McCracken was more interested in the Clint Eastwood film *In the Line of Fire*, which I'd seen on my flight to California. The fact that this was a drama employing Silicon Graphics digital technology, rather than a science fiction fantasy, signaled another breakthrough. Campaign footage used in the film about an assassination attempt on a U.S. president came from the Clinton presidential campaign. The machines were able to deftly remove Bill and Hillary from the crowd and parade scenes and replace them with the film's actors. The naked eye can't detect that the scenes have been altered. This saved the cost of having to re-create all those scenes with camera crews and an army of extras.

McCracken now wishes to expand that concept to all films so the company no longer has to wait for science-fiction or fantasy productions. "The next logical step would be to use a computer to simulate all of the shots needed in any movie, then go out and do the movie, saving money by not wasting so much film on shots that aren't used," explained McCracken.

Because Silicon Graphics technology is based on the ability to design specialized microprocessor chips, its first clients were research-oriented people who could quickly see the potential for such graphic precision in their businesses. A few years ago, the military was its top customer, using the machines to envision various installations and equipment. A decline in defense spending made the entertainment market more attractive, however, with folks like George Lucas and Steven Spielberg finding the high-tech machines to their liking. To understand exactly how far this technology has come in the past decade, take a look at the first *Star Wars* film, or perhaps go back even further to *2001: A Space Odyssey* and watch how slow or artificial much of the movement seems to us today.

Hollywood accounts for only about 15 percent of Silicon Graphics' rapidly growing revenues. One of the biggest markets for the company's computers is the automotive companies. Before spending $1 million to make a clay model, they can test the design on Silicon Graphics systems. It's possible on the screen not only to design and structure a vehicle, but to ram it into a brick wall to see how it crumbles. Theme park rides are another growth area, with Silicon Graphics magic capable of transporting the individual through unforgettable adventures, terrors, and fantasies. You once thought the revolving Tilt-A-Whirl or the roller coaster at the local carnival were really something? Try flying wildly into intergalactic space while dodging realistic 3-D asteroids. That will get your heart pumping.

Biotechnologists employ the machines to model molecules and for computational chemistry. The company's goal is eventually to put a $5,000 supercomputer on the desk of every scientist and engineer. During my visit to the headquarters, demonstrations of new graphics equipment were being made to small groups of industrial clients and television network executives. There were clusters of three or four people in front of each machine as staffers explained and demonstrated. In the office hallway beside the demonstration area, 3-D pictures seem to jump out at the casual visitor. These include dramatically realistic depictions of an astronaut, the human inner ear, and the AIDS virus.

"The only way for us to keep growing 30 percent a year is to be innovative and responsive to change," said McCracken, who believes that the fastest competitors will always win. "High technology is one of the more volatile industries, but with risk there is potential payoff as well, and we're very conservative in our financial management to avoid risks."

James Clark, the former chairman of the company, who resigned to start up Netscape Communications Corp. in 1994, founded Silicon Graphics in 1982 after big computer companies showed no interest in his theories. His research as an associate professor of electrical engineering at Stanford University had centered on designing specialized microprocessor chips that calculated the geometry of light reflected off moving and rotating shapes. Three-dimensional graphics on computer screens, he was convinced, were destined to surpass the two-dimensional technology that was the industry norm. He added digital audio and video capabilities to his machines as well. Since all these capabilities require the crunching of overwhelmingly complex algorithms, Clark's computers did it faster by putting the graphics code right on the silicon chips, hence the firm name Silicon Graphics. And, by starting up Silicon Graphics with venture capital he raised on his own and using former graduate students to start the company, Clark now owns stock worth more than $40 million. Thank heavens the big companies weren't interested in his futuristic ideas.

Of course, other firms in the computer industry have had rags-to-riches success stories, too. Some of them have also had their profitability and turf taken away by other upstart companies who came up with their own bright ideas. The key to maintaining competitive advantage in the future, McCracken believes, is in making customers feel that you have designed a product specifically for them, with features or capabilities for which they will pay a premium. Once a company is no longer on the leading edge of technological change, its gross margins shrink, he notes. The performance, or computing power relative to price, in the computer industry is now increasing tenfold every 3½ years, he said, compared to a tenfold increase every 7 years in the 1980s and every 10 years in the 1970s. So, unless there are some significant changes in your product, it can become a commodity offered by everyone rather quickly.

Now that Silicon Graphics has revenues of more than $1 billion annually, it must stay ahead of the game so that neither upstarts nor larger megabillion-dollar giants will pass it by. There is definite risk, but thus far its execution has been flawless. It is taking on a lot of competitors in different computer markets by offering innovation at a good price. Product and market momentum, higher profit margins, and expansion into new markets such as digital editing, supercomputing, and desktop publishing all look promising for the future.

The worldwide market opportunity for digital editing in cable and television, an estimated $3 billion, currently is highly fragmented. Silicon Graphics has just begun to penetrate the digital editing markets, but has a strong position because it is viewed as a low-cost solution. Meanwhile, the supercomputer market represents more than $1 billion and is dominated by Cray Research, Convex Computer at the minisupercomputer level, and other small vendors. The Silicon Graphics strategy is to sell lower-cost, flexible solutions.

The high-end desktop publishing market, representing $1 billion in hardware and software sales, is dominated by Macintosh and other personal computers. Frequently, however, high-end users demand faster graphics and are unhappy with the slow imaging now available. Silicon Graphics would only have to snare a small portion of the PC desktop publishing market to be successful. In addition, a multibillion-dollar market for video jukebox services that dispense video on demand and interactivity is expected as the multimedia interactive networks of the 21st century take shape. As designer of the technology underlying video jukeboxes, Silicon Graphics could capture a significant portion of this high-margin business as it unfolds.

The company has received a strong flow of orders, with customers frequently indicating they want to increase their spending on Silicon Graphics systems beyond their initial intentions. Its graphics computer systems range from the Indigo series of workstations and servers, including the Indy desktop workstation, through the IRIS Crimson workstations to the Onyx systems, a family of advanced graphics supercomputers that are 10 times more powerful than any previous Silicon Graphics workstation. To complement the visual computing systems, the company offers the Challenge and PowerChallenge systems, ranging from entry-level single processor servers to enterprise-wide symmetric multiprocessing supercomputers. The flexible Challenge lines let users create technical computing scenarios that specifically fit their individual application needs.

All of these computers use microprocessors developed

by MIPS Computer Systems, a firm that Silicon Graphics acquired in 1992. Software, it is important to note, can be run without modification across its entire product line. IRIS workstations use IRIX, an enhanced version of UNIX, as their operating system software. More than 1,500 application software programs are available for use on Silicon Graphics workstations.

The company's new Indy desktop system with digital color camera for videoconferencing starts at under $5,000. It is the first family of high-performance, color desktop systems that integrate fast processors, graphics, and digital media capabilities into the fastest desktop line. It's an important entry into the low end of the market and expected to be the prime mover behind a huge increase in Silicon Graphics' unit volumes and market penetration. One of the higher-priced Indigos, the XZ, was heralded by *PC* magazine as "the champion of 3-D graphics" and, at just over $30,000, excellent for users who "absolutely must have" top performance.

An interesting sidelight about the Indy, which took two years to develop, is that had the company started developing it three months before it actually did, there likely would have been no digital camera included. Customers had been telling the company that they wanted videoconferencing capabilities, and the technology became available just in time. The low end of the company's market is growing the fastest, aided by the addition of more and more software. The company hired Kirk Loevner, formerly a vice president with Apple Computer who brought more than 10,000 new software and hardware products to Macintosh, to help add to its third-party software partners.

Silicon Graphics' high-end systems contribute about 40 percent of revenues, with selling prices starting at around $88,000 going up to hundreds of thousands of dollars. The company's Reality Station, costing $94,900 and up, has the world's fastest graphics, able to process 320 million pixels (picture elements) a second, or three times as many as a quality PC. High-end workstations and servers provide support for gross margins and give the company an opportunity to move its customers up the power curve. They also permit the company to compete in entirely new markets. Over the past year or so, it has entered the minisupercomputer market, posing a threat to companies such as Convex Computer. It has recently competed successfully against Cray and Thinking Machines on some orders, with its high-end 36-processor–type systems giving it the performance to move into even higher-end markets.

The company has taken growth slowly so it doesn't fall prey to the massive layoffs of so many high-tech firms. In 1976, when Hewlett-Packard was the same size in terms of sales, it had about 18,000 employees versus the current Silicon Graphics size of around 4,000, McCracken noted. Often one or two people will be put on a project that might involve as many as 50 at other companies. It never has two competing teams work to develop the same product, as IBM and some other companies do, because McCracken considers that a waste of time when those workers should instead be focused on real competition with other companies.

A walk through the assembly area indicates the exacting way in which technicians test, put together, and package these units. It takes 14 hours, including testing, to put together an Indigo system. Silicon Graphics' employee turnover rate of about 10 percent is one-third the typical rate among competitors. Every year, about 35 people who have broken organizational boundaries to generate a good idea or solution are nominated by colleagues for representing the entrepreneurial spirit of the company. The finalists and the winner of the "Spirit of Silicon Graphics" award are announced at the company holiday party. They and a loved one receive a trip to Hawaii.

"I believe there's room for an innovative, fun company that doesn't have to be old and boring," asserted McCracken, relaxing in the *Total Recall* conference room.

Investment Close-Up: Silicon Graphics Inc.
2011 N. Shoreline Blvd., Mountain View, California 94043
(415) 960-1980

Silicon Graphics makes high-performance workstations and computing systems for design, analysis, and simulation of three-dimensional objects.

Chairman, president, and CEO: Edward McCracken
Investor contact: Marilyn Lattin
Total employees: 5,000

Stock: Traded on the New York Stock Exchange under the symbol "SGI." Price of $37¼ a share (5/16/95). No dividend. Price-to-earnings ratio of 29.

Sales and Earnings: Sales of $1.48 billion in 1994, with earnings of $140.7 million. Five-year annual sales growth of 33 percent, with earnings growth of 86 percent.

Earnings per Share Growth: Five-year earnings per share annual growth rate of 25 percent. Projected (Institutional Brokers Estimate System) five-year earnings per share annual growth rate of 26 percent.

Data from Bridge Information Systems Inc.

Silicon Graphics Inc.

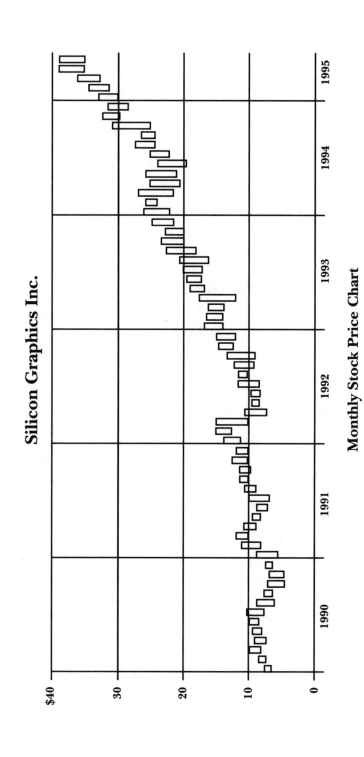

Monthly Stock Price Chart

2

International Investing

Much like the exotic Orient Express barreling full tilt along the rails of Main Street USA, international investing has abruptly captured the undivided attention of average American investors.

The ride may take your breath away, but the returns and romance are well worth the ticket price.

As we enter the 21st century, average investors will own equities from exchanges in once unthinkable places such as China, India, Russia, and Eastern Europe. The overwhelming momentum of new economies and their massive populations, coupled with the desire of U.S. investors to diversify into faster-growing markets, will make it happen. Foreign investing also serves as a hedge against downturns in the U.S. market. After all, the U.S. market now accounts for only 33 percent of the world equity market.

Over the past 10 years, many foreign markets have handily outperformed the average annual U.S. market gain of about 13 percent. Over that same time period, the stock market in Hong Kong averaged a 27 percent annual increase, France 21 percent, Spain 20 percent, Japan 20 percent, Switzerland 17 percent, the United Kingdom 16 percent, and Germany 14 percent.

Stock mutual funds are the easiest way to initially invest internationally, since all the complex legwork of finding a diversified mix of foreign countries, industries, and companies is done for the investor. There are global funds that invest throughout the world, including the United States, as well as international funds that invest in markets outside the United States and targeted funds that invest in a specific region or country. It's rather difficult to buy stocks of foreign companies yourself, although a number are available for purchase in the United States as American Depositary Receipts, discussed later in this chapter.

Betting on individual markets can be a tricky business. For example, the star world markets of 1993, Hong Kong, Indonesia, and Thailand, fell back to earth in 1994. The stellar performers in 1994 were Brazil, up 64 percent; Peru, up 45 percent; Finland, up 43 percent; Chile, up 41 percent; and Colombia, up 29 percent. There are about 300 stock funds emphasizing overseas investment, 100 more than a year ago. Following the trend, many familiar domestic funds are tossing a few overseas issues into their portfolios as well these days.

U.S. investors accounted for $66 billion, or 42 percent, of the new money that foreign investors poured into the world's equity markets in 1993. That helped push up stock prices in some developing countries.

Despite such explosive growth, American investors still have just a fraction of their money invested overseas. Less than 9 percent of money in stock mutual funds is in international funds. While that's double the amount of a year ago, it's still less than the 10 to 30 percent recommended for proper diversification of an individual's portfolio. Countless investment firms and managers are getting into the act. There are also plenty of emerging markets with powerful growth rates if you're willing to assume some risk.

Be forewarned: International investing is not without its volatility, whether sparked by economic or political events. For example, when peasant attacks on government facilities occurred in the Mexican state of Chiapas early in 1994, the fast-rising Mexican stock market suffered a quick temporary drop as foreign investors who knew nothing about Chiapas received a jolt they hadn't anticipated. A significant market decline also followed the assassination of Mexican presidential candidate Luis Donaldo Colosio. In addition, once-revered Japan's complex political and economic woes have taken their toll on its market and frightened many foreign investors completely away.

Proven portfolio managers such as J. Mark Mobius, who emphasizes undervalued stocks and runs the Templeton Developing Markets Trust, and Ralph Wanger, who enjoys uncovering little-known firms and manages the Acorn International Fund, offer long-term track records rather than a sudden emphasis on what's fashionable. They'll show ingenuity in their stock selections rather than simply tossing "the world's greatest hits" into their portfolios.

Both funds, holding many stocks from less developed nations, are ready for the dramatic growth of world markets in the 21st century as free market economies flex their muscles. Both managers point out that their jobs are being made easier by the advent of communication tools such as facsimile machines, plus the many market reforms around the globe designed to improve disclosure and accounting procedures and open trading to foreigners.

"You simply must have faith in all the people around the world before you're willing to invest in higher-risk areas," the enthusiastic Mobius explained in a telephone interview from a restaurant in Djakarta, Indonesia. "There's a philosophical change as governments of the world seek to move to market economies, which will result in more stock exchanges and much faster growth."

Mobius, who has lived in the Far East since the early 1960s and run the Templeton Developing Markets Trust since it was started up in the fall of 1991, was dining with local Indonesian executives following tours of three factories. He'd just taken a helicopter ride over thick forest to better understand a paper products company's environmental procedures. Eighty percent of his time is spent visiting companies, and he has a team of young analysts over whom he says he "cracks the whip."

"Ever since the 1989 revolutions destroying socialist thought, there have actually been more investment opportunities in Latin America than in Eastern Europe or Russia, but we can generally expect to see many new areas of high growth," predicted Ralph Wanger as he leaned back on the blue sofa in his downtown Chicago office in a modern high-rise. "The fact is, the United States is a mature industrial economy with 2 to 3 percent growth, so other parts of the world offer considerably greater growth potential, in some cases 6 to 10 percent."

Well known for his long-term success with the Acorn Fund, which includes international equities in its portfolio, Wanger started the Acorn International Fund in the fall of 1992. Responding to a massive influx of money into Acorn International, Wanger in early 1994 closed the fund to new investors for the time being so he could better manage it. He finds that small foreign stocks sometimes aren't understood or well followed even in their home countries, where the emphasis quite likely is on larger capitalization issues That means they're often undervalued as well. Looking toward the 21st century, he sees China, India, Russia, Eastern Europe, and Latin America offering significant opportunity. Ready for that challenge, he refers to himself as the "generalissimo," doing little international travel but depending on the research turned up by four globe-trotting analysts.

"You must invest in emerging markets with at least a five-year time horizon, for you'll have losses along the way, even though a patient investor really can't go wrong in the long run," advised Mobius, whose Templeton Developing Markets Trust declined in 1992 due largely to political turmoil that affected his holdings in Turkey. He recommends that investors first put money into a diversified global fund, then delve into the emerging markets if they are willing to be more patient.

A native of New York who received his Ph.D. from Massachusetts Institute of Technology, Mobius became interested in the Far East when he studied at Japan's Kyoto University. He launched his own regional economics and research consulting firm in Hong Kong in 1970. After a subsequent investment career with Vickers da Costa and later as president of International Investment Trust Co. in Taiwan, he joined Templeton in Hong Kong in 1987. There he introduced the first New York Stock Exchange–listed emerging markets fund, one of a number of Templeton funds he now oversees. The most recent addition is the Templeton China World Fund, designed to take advantage of the boom in China and Hong Kong. In recent years Mobius has become Templeton's international ambassador in place of founder Sir John Templeton, who has curtailed his travels.

Recently, Mobius's favorite investment areas for both Templeton Developing Markets Trust and his Templeton Emerging Markets closed-end fund include Brazil, Portugal, Hong Kong, and Turkey. Some individual stock favorites include Telebras (Telecommunicacoes Brasileiras SA), one of Brazil's largest suppliers of telecommunications services, and Cukurova Elektrik AS, Turkey's privatized hydroelectric power firm.

It's worth noting that the winners in emerging markets keep rotating. Because it's so difficult to predict consistently which market will be the next top performer, diversifying across various emerging markets makes the most sense. For example, the top markets in 1987 were Greece, Taiwan, Zimbabwe, Venezuela, and Turkey, with Brazil, India, and Nigeria the biggest losers. In 1989 the winners were Turkey, Argentina, Thailand, Taiwan, and Mexico, with Venezuela, Jordan, and Korea the losers. For 1992, Thailand, Colombia, Malaysia, India, and Jordan led the way, with Zimbabwe, Turkey, and Venezuela at the bottom. Other special considerations with developing markets include risks related to market and currency volatility, adverse social and political developments, and the relatively small size and lesser liquidity of these markets. For those willing to hang in there, the promise is great.

An interesting aspect of international investing is that there's often little correlation between markets. For example, when Japan's speculative bubble burst, it didn't affect other Asian markets or slow down Wall Street. This concept, which has held true for the past two decades, isn't likely to change significantly as more emerging markets enter the investment fold.

Taking a world view can open an investor's eyes. When the relative sizes of different economies are considered, results are often surprising. New data on gross domestic product from the World Bank indicates that China already has the world's third largest economy, and, if its growth rate holds at current levels for another three decades, it will have the largest economy. In addition, developing countries now account for more than one-third of the world's gross domestic product. The top 25 world economic rankings, in order, are the United States, Japan, China, Germany, France, India, Italy, the United Kingdom, the Russian Federation, Brazil, Mexico, Canada, Indonesia, Spain, the Republic of Korea, Thailand, Australia, Turkey, Iran, the Netherlands, Pakistan, Ukraine, Egypt, Colombia, and Argentina.

"The Chinese and Indian stock markets will become two

of the largest in the first part of the 21st century, and Brazil, Nigeria, and South Africa will also be strong," Mobius predicted, pointing out that emerging market capitalization has grown from $100 million in 1987 to $3.8 billion today. "I'd like to see more international investing because it means more opportunity for me to buy and sell."

Though it requires a strong degree of confidence, Mobius recommends buying into his fund when things look bad and net asset value is down, so that there will be greater forward momentum in the future. His favorite investors are couples setting money aside for their children's educations or their own retirements.

As Wanger sees it, there's an inevitability to the economic growth of emerging countries because they're finally developing a middle class. "As these countries 'come out of the swamp,' they realize they need a telephone system, electric power, and, eventually, broadcasting and cable, all of which offer investment opportunities," Wanger noted. "Some of these countries need virtually everything."

Wanger currently has the largest portion of his money in Asia, primarily the Japanese, Hong Kong, and Malaysian markets, as well as significant holdings in Europe, with the greatest chunk in Germany and Scandinavia. Some favored individual stocks include Spanish sausage makers Conservera Campofrio and Oscar Mayer SA and the Portuguese media firm Filmes Lusomundo. In Hong Kong, he likes the Wo Kee Hong firm in distribution of laser discs and air conditioners, as well as Television Broadcasts Ltd. and China Bicycle. Other picks are Philippine Long Distance Telephone and the Mexican media firm Grupo Radio Centro.

International investing was once considered somewhat "un-American," although recent investment in this country by foreigners has blunted that belief. Nonetheless, there is an undeniable impact from all that money flowing overseas. "One negative aspect of international investing is that it puts more U.S. money outside of the United States and into other competing markets, so the U.S. market won't be able to go up as much," explained Wanger. "It also ultimately makes it easier for other countries, where people work much cheaper, to compete against U.S. companies."

Templeton Developing Markets Trust, based in St. Petersburg, Florida, requires a 5.75 percent load (initial sales charge), which can be defended in light of Mobius's extensive background and past success, while the currently closed Acorn International in Chicago is a no-load fund.

Keep in mind that currency fluctuations in the value of the U.S. greenback can make a difference in overseas investments. For example, if your Japanese stocks rise 12 percent and at the same time the U.S. dollar moves up 4 percent against the yen, your net gain is only 8 percent. The dollar's fall against the yen in 1993 created good fortune for some U.S. investors, turning a 24 percent gain in Japanese stocks into a 46 percent increase when gains were figured in dollars. On the other hand, the British pound's 1992 devaluation turned a 25 percent gain in sterling on the London Stock Exchange into a slight decline when translated into dollars. It's expected that the dollar will get stronger against European currencies as the U.S. economy improves, so some fund managers have been protecting against losses on European holdings by selling the German mark and French franc. However, a great many money managers who hold for the long haul don't hedge at all because they believe all the fluctuations average out in the end and the cost of hedging therefore isn't worth it.

Focusing on the 21st century, many foreign markets offer promise. It's probably a good idea to have the international portion of your personal portfolio consist of about 70 percent developed markets and 30 percent emerging markets, since the latter are far more likely to encounter volatility. Invest for the long run, without concern for the economic and market bumps of a few months or a year. You will experience some down years. Don't invest internationally if the first hint of negative trends or volatility will send you running. Also realize that each region and country has its own personality that can't simply be lumped together with all other non–U.S. areas.

The Asia-Pacific region offers enticing emerging growth prospects. The privatization of the telecommunications industry in Singapore and the ability to invest in China's growth through the Hong Kong markets lends economic importance. Rebounding exports, falling interest rates, and hopes for a significant easing of restrictions on foreign investments have been pluses for the South Korean market. Also popular is Taiwan, whose electronics companies are much admired. This region's use of formal and informal U.S. dollar pegs also helps minimize the currency risk in U.S. terms. Hong Kong and Malaysian markets offer opportunity due to price declines. Overcoming a long period of economic strain, the Japanese market has rebounded.

South of the border is attracting more investors. In Latin America, Mexico has been buoyed by approval of the North American Free Trade Agreement. Mexican firms that should prosper are those that can compete successfully in international competition. While its economy remains slow moving, and much depends on current government policies remaining in place long-term, it has done a great job the past five years of bringing inflation to less than 10 percent annually and keeping interest rates steady. Argentina, aggressive in its privatization programs, remains fairly inexpensive despite strong underlying earnings growth. Reform in Chile has been quite effective, with its gross domestic product growth averaging 6 percent annually the past four years, but it has made its shares expensive. The Brazilian market has undergone a recent revival based on rising confidence in the economic moves of its government.

An investment flight across the Atlantic may also make sense. In Europe, the United Kingdom appears headed toward a period of modest economic growth, low inflation, and low interest rates much like those of the 1960s. Despite recent disappointments, France is likely to experience an economic turnaround, and its markets should benefit from privatization programs. Italy's volatile yet rising markets also should be helped by privatization, though the zigzag movement of the lira understandably gives investors pause. The new Germany has been attractive to foreign investors, though its expected economic recovery is already priced into its stock market. A stronger dollar, making German stocks relatively cheap for U.S. investors, has boosted foreign investment in that market to about 20 percent. Spurred by higher corporate profits, the Spanish market's gains should continue. Interest rate declines have assisted the market in the Netherlands, where there's also hope for an improved economy. Additional attractive and reasonably priced investments are available in Sweden and Denmark.

The land "down under" is on a roll. Australia, scheduled to host the summer Olympics in the year 2000, has seen its market prosper with low rates and solid corporate earnings. Up north, Canada's market has been helped by low rates, but unemployment and weak corporate profits linger. In Switzerland, higher profits are attracting both foreign and domestic investors. Emerging market opportunity is strong in South Africa, with strong growth expected following its market liberalization. Both Turkey and Finland, helped by U.S. investment, have experienced strong market gains.

All the twists and turns of these world economies underscore why average investors usually decide to go with stock mutual funds run by managers who are more than willing to lie awake at night wondering what all those nations are really going to do next.

Some other foreign stock funds that have been around longer than either Templeton Developing Markets Trust or Acorn International mentioned earlier are worth noting.

The $5.53 billion–asset T. Rowe Price International Stock Fund of Baltimore is a no-load fund whose relatively low risk and consistency have been admirable. It has turned in solid long-term returns, never sliding into the lower rankings among international funds. Its five-year average annual return is about 8 percent, while its 10-year average is above 17 percent. Although the fund tends to overweight some countries in favor of others, its management team keeps assets diversified among 27 countries. The portfolio contains nearly 300 names, further spreading risk. Recent largest holdings included Telefonos de Mexico, Elsevier, Royal Dutch Petroleum, and United Overseas Bank. While the fund generally invests in common stocks or other equity securities, it may invest up to 35 percent in any other type of security.

The $2.14 billion–asset Scudder International Fund of Boston is a no-load fund that has had consistently good returns and whose value emphasis and occasional moves into bonds or cash have kept its risk below average. Its five-year average return is about 6 percent, and its 10-year average is more than 15 percent. Management makes decisions from a "top-down" view of regional markets and economies; a "bottom-up," value-oriented analysis of individual stocks; and a global industry analysis to find timely investment themes. Recent large holdings included Aoyama Trading, Credit Nationale, Federation of Malaysia bonds, Cetelem, and Carter Holt Harvey. It is willing to buy small, relatively unknown companies and bet on regions that aren't currently popular.

The $537 million–asset Merrill Lynch Pacific Fund Class "A" of New York, which requires a 5.25 percent load, can boast of a 10-year average total return that ranks in the top 1 percent of all equity funds. It has steered successfully through a variety of market conditions. Its five-year average annual return is 10 percent, and its 10-year return is 18 percent. Big holdings recently included China Light & Power, Toyo Seikan Kaisha, Tokio Marine & Fire Insurance, Dai-Tokyo Fire & Marine Insurance, and Nichido Fire & Marine

Insurance. Recent difficulties in the Japanese market have taken their toll, but its large positions in the Hong Kong and Malaysian markets have made up for it. For someone interested in investing in the Pacific region, this veteran fund offers an unparalleled long-term track record.

The $6.6 billion New Perspective Fund of Los Angeles, which has a 5.75 percent load, places heavy emphasis on the concept of the information superhighway. It recently had 20 percent of assets in telecommunications and media companies. Telecom New Zealand, Vodafone Group, and News Corp. are examples. But it isn't just jumping on a trend, for only two of its holdings in this area have been acquired since 1990. Its five-year average annual return is more than 10 percent, and its 10-year average return is 15 percent. The fund has been a dependable "all-weather" holding for two decades.

Yet another way of investing internationally is through American Depositary Receipts (ADRs). These ADRs are for investors who still like the idea of selecting a specific company in which to put their money.

By definition, an ADR is a negotiable certificate that represents and is interchangeable with shares of the publicly traded securities of a foreign corporation. The underlying shares remain on deposit in a local custodian bank while the ADRs trade in the United States either on an exchange, in the over-the-counter market, or through private placements. Included in the ADR's price are the custodial bank's charges for functions it performs, such as holding securities, handling currency exchange, distributing dividends, and managing tax issues.

About three-fourths of the 1,500 ADRs available in this country trade over the counter. ADRs may be issued on a one-to-one basis to the underlying shares or may represent a fractional share or multiple shares of the foreign firm. While exchange rates will still affect share prices and dividend yields, currency exchange problems are minimized because ADRs trade through U.S. dollar–denominated quotes. Dividends and interest are also paid in U.S. dollars. The ADR settles trades according to U.S. trading rules with settlement occurring in five business days.

Record levels have been set in the depositary receipt market in recent years, with the $248 billion in ADR trading volume in 1994 a gain of more than 23 percent, according to the Bank of New York. A total of 289 new publicly traded sponsored ADRs were established from 44 countries in 1994, up 130 percent from the prior year. From China, Shanghai Petrochemical has listed its ADRs on the New York Stock Exchange, while Shanghai Erfangji and Shanghai Tyre and Rubber established over-the-counter programs. A significant number of new ADRs are expected from China as we approach the 21st century. United Kingdom (which has the most ADRs traded in the United States), Mexican, and Dutch firms have been the most actively traded. South Africa, France, Argentina, and Hong Kong have also shown impressive gains.

There are plenty of countries and companies to choose from. The top ADRs in NYSE share volume recently were Telefonos de Mexico; Glaxo Holdings of the United Kingdom; Hanson PLC of the United Kingdom; Royal Dutch Petroleum of the Netherlands; British Petroleum PLC; YPF Sociedad Anonima of Argentina; SmithKline Beecham of the United Kingdom; News Corp. of Australia; Wellcome PLC of the United Kingdom; Unilever of the Netherlands; Repsol of Spain; Philips of the Netherlands; Tiphook PLC of the United Kingdom; Vodafone Group of the United Kingdom; and Imperial Chemical Industries PLC of the United Kingdom.

Meanwhile, the most popular ADRs trading over the counter here have been L. M. Ericsson Telephone "B" shares of Sweden; Senetek PLC of the United Kingdom; Memorex Telex of the Netherlands; Reuters Holdings of the United Kingdom; and Teva Pharmaceuticals of Israel.

Select an ADR as you would the stock of a domestic company, taking into account its long-term fundamentals and not simply its geographic location.

Some examples of ADRs worth considering for investment include Bank of Singapore, a large bank well positioned in a number of Asian markets and featuring a likely five-year annual earnings growth rate of 17 percent; Cable & Wireless, the U.K. telecommunications firm that owns a large chunk of Hong Kong and Australian telecommunications companies and has an expected five-year annual growth rate of 16 percent; Fletcher Challenge, a New Zealand forest products company that is that nation's largest firm and expected to have a 20 percent five-year earnings growth rate; Telecommunicacoes Brasileiras (Telebras), the Brazilian telecommunications company that could have a 30 percent growth rate over the next five years; British Steel, the United Kingdom's only integrated steelmaker and a company likely to benefit from a turnaround of the European economy; Campanias de Telefonos de Chile, the Chilean telecommunications firm that should have a 30 percent annual growth rate for the next several years; and Ek Chor Motorcycle, a Chinese motorcycle manufacturer expected to grow at a 25 to 35 percent annual rate.

Yet another way to play international investing is through closed-end funds traded on U.S. stock exchanges that emphasize specific countries or regions. They're discussed in the chapter on closed-end funds.

As all of these examples point out, investing is no longer simply a domestic pursuit for American investors. Climb on board the Orient Express and get to know the world.

Investment Close-Up: Templeton Developing Markets Trust

700 Central Avenue, St. Petersburg, Florida 33701
(800) 292-9293

Templeton Developing Markets Trust seeks long-term capital appreciation, normally investing at least 65 percent of assets in equity securities of countries with developing markets. For capital appreciation, it may invest up to 35 percent of assets in debt securities rated at least "C" or judged to be of comparable quality.

Portfolio manager: J. Mark Mobius
Fund inception: 10/17/91
Total assets: $1.9 billion
Distributor: Franklin/Templeton Distributors

Shares: Traded under the symbol "TEDMX." Net asset value of $12.69 a share (3/31/95). Initial sales charge of 5.75 percent. Management fee of 1.25 percent. Minimum initial purchase of $100.

Performance: One-year total return a negative 9.25 percent (through 3/95) and three-year average annual return of 12.91 percent. In 1994, fund value was down 4.21 percent in the first quarter, down 5.64 percent in the second, up 10.57 percent in the third, and down 8.53 percent in the fourth. First quarter 1995 was down 4.91 percent.

Portfolio: Composition was recently 63.9 percent stocks, 35.9 percent cash, and 0.2 percent other securities. Heaviest stock weightings were financials, utilities, and industrial cyclicals. Regional exposure was greatest in the Pacific Rim and Latin America.

Data from Morningstar Inc.

Templeton Developing Markets Trust

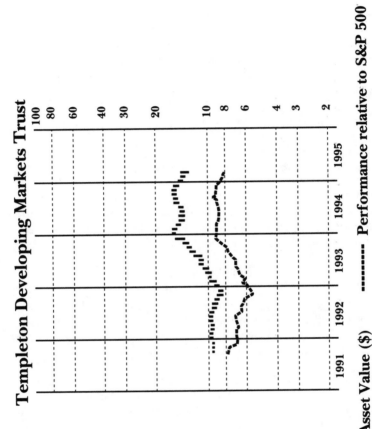

IIIIIIIII Net Asset Value ($)   ------- Performance relative to S&P 500

Investment Close-Up: T. Rowe Price International Stock Fund

100 E. Pratt Street, Baltimore, Maryland 21202
(800) 638-5660

T. Rowe Price International Stock Fund seeks total return on its assets from long-term growth of capital and income, investing primarily in stocks of established non–U.S. issuers. While it generally invests in common stocks or other equity securities, it may invest up to 35 percent in any other type of security.

Portfolio team leader: Martin Wade
Fund inception: 5/09/80
Total assets: $5.5 billion
Distributor: T. Rowe Price Investment Services

Shares: Traded under the symbol "PRITX." Net asset value of $11.20 a share (3/31/95). No initial sales charge. Management fee of 0.35 percent of average net assets plus 0.48 percent group fee. Minimum initial purchase of $2,500.

Performance: One-year total return of 0.59 percent (through 3/95), three-year average annual return of 10.81 percent, and five-year average annual return of 7.65 percent. In 1994, fund value was down 2.39 percent in the first quarter, up 0.85 percent in the second, up 5.26 percent in the third, and down 4.23 percent in the fourth. First quarter 1995 was down 1.06 percent.

Portfolio: Composition was recently 93.6 percent stocks and 6.4 percent cash. Heaviest stock weightings were in industrial cyclicals, financials, and services. Regional exposure was greatest in Europe, Japan, and the Pacific Rim.

Data from Morningstar Inc.

T. Rowe Price International Stock Fund

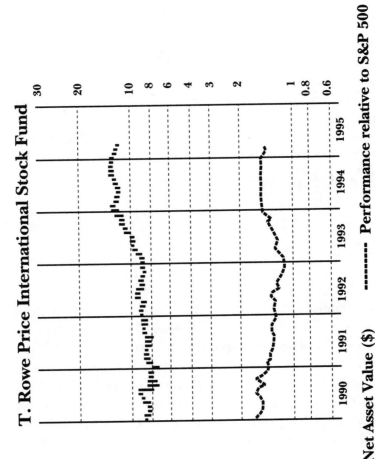

30
20
10
8
6
4
3
2
1
0.8
0.6

1990 1991 1992 1993 1994 1995

IIIIIIII Net Asset Value ($)   -------- Performance relative to S&P 500

3

Bell Sports

It's the law.

California's mandatory bicycle helmet law for riders under the age of 19 went into effect January 1, 1994. For the first year, police are given only the authority to stop and warn youths, but starting in 1995 young riders without helmets face $25 fines. As Governor Pete Wilson signed the bike helmet law, he cited the nearly 18,000 youngsters treated for bicycle-related injuries in California each year. Children also accounted for at least half of the state's cycling fatalities.

It's an idea whose time has come. The owner of The Attic, a video arcade and card shop in the town of Tiburon, who had seen the results of bike crashes involving his young patrons, posted the sign: "No shoes, no shirt, no problem. No bike helmet—no service."

Helmet laws, coupled with the expected dramatic growth of helmet use overseas for decades to come, perfectly position helmet maker Bell Sports Corp. for the 21st century and provide an opportunity for investors in the company's stock.

At Mike's Bikes in downtown San Rafael, there is a wall of colorful and aerodynamic lightweight helmets for those seeking to fulfill the legal requirement. Owner Dave Kaplan, who sold 600 helmets the year before the new legislation went into effect, estimates that his sales of helmets for youngsters have risen 25 percent. Among the choices hanging in his shop is a Bell Image, advertised as "the No. 1 microshell helmet in the world," retail price $79.99. Its color is black, spattered with yellow, purple, and raspberry. "Pretty cool," a young customer told me. There's a Bell Quest softshell helmet that retails for $59.95. From Bell's Pro Series, the $114.99 Pump Razor utilizes Reebok technology to pump up an inner inflation device so the helmet fits your head exactly. A Bell Cruzer helmet for rollerblading and skateboarding goes for $59.95. Kaplan's sale prices were $10 to $30 below the manufacturer's suggested retail prices.

Helmets are big business and getting dramatically bigger. Mandatory helmet legislation is on the rise in the United States, with more than 20 million youngsters in nine states already covered. Safety awareness groups around the country and Congress have also taken up the cause. As was the case with protective child seat legislation several years ago, it's expected that youngsters in virtually all states will be covered within a relatively short period of time as bicycle safety continues to be a growing concern. Safety is a worthy concept that sells and a trend the investor can easily monitor by watching the bicycle riders cruise through the neighborhood.

"As kids get used to bicycle helmets, they'll definitely be using them when they grow into adulthood," predicted Terry Lee, chairman and chief executive of Bell Sports, which holds 50 percent of the U.S. bicycle helmet market.

"It's also true that many parents who are asking their children to wear bicycle helmets feel they must lead by example and therefore wear helmets themselves."

Bell Sports is a high-quality growth company with excellent financial returns that include an operating margin of more than 17 percent. It's quite likely the company can continue its record of consistent growth of 20 percent or more in operating income in the U.S. market while experiencing explosive growth overseas. Its marketing-oriented management is geared toward profits and acquisitions of other companies. The annual report, or "performance report" as the company calls it, is filled with action bicycling photos as colorful and grabbing as anything put out by Nike. These executives should be able to maneuver the company capably no matter how much bigger it grows. In addition, there's no risk of the product being supplanted by technology, and sales should hold up well even in recessionary periods.

To understand the creative nature of this firm, which has manufactured helmets for 39 years, consider its unusual development of a recent product.

Small blinking lights implanted in the heels of the athletic shoes worn by several youngsters playing in his seven-year-old son's basketball game caught Lee's eye last year. All the kids seemed fascinated with this simple concept heavily advertised by shoe manufacturer L.A. Gear. But for Lee, the interest went a step further. The next day he met with members of Bell Sport's research and development group at the Rantoul, Illinois, headquarters.

The result of that brainstorming session, thanks to fiber-optic technology, was the Dino-Light multisport hardshell helmet for kids ages four to eight, which features a large blinking light on the back. To add to the "coolness" factor and sales appeal, a big orange Tyrannosaurus is depicted on that battery-powered light. Also included are neon dinosaur stickers that can be plastered all over the helmet. It's a slick case of L.A. Gear shoes (given credit on the helmet's box for the technology) meets *Jurassic Park*. But this is serious business, too. Included is an owner's manual that explains the need to position the helmet on the child's head, fit it properly, adjust straps, check the adjustment by grasping the helmet as you roll it forward and backward, and, finally, take a test ride. Of course, lights also make a small child more visible after dark, which is another safety feature.

Bicycling is currently one of the most popular exercise activities in this country, eclipsed only by walking and swimming, and involves nearly 100 million riders. More than half of those are serious participants, the kind most likely to use helmets. Bell Sports, which introduced both the first protective bicycle helmet and the first toddler helmet, states its strategic corporate mission as an intent "to dominate the global bicycle helmet market and lead select categories of the bicycle accessory market."

It has a good start. Check out the stores in your community. With helmets in the infant, youth, and adult categories, the Bell brand name now is offered in the mid-to-premium price range (retail prices are generally from $39 to more than $100). The company is proud of the fact that *Consumer Reports* rated Bell helmets as the top choice in all three age categories. Its BSI brand in the economy category ($20 to $40) is sold at high-volume chains such as K mart, Wal-Mart, Target, Toys "R" Us, Sears Roebuck, and Sam's Warehouse Clubs. BSI has been dramatically successful, the fastest growing portion of the company with revenue gains of more than 50 percent in some quarters. Industrywide sales of less expensive models will likely increase the most as all children are eventually required to wear helmets. The only negative in that is BSI profit margins aren't as much as for Bell brand helmets.

The firm also designs, manufactures, and markets other bicycle accessories. Its Rhode Gear brand is a leader in bicycle carriers, child seats, and locks, while its BSI brand markets bicycle carriers and child seats to mass merchants. The company in 1992 acquired Blackburn Designs, a producer of accessories such as bicycle luggage racks, tire pumps, bicycle bags, water bottle cages, and work stands.

In early 1994, Bell Sports acquired VistaLite, a small bicycle accessory manufacturer specializing in safety lights and halogen headlights, which had revenues of $6.5 million the prior year. This new addition is about half the size of Blackburn. With plenty of cash on hand, the company is definitely on the trail of buying additional firms that fit well with its existing businesses. Bell has also signed an agreement with First Team Sports, which will market Bell-produced helmets for rollerblading under the Ultra-Wheels and Skate Attack brand names.

Some other types of Bell helmets travel by so fast that you'll have to watch very closely for them. Bell Sports has long been a leading name in auto racing helmets, with two-thirds of the drivers in the recent Indianapolis 500s wearing them. Emerson Fittipaldi won the race wearing the Vortex SS, an innovative design developed by Bell in just three months that significantly reduces the helmet buffeting and lift found in open-cockpit cars at high speed.

About 72 percent of Bell Sports sales currently come from bicycle helmets, 25 percent from bicycle accessories, and 3 percent from racing helmets. Nearly one-third of its sales come from international markets. While helmet usage is growing, there's plenty of room to expand. At this point, only 17 percent of all U.S. riders—up from 15 percent a year ago—and only 10 percent of U.S. children under the age of 16 wear helmets, a situation that offers considerable potential. Based on its dominant market share, each 1 percent increase in helmet usage has the potential to translate into as many as 600,000 helmets for Bell Sports. The growth in sales of mountain bikes, now comprising 67 percent of all bicycles sold, is another positive factor. Nine out of 10 mountain bike owners wear helmets because they realize their importance when a tumble occurs.

Bell is the only big domestic manufacturer of the type of helmets that use a polystyrene core as cushion. It employs a heat and pressure process to actually mold the polystyrene, while other domestic makers attach their components to cores they buy elsewhere. The weight of the helmets ranges from a mere 6.6 ounces to about 9.9 ounces. Typical color choices include purple and orange spider, mako blue, violet dusk, water drop blue, and magenta. Since helmets don't really wear out in normal use, upgrading the style, fit, colors, and basic design of the product line on a regular basis might entice a customer back after two or three years instead of the traditional four-year period.

I had the opportunity to play around a bit with the company's Pump Avalanche mountain biking helmet, featuring an iridescent shade called "Mud Splat." Besides the clever Reebok pump design, there's a removable visor to reduce glare and shade the eyes, 10 vents for "massive air-grabbing ventilation," and an ultra-thin ⅜-inch strap with buckle system to keep the helmet on your head. Yes, I was able to figure out how to operate everything, but helmet technology is obviously advancing significantly. Tucked in the helmet was a lifetime crash replacement policy with the following explanation: "As the inventor and world's leading manufacturer of bicycle helmets, Bell knows the major role helmets play in injury prevention. Frequently, helmets are damaged in accidents as they do their job in protecting us. This means the helmet must be replaced. Bell is sincerely interested in your safety, and in advancing the state of the art in head protection. If your helmet is damaged in an accident during its lifetime, Bell will replace it for a nominal fee."

International opportunity, the key to success in the coming century for so many firms, is knocking.

Helmet usage will be growing overseas, with no end in sight. A decade ago, virtually no one outside the United States—except for bicycle racers perhaps—wore helmets. Even the Tour de France didn't require them until 1992. In Europe, considered to be about four years behind the United States in acceptance of helmets, less than 10 percent of 110 million riders now wear helmets. Bell Sports ranks second in sales there and has set the goal of becoming number one. After offering the Bell brand name, it has since introduced Rhode Gear and BSI. The United Kingdom is gradually following the U.S. pattern of helmet use. Other countries such as Germany, Luxembourg, and Belgium are also starting to accept the concept, with the mass merchandising possibilities expanding. It's expected that France, Italy, and Portugal will follow next, eventually to be joined by Eastern Europe. Bell Sports recently opened a manufacturing facility near Etienne in central France, increased its sales and marketing staff in Paris, and began designing helmets specifically for Europe. Its experience thus far with this small operation seems to be considerably more positive than that of Walt Disney Co. with its financially-troubled Euro Disney outside Paris.

In the Pacific Rim, Japan is developing as a strong market for helmets, and the potential of China is impressive. Interestingly, Australia has helmet laws for adults, and more than a million helmets are sold in that country annually. Bell Sports is interested in making an acquisition there and expects to generally intensify its acquisition strategy as it grows worldwide.

"In most new markets, we typically find that a small initial order is made by merchandisers, and, once it's sold out, another cautious order is made," Lee explained. "From that point on, the size and regularity of orders grows significantly."

It is worth noting, however, that despite compounded

annual revenue gains of 150 percent overseas in recent years, the company's efforts in that immature market will probably continue to face lulls from time to time. European sales, for example, unexpectedly suffered a slowdown in 1993 after several years of major gains. The culprits were consumers' economic concerns and the learning curve about helmet usage. Research by the Goldman Sachs investment firm found that, despite such temporary setbacks, the European movement to increased helmet use appears unabated. A positive possibility for the company is that, whenever weakness occurs in foreign countries, it may lead to a shakeout of smaller or weaker competitors and give Bell Sports the opportunity to acquire companies at more favorable prices. Although Bell Sports does take a long-term view of expansion, the unpredictability of overseas economies can cause volatility in the stock price.

At home, perhaps Bell Sports can continue to be all things to all bicyclists. Despite the emergence of more than 15 new manufacturers over the past five years, it remains dominant in the United States as a high-quality low-cost producer with a nationally recognized brand name, according to a research study by the William Blair & Co. investment firm. Bell is the only competitor offering a full product line in terms of price ranges and age categories. Furthermore, it boasts a long-time successful track record in product liability, which is significant with so many new arrivals in this field in which safety concerns are preeminent. Helmet industry competitors Troxel, Cycle Products, Giro, All American, and Huffy have market shares ranging from 10 percent to 3 percent, with a number of smaller niche companies holding the remaining portion of the market. Troxel is a strong competitor, but only in the low-priced infant and youth helmet market. Giro has significantly increased its share of the premium adult helmet business by offering some hot new helmets and inking a successful endorsement deal with popular U.S. cyclist Greg LeMond, but it doesn't seem to be aiming toward capturing the same broad mass market that Bell dominates. Perhaps a greater threat would be if some major company with nationwide marketing strength in other related products decided to enter the helmet market, the Blair report speculates.

"Bell is the only widely recognized brand, and I view all of the others as upstarts," asserted the scrappy Lee, who was head of sales for Wilson Sporting Goods before he joined Bell Sports in 1983 and became its CEO in 1989.

Bell Sports' sales channels are broad-based through independent bicycle dealers, sporting goods retailers, mass merchants, warehouse clubs, and discounters. A transformation to direct sales of its products to independent bicycle dealers, eliminating distributors, should increase the number of outlets served and improve delivery times. As Bell Sports grows, it will be crucial that it is able to manage its inventory and distribution systems effectively so the needs of dealers and retailers are met. Any company that lets that slide is in big trouble.

Lee emphasizes several important areas in which Bell Sports must excel:

- Offering a multibrand product line. When finding a new need, such as its recent move into the burgeoning market of helmets for in-line skaters, the company has the ability to offer a product under one of several brand names and prices.

- Employing innovative new technologies. The company was the first to use expandable polystyrene as helmet liners, providing strength and lightweight design. It's used in conjunction with the company's unique lightweight microshell outer covering.

- "Vertically integrating" the production process. Doing it yourself from top to bottom can clearly pay off. For example, by employing its own testing lab, the company improves quality control, speeds up response times, and cuts costs.

- Avoiding potential lawsuits. The strategy for getting that done is making sure bicycle helmets are produced using the highest quality manufacturing with extensive safety testing before they leave the factory. Bell's helmets exceed independent industry safety standards. (It's worth noting that, although Bell Sports no longer makes motorcycle helmets, it still faces some risk from lawsuits involving the large number of its motorcycle helmets still in use.) The company's aggressive defense strategy toward lawsuits, in which it has successfully defended itself hundreds of times and suffered only one adverse verdict 16 years ago, should help offset possible future negative judgments. A $10 million product liability insurance is yet another company precaution.

     Nonetheless, investors must keep in mind that product liability is always a consideration with any safety-related product. The more Bell bicycle helmets of all types being used by kids these days, the greater the chance for lawsuits.

Bell Sports was formed in 1989 through the combination of four existing companies. Senior management and several institutional investors took over ownership, and the initial public offering was made in April 1992. The previous companies included Bell Racing Inc., a marketer of auto racing helmets, suits, and accessories; Bell Helmets, a marketer of motorcycle helmets; Echelon Sports Inc., which consisted of both the Bell Bicycle marketer of bicycle helmets and the Rhode Gear marketer of bicycle helmets and accessories; and the Look America Corp., a marketer of bicycle accessories. In early 1995, Bell Sports and American Recreation Holdings Inc. entered into a merger agreement.

American Recreation, a maker of bicycles and helmets, became a Bell Sports subsidiary.

All of those deals permitted Bell Sports to concentrate on its core bicycle helmet and accessory businesses, which afford it the greatest opportunities for global achievement in the 21st century.

Investment Close-Up: Bell Sports Corporation
Route 136 East, Rantoul, Illinois 61866
(217) 893-9300

Bell Sports, the leading manufacturer and marketer of bicycle helmets, also makes sports accessories and helmets for automobile racers.

Chairman and CEO: Terry Lee
Executive VP, CFO, and investor contact: Howard Kosick
Total employees: 800

Stock: Traded on NASDAQ under the symbol "BSPT." Price of $14 a share (5/16/95). No dividend. Price-to-earnings ratio of 25.

Sales and Earnings: Sales of $116 million in 1994, with earnings of $10.5 million. Five-year annual sales growth of 36 percent, with earnings growth of 296 percent.

Earnings per Share Growth: Five-year earnings per share annual growth rate of 17 percent. Projected (Institutional Brokers Estimate System) five-year earnings per share annual growth rate of 16 percent.

Data from Bridge Information Systems Inc.

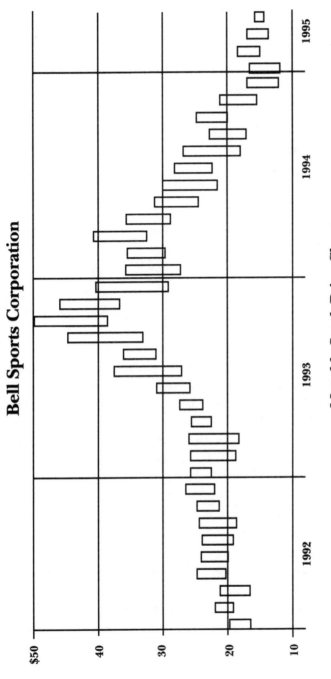

Bell Sports Corporation

Monthly Stock Price Chart

4

AT&T

The main AT&T Corp. network operations center in Bed-minster, New Jersey, looks like a darkened war room, with a wall of 75 projection screens featuring maps of the United States and the world.

Colored lines depict flows of incoming and outgoing calls, while sophisticated alert systems automatically pop any exceptions to the norm onto the screen. To better handle the 185 million daily calls going through the trunk lines connecting AT&T offices, specialists sit at computers typing in the necessary commands to assist trouble spots or reroute calls for areas with extreme call volume. In emergencies, the company assigns a higher priority to phone calls originating from a trouble area than those flooding in.

AT&T technology, with a network that carries voice and data calls through 2.5 billion circuit miles of transmission facilities, has come a long way since the company was incorporated in 1885.

It is enjoying across-the-board growth in its businesses while generating strong revenues and profits. Prospects for those who buy its shares are excellent. But progress to this point will seem like a few quick seconds of busy signal when viewed from the vantage point of the 21st century. There's a whole lot more on the drawing board.

From the first trans-Atlantic telephone service in 1927 to the invention of the transistor in 1947, the laser in 1958, and the Telstar communications satellite in 1962, Ma Bell as a regulated monopoly had plenty to show for its efforts. But it was still basically a telephone company. Since AT&T's court-ordered divestiture of the regional Bell telephone companies in 1983, however, this smaller, leaner company has been attempting to turn up the pace to light speed. It's still considered the world's most successful high-technology corporation. But, while fighting the ongoing brutal battle of long-distance market share, it has taken aggressive steps to attain a leadership role in the communications revolution. The company's formal name change from American Telephone & Telegraph Co. to AT&T Corp. in 1994 symbolized a new era in its history.

When Robert Allen, AT&T chairman and chief executive, looks out of the corner window in his Basking Ridge, New Jersey, headquarters office these days, he sees the rolling hills and trees surrounding the huge concrete complex. But his mind is conjuring up a lot more.

"We'll have low-cost Videophone service within the next five years, but in the next century it will be much more prevalent," the slim, gray-haired Allen said in his softspoken but confident manner as he glanced out that window. "Now, I'm not a crystal-ball gazer, and you can sometimes let technology run away with you, but we can expect a world that will give people the capability to access virtually any information from any place they want to be."

Working toward that ambitious goal, AT&T has lately

snared a string of multibillion-dollar deals that mark it as the prime contractor for the building of the information superhighway. In the largest deal, Bell Atlantic chose AT&T to help construct an advanced video and data network to bring items such as interactive video and films to eight million mid-Atlantic homes. The agreement will net AT&T $8.5 billion over five years. Meanwhile, Pacific Telesis awarded the company a $5 billion contract to put together a California network; Saudi Arabia gave it a $4 billion contract to rebuild that nation's telephone system; and Southern New England Telephone will spend $1 billion to improve its technology using primarily AT&T.

Innovation doesn't come without its trials and tribulations. When I asked Allen about products with future potential, he pointed to the recent $1,000 AT&T Videophone, which works on a regular phone line, as the beginning of a long line of products. He also mentioned the new class of wireless, handheld communications devices based on the AT&T Hobbit microprocessor and the PenPoint operating system. Having previously used the Videophone myself, I considered the slow-moving snapshotlike image unlikely to wow any sophisticated high-tech consumer who thrives on motion and color. Even AT&T commercials present a view of the future characterized by super-sharp interactive video telecommunications that aren't yet available from the company. As a result of its lack of sophistication, the initial Videophone has had few sales. In the same vein, the $2,500 Model 440 handheld wireless model made by AT&T's Eo Inc. business that Allen was talking about was withdrawn after fewer than 10,000 were sold. Eo was permanently closed down by AT&T, an acknowledgment that not all bright ideas are immediately workable.

"The Videophone idea may have been oversold a bit, and we knew that in this form it would have limited application," responded Allen. But he patiently emphasized that "compression of a video signal through conventional phone lines is nonetheless a considerable technological breakthrough" and that both it and the handheld wireless communications devices will only get better. Unlike a smaller company, which has everything riding on the success of each new device, giant AT&T's financial might in other areas affords it the chance to be patient.

AT&T's new WorldWorx video conferencing service, which uses desktop computers, is another ambitious attempt to put pictures with words. This could place AT&T in the forefront of standards for video phones. Computer companies such as Apple, IBM, and Sun Microsystems have pledged to design their products to be compatible with it.

One unanswered question, as Allen sees it, is how much people really need to get together to see each other. For if video conversations will suffice, travel will be completely revolutionized in the future. Of course, perhaps the most crucial unanswered question is whether people will be willing to pay for the enhanced ability to communicate. If they are, he believes AT&T is perfectly positioned. "Data carried by superior communications and information networks is the key," said Allen, who testified before Congress that he'd like to see a "seamless web" of connected but competing networks that build on existing lines run by the nation's phone companies. "But whatever the technology of the future, AT&T will be a worldwide, major part of it."

To make that point clear, Allen has taken some risks. He not only put together the agreement in principal to buy McCaw Cellular for $12.6 billion, but engineered the $7.5 billion buyout of computer firm NCR Corp. in 1991. Both are key to the new "anywhere, anytime" communications. NCR, which underwent a name change to AT&T Global Information Solutions in early 1994, didn't turn a profit until the second quarter of 1994. It has gone through a restructuring and elimination of 7,500 jobs, downsizing and aiming this large computer business more toward the specific needs of its customers. Allen considers it a solid long-term acquisition that will help AT&T cut its own previous losses in the computer field, though profitability is dependent on improvement in lagging overseas economies and the success of those changes now under way. The McCaw acquisition makes up for AT&T's initial mistake of not actively pursuing the cellular market and also makes possible nationwide cellular-phone services marketed under the AT&T brand name.

Allen's dramatic actions led to a *Business Week* cover story on AT&T bearing the headline: "Dial 1-800-GUTS." A *Fortune* magazine cover story posed the question: "Could AT&T Rule the World?" Actually, his quiet demeanor really isn't that of a General Patton or a Road Warrior, though the fact that he runs for long stretches each day does underscore that his physical stamina matches up to his mental toughness.

Adding to his arsenal for the future, he has also bought or invested in a dozen start-up companies to obtain hardware and software for the new communications. They represent a little bit of everything. Some examples include stakes bought in the General Magic consortium, developing the Telescript communications language that enables different brands of personal communicators to exchange messages; the ImagiNationNetwork Inc. on-line computer service, which provides networked interactive multimedia entertainment over regular telephone lines; 3DO Co., which will create home multimedia systems using AT&T–licensed technology; and Knowledge Adventure, a multimedia educational software company.

Yet another advanced AT&T system reportedly under study would use the telephone as central controller to funnel information to and from the TV, video-game player, personal computer, facsimile machine, video cassette recorder, answering machine, and video camera. Electronic plug-in cards would change functions based on the consumer's desires. AT&T's team of high-tech companies would again make it happen.

The company has also formed alliances with Lotus Development Corp., Novell Inc., and Xerox Corp. for software applications to improve communications for millions of computer users through AT&T's public network. It is joining forces with Motorola, IBM, and Loral to develop a process using x-rays instead of ultraviolet light to create semiconductors vastly more powerful than those in use today. Through an alliance with Liberty Media Corp. and the Allen & Co. investment-banking firm, it is launching a national cable network of sports documentaries, films, and talk shows called Classic Sports Network.

The five areas that make up AT&T's overall technology strategy for the 21st century include: (1) networked computing, with its computer capabilities, long-distance networking abilities, and research and development together linking powerful computers and databases to networks on a global scale; (2) wireless technology primarily through McCaw Cellular; (3) messaging, with wireless personal communicators making it possible to drop a line, written or oral, to a colleague, with the network finding the person and delivering it; (4) visual communications, with the Videophone expanding to make desktop videoconferencing a common event; and (5) voice and audio processing, with which people will be able to talk to machines that understand them and respond to their spoken commands.

Global implications are a part of any product decisions. In early 1994, AT&T set up foreign units, each with its own executive, to go after the promising markets of Asia, Europe, and Latin America. It already employs more than 50,000 workers in foreign markets, half in traditional AT&T equipment and services and the rest in Global Information Solutions.

"I've never seen anything occur so quickly as what has happened in the past two years with everyone suddenly talking about globalization," said Allen, who wants to see overseas revenues rise from the current 24 percent to more than 40 percent by the turn of the century. "This is also entwined with the democratization of the world, because people know more through greater communications, so they learn about countries outside their own and events such as Tiananmen Square don't go unnoticed."

AT&T is a growth stock that will continue to meet its goal of at least 10 percent earnings growth annually, Allen vowed. To reach that goal, strong international expansion will be required. Because the company has the know-how to sell its rapidly changing products and services in new markets, he believes AT&T revenues can more than double to $150 billion to $200 billion in the first part of the 21st century. While AT&T's U.S. business grows at about 6 percent a year, China, other nations in Asia, and countries in Latin America and Eastern Europe are modernizing archaic phone systems and can make big orders. For example, China is expected to acquire $1.2 billion in new switching gear every year for the next three decades. AT&T has signed a memorandum of understanding with China that covers the provision of a large range of communications products from switching, microelectronics, fiber-optic cable, and telephones to network management, research and development, and training of personnel. The company will build three manufacturing plants in China and triple its workforce there to 800 by 1997.

"We have the capability to build the necessary infrastructure on a global basis, and we'll have enough advanced personal communications products to enhance the return," he said. "How all of the information superhighway situation will sort out in light of all the mergers and alliances going on I wish I knew, but I do know that I want to be the supplier to those who build that broad superhighway."

AT&T successfully bid for 21 personal communications service licenses for $1.68 billion at federal auction in early 1995. When asked whether the new wireless system, called PCS, with its inexpensive handsets, low-powered transmitters, and longer battery life, could become a major rival to cellular, Allen measured his words carefully: "It has a different cost structure and could be a competitor for various levels of service, but we'll just have to see how it works out."

AT&T's basic long-distance business is a concern, for the company's 90 percent share of the market a decade ago has eroded. While it's true that its recent 60 percent share is now part of a much larger long-distance market of $60 billion, compared to only $39 billion a decade ago, long distance remains a dog-eat-dog business with aggressive advertising and competitive pricing. MCI has a 19 percent market share, increasing 1 percent each year due to successful promotions such as its special "Friends and Family" rates. Generally considered to have been outmarketed by MCI, AT&T responded more aggressively with several plans, including "True Rewards" in which customers earn points toward frequent flier miles, cash, or free minutes on subsequent calls. AT&T added one million residential customers in 1994.

"Long distance will be a solid business for a long time," said Allen, insisting that the company's new marketing plans will enable it to grow. "The competition will be as heated as it can be, and we intend to emphasize real value in our sales campaigns."

AT&T in February 1994 announced that over two years it would cut as many as 15,000 jobs in long-distance services, or 15 percent of the workforce in that area, to try to boost profits in this slow-growth business. Further cuts haven't been ruled out as the company seeks to boost the almost flat long-distance revenue growth to at least the industry rate of 4 to 5 percent. The company estimates that it can save about $900 million a year through the cuts by installing new technology in its long-distance network and with other streamlining.

Thanks to its Universal Cardholders business, AT&T's financial services are providing strong profits. It now ranks as the second largest credit card issuer in this country after Citicorp. A discount from standard calling-card rates and aggressive marketing are what set it apart. But there's more to AT&T than that. Besides operating interstate and international toll networks and portions of intrastate networks, AT&T owns local on-premises equipment, Western Electric, and Bell Laboratories. It's the only big telecommunications service firm that makes telephones, computers, and PBXs (private branch exchanges that route calls within a company). It is the U.S. market leader in answering machines and cordless phones, and its PBX business has recently become profitable.

AT&T's corporate groups are composed of the following categories:

- Communications Services, which markets global long-distance and electronic messaging services for business and residential customers; manages the AT&T worldwide network and private corporate networks; installs undersea fiber-optic systems; provides operator, directory, and interpretation assistance; and handles voice and electronic mail, teleconferencing, and the consumer credit card.

- Communications Products, which develops, manufactures, markets, and services telecommunications products for consumers, businesses, and governments around the world. Included are cordless, corded, and cellular phones; the Videophone and personal communicator; FAX machines; answering machines; home security systems; and video-conferencing products. While the company considered selling off this group a while ago, its decision to stick with it has proven to be a profitable move.

- Network Systems, which manufactures, markets, and services network software and equipment for telephone companies, governments, private network operators, cable television operators, and wireless service providers. Once a drag on the company but now quite profitable, this division includes cable, switching, transmission, and wireless systems.

- Global Information Solutions, with the former NCR name retained on certain of its products, a computer maker that links departments, buildings, and global locations through servers and client computers and offers hardware, software, and services for networking.

- AT&T Capital Corp., which provides customers with leasing and financing services for telecommunications equipment, complex computer systems, office and manufacturing equipment, and automobiles.

With 2.3 million shareholders, AT&T has the most stock-holders of any stock in America. Its market value ranks as fourth in the world, behind only Nippon Telegraph & Telephone, Exxon, and General Electric. Despite its generally strong performance, any slippage in share price always draws widespread anguish among shareholders. Allen takes the concept of bolstering shareholder value very seriously.

One means of bolstering shareholder value has been the company's ambitious "economic value added" (EVA) program, which is a way of measuring an operation's real profitability. Allen has become one of the major spokes-people for the viability of this approach. Taking into account the total cost of the operation's capital, it represents the af-ter-tax operating profit, minus the total cost of capital. If a firm's EVA is positive, it is creating wealth, while a negative EVA indicates the operation is actually destroying capital. In 1992, Allen had AT&T managers divide their various businesses into profit centers resembling independent com-panies. All the capital each one uses now goes on its bal-ance sheet. Some businesses discovered they've been posting negative EVAs for years. "EVA requires more discipline, but we spend a lot of capital in this company each year, and it puts a premium on value over capital," Allen explained.

Allen's open manner and clear vision set him apart from many bosses of enormous companies. He's more than happy to be a national voice on technological change, and his man-agement style, while far from bombastic, nonetheless asserts that he is in charge. A career AT&T manager who became chairman and CEO in 1988 after James Olson died, Allen generally lets the strong executives he puts in charge of ma-jor business groups call their own shots. But he'll quickly remove a manager if goals aren't being met. He has also brought in managers from outside the company, a concept alien to AT&T. He has improved discussion between differ-ent groups within the company and set up special teams to develop areas of opportunity, such as video, wireless, data transmission, and voice recognition and processing. Team leaders often are not the actual top bosses in charge of the areas in question, which is an Allen strategy to stir things up and help the company think about how it will handle new future businesses.

AT&T has cut more than 150,000 jobs since the U.S. government made the then-monopoly divest the seven re-gional Baby Bell operating companies in 1984. Yet, with that ongoing employment decline firmly in mind, AT&T's 1992 contract with the Communications Workers of America and the International Brotherhood of Electrical Workers broke new ground in cooperation. Unions are now brought into planning sessions and have a voice in decisions that affect jobs. Spending on training laid-off workers has also been increased.

In a recent AT&T annual report, Allen said the company will, first, work toward the elimination of regulatory restrictions, which it considers unnecessary in a highly competitive long-distance market. Second, it will support legislation that makes local exchange competition a condition for regional Bell companies entering the long-distance or manufacturing business.

Though AT&T was the first company to be a triple winner of the Malcolm Baldrige National Quality Award, it must nonetheless be nimble these days. Allen, expected to continue as CEO until he turns 65 in the year 2000, wants to be around to make sure AT&T is just that. "With all of the changes going on, we have to be quick to change or fine-tune our strategy so changes don't leave us high and dry," concluded Allen, who believes once-mighty IBM didn't realize how frail its mainframe business really was. "Companies get into trouble because they're not quick on their feet."

Investment Close-Up: AT&T Corporation

32 Avenue of the Americas, New York, New York 10013
(212) 387-5400

AT&T is the largest U.S. long-distance company. It also manufactures telecommunications equipment and computers and provides financial services.

Chairman and CEO: Robert Allen
Investor contact: Glenn Swift
Total employees: 304,500

Stock: Traded on the New York Stock Exchange under the symbol "T." Price of $50⅞ a share (5/16/95). Dividend of $1.32 a share. Price-to-earnings ratio of 17.

Sales and Earnings: Sales of $75 billion in 1994, with a profit of $4.7 billion. Five-year annual sales growth of 5 percent, with earnings decline of 63 percent.

Earnings per Share Growth: Five-year earnings per share annual growth rate of 7 percent. Projected (Institutional Brokers Estimate System) five-year earnings per share annual growth rate of 12 percent.

Data from Bridge Information Systems Inc.

AT&T Corporation

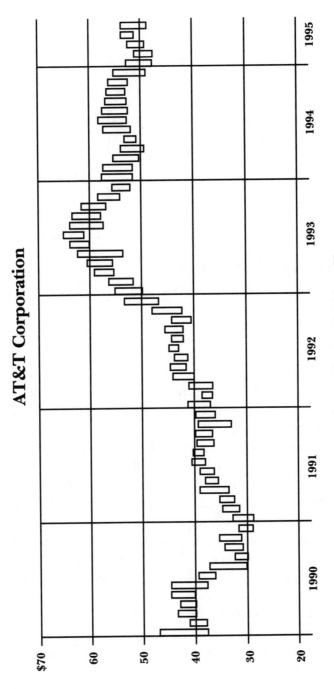

Monthly Stock Price Chart

5

Booming Brokers

Changing U.S. demographics that include a growing number of Asians and Hispanics represent just one of many areas in which financial firms are aiming to please investors as we near the 21st century.

Traders and marketers wearing headsets were speaking either Mandarin or Cantonese, depending on the call-in investor's preference, as they fielded phone inquiries at the Asia Pacific Center of Charles Schwab & Co. on San Francisco's California Street during my visit there. Another center has opened outside Los Angeles. They feature Chinese-language literature and are designed to handle business primarily from U.S. citizens who simply prefer doing business in Chinese.

In Miami, the Schwab Latin American Center concentrates on Spanish. The goal of the centers is to cater to this nation's rapidly expanding Asian and Hispanic populations, both of which are expected to increase significantly in numbers and financial clout in the coming century.

The explosion of financial services as we enter the next century is well under way. An aging, more affluent, and diverse investing public is looking for better returns combined with greatly improved technology and expanding investment opportunities here and abroad. Baby boomers want to send kids to college and plan for retirement.

You're never too old to be an investor. Over at Schwab's corporate headquarters on Montgomery Street, several rows of senior citizen investors sat in the lobby scanning the moving stock ticker as they razzed each other about the quality and performance of their respective holdings. Just upstairs, a demonstration of Schwab's new StreetSmart on-line trading software was under way. Designed to bring trading and banking transactions to the home, it's yet another means of making financial services available to everyone.

The stocks of financial services giants Charles Schwab in discount brokerage, Merrill Lynch & Co. in full-service brokerage, and T. Rowe Price Associates in mutual funds have become admired growth investments.

The decline of bonds and bond mutual funds in 1994 is an example of the vagaries that can cut profits in any given year. These companies are going all out to build strong customer loyalty to ease them through the unavoidable cycles when markets are down. Each presents a different piece of the rapidly expanding financial pie, split between the competing do-it-yourself and trust-an-expert philosophies. All three have crack marketing efforts and service to back them up, providing the potential for powerful earnings movement now and in the future as investors continue to expand beyond traditional bank instruments.

"The consumer of today and tomorrow wants it all, with instant transactions and instant information 24 hours a day," said Charles Schwab, chairman and chief executive of the 208-office discount brokerage that bears his name. "We've done well with instant information at Schwab and we want to do even more now, in a sense becoming more like a McDonald's with a constant level of service."

Looking out at the Transamerica pyramid, Schwab's office features a modern painting and print on its wall, both indicative of forward thinking. A thoughtfully introspective, almost shy man, Schwab carefully weighs each word as he speaks of innovations such as the OneSource program, which provides 340 "no-load" (no initial sales charge) mutual funds with no transaction fees for investors looking to change funds. Such funds have an arrangement with Schwab whereby they pay a fee for their inclusion. In market downturns, investors switching out of those funds tend to move into Schwab's money market funds, yet another financial plus for the company.

Like former Chrysler boss Lee Iacocca, Schwab personifies his company by serving as spokesperson in all of its advertising. He projects the image of a concerned "everyman" who wants to save investors some money by encouraging them to buy stocks, bonds, and mutual funds through a lower-commission company. While it doesn't offer investment advice, it does feature efficient, courteous service.

The business didn't start out as a sure thing, but as a very small operation in 1971. Three years later, it took part in a groundbreaking Securities and Exchange Commission trial period in which discounts were offered on very large and very small transactions. Then all hell broke loose. In its famous action of May 1975, the SEC mandated an end to all fixed commissions, opening the door wide for discount brokerage firms to rush in. Still the visionary who founded this company, which now holds three million active accounts, Schwab retains his competitive bent. After all, his empire is built on the concept of discount commissions for investors doing their own homework, so full-service brokers are the enemy.

"I look at Merrill Lynch and wonder how it will deal with changes on the transaction side, for I see a conflict in that their broker basically holds the information and then presents it again," Schwab said with a frown as he folded his hands in front of him. "Ours is a more open culture."

It's a culture built around some basic services. The Schwab brokerage account offers fast transactions and 24-hour service, while the TeleBroker Services Touch-Tone telephone program can save the investor 10 percent in commissions. Keogh accounts for the self-employed, custodial accounts for children, and trust brokerage accounts for individuals who manage their own trust assets are also important contributors to Schwab's bottom line.

Innovation is necessary to snare the price-conscious do-it-yourself investor who doesn't plunk down money for anything simply based on a famous name. Besides offering no-load funds without transaction fees, another new wrinkle is the no-fee individual retirement account guaranteed for life on accounts of more than $10,000. The company believes the customer commissions and additional business attracted by this offer more than offset the processing and other costs. Investors can leave Schwab without paying an exit fee.

All the numbers seem to add up for Schwab. For five years, Schwab's total trades per quarter have increased at a compound annual rate of nearly 30 percent, reflecting not only rapid gains in New York Stock Exchange and NASDAQ volume, but large market share gains as Schwab attracted new accounts. Strong growth is expected to continue as mutual funds and other professional investors actively manage growing pools of money. Schwab is by far the largest discount broker, with a 45 percent share of that market. It's possible that Schwab may lose some market share due to competition from a variety of new discounters, among them banks, but Schwab's advanced technology and ability to adjust costs should keep it on an upward course. Its institutional division, which caters to independent investment managers who advise investors, increased nearly 80 percent in one year and now has more than $36 billion in client assets. In early 1995, Schwab acquired ShareLink Investment Services PLC, Britain's largest discount broker.

Schwab's ambitious but achievable goal is to increase the value of the company by attaining over the long haul a 20 percent annual net revenue growth, while maintaining an after-tax profit margin of 10 percent and a return on stockholder equity of 20 percent. Investors must remember that, because earnings are tied to market volume, Schwab stock can be volatile at times. Founder Charles Schwab, who had sold the company to BankAmerica Corp. but then headed a buyout seven years ago, controls about 23 percent of the company's stock, management and the ESOP (employee stock option program) about 50 percent.

"This company spends a lot of its energy and cash flow on technology, which is a critically important factor as we enter the 21st century in that it lets you customize your services," Schwab said proudly. "The customer of the future will want not only a convenient location where he can see someone face-to-face, but 24-hour transactions like an automated teller machine."

With technology a high priority, a five-year, $100 million updating project was begun several years ago. It has played a big role in reducing processing costs and the time needed to program new products and services. Schwab operations aren't capital-intensive, its greatest investment in the business being computer software. In addition, a fourth regional telephone service center in Orlando was recently added to help handle the greater business generated by programs such as OneSource and the growing branch network.

The rampaging Merrill Lynch & Co. bull takes a very different, but successful, approach to its business.

It's the nation's largest brokerage business, with 500 offices in the United States and 30 foreign countries built on the concept of "value-added" full service rather than price savings. The reward for this strategy is a mind-boggling $568 billion in client assets and more than six million client accounts. It has nearly 13,500 financial consultants. For seven straight years it has been the top underwriter of debt and equity in this country.

It also boasts a name and image synonymous with investing, as it goes about serving investors, corporations, and governments worldwide.

"With the complexity of world markets, I believe professional advice and counseling are becoming more important, and I believe the answer to the question of how many people truly understand markets and investments is 'not many,'" declared Daniel Tully, chairman and chief executive of Merrill Lynch, whose top priority is to strengthen personal relationships with clients that will last many years. "Our marketing in the past estimated that the do-it-yourself discounters would account for a 25 percent share of commission products and that's about where it has stayed."

The gregarious Tully, a New York Irishman and son of a dockside steam fitter from Queens, is blessed with an ability to tell stories to back up virtually every point he makes. A lifetime Merrill Lynch executive, he's proud of its past innovations, such as the Cash Management Account and zero-coupon convertibles, and believes the company's future is bright because of its research capabilities, asset allocation advice, and managed products such as mutual funds and variable annuities. He resents the experts who once declared the full-service brokerage industry old-fashioned and doomed, and his view of the investment future differs considerably from that of Schwab. Tully relates the story of an Indian tribe that kept intentionally destroying the water pipe a helpful "technocrat" had installed so tribe members wouldn't have to walk all the way down to the stream to bring back water every day. "While the water pipe was more efficient, it didn't take into account the social aspect that the people simply wanted to get together at that stream every day," he said, underscoring what he feels are the positive social aspects of dealing with a broker.

Three hundred full-service NYSE firms have gone out of business since 1975. Merrill Lynch, featuring a zeal for selling without the snobby attitude of some competitors, remains an exciting place to be on Wall Street. "The 76 million-member baby boom generation is saving at only one-third the rate necessary to finance the kind of retirement it expects," said Tully. "As they awaken to this problem, it's logical to assume that saving and investing will become an even stronger growth industry."

Aided by the low interest rates offered on competing investments, all of Merrill's businesses—which include securities brokerage, investment banking, asset management, and life insurance—have been booming. With client transactions increasing at a rapid 30 percent clip, Merrill has taken steps to strengthen its organization and better manage its risks and costs. It is emphasizing asset gathering and the sort of fee-based products that encourage long-term customer relationships. This strategy should help in market downturns. One such product is the Merrill Lynch Consults "wrap" account, which invests client assets with outside money managers and provides account information. Increasingly, the percentage of Merrill Lynch revenues from fees, as opposed to commissions, is growing. Tully predicts consumer holdings of securities will continue to grow much faster than the economy as a whole, as bank deposits and loans are further eroded.

In the late 1980s, Merrill Lynch was in big trouble, hurt by ballooning costs and poor investments. The company was smart enough to sell its underperforming real estate brokerage and telecommunications operations. Much more

painful was the dismissal of about 20 percent of its employees over the past several years. Today it's a much tighter ship with a superb balance sheet. It has lately averaged nearly one-half of the net profit of the nation's seven leading securities firms. While it will be difficult to continue the strong earnings and stock price momentum of recent years, Merrill Lynch is building a future that intelligently takes into account all of the major demographic, economic, and global trends. It has begun to originate large commercial loans, thereby moving onto the turf of commercial banks as well.

The thought of the 21st century is an exciting one for Tully, who predicts that the portion of client assets invested internationally will grow from the current 7 percent to more than 20 percent by the year 2000. Merrill Lynch is making long-term global opportunities a theme in all of its presentations to clients, which is helped by excellent results from products such as the Merrill Lynch Pacific Fund. Improving prospects in worldwide investing will be more consistency among nations in regard to accounting and financial reporting, securities issuing and registrations, capital standards for financial services companies, and greater access to information about trades that have been completed. Securities firms that do not function globally will be at a disadvantage in the coming century, Tully believes. His company has also become a force in helping overseas corporations, financial institutions, governments, and affiliates raise capital globally. It's playing a growing role in helping foreign governments privatize their state-owned industries, with some key examples in Latin America being Telecom Argentina, Telefonica de Argentina SA, and Telebras of Brazil.

"We're going to manage this firm for the next generation and are poised for unprecedented global growth," Tully said forcefully. "We have powerful franchises in serving corporations and governments worldwide."

The booming mutual fund industry is showing no sign

of slowing down. Industry assets are projected to grow beyond $4 trillion before the turn of the century. Just ask George Collins, president and chief executive of Baltimore-based T. Rowe Price Associates, which manages the respected no-load (no initial sales charge) fund family, how popular funds have become.

"I moved five years ago into a new neighborhood and kept my mouth shut about what I do for a living," said Collins, who has been in the fund business 22 years. "Now the word is out, and I'm getting an amazing number of referrals from people with $500,000 to $2 million in assets who have pension, termination, or rollover money to invest and are looking for help."

Not only are those neighbors going right to the top, but they're also dealing with a company admired not only for its service, but also for the performance of its funds and the returns from its own stock. The firm was founded in 1937 by Thomas Rowe Price, who pioneered the growth stock theory of investment and entered the no-load mutual fund business in 1950.

Earnings of T. Rowe Price Associates, with nearly $60 billion under management that includes almost $40 billion in 65 mutual funds, have continued to beat the expectations of analysts. It has more than 3.5 million investor accounts, and its assets have tripled since 1986. Explosive increases in international and global stock funds, accounting for more than half of the firm's new investment money, improves operating margins because such funds tend to have somewhat higher management fees than do regular domestic funds. The company is benefiting more than most mutual fund companies from the international boom, for it has been long involved in the international sector through its joint venture with London-based Robert Fleming Holdings. Its group of 12 international and global funds for U.S. investors features attractive and proven long-term choices such as the

T. Rowe Price International Stock Fund. In light of the hike in the top individual tax bracket and possible additional increases in the future, the company's strong position in tax-exempt bond and money-market funds is also a plus. Investors who track fund performance clearly know a good thing when they see it.

In addition, Price serves as investment advisor to sponsored real estate partnerships and institutional and individual accounts. It has sold a $34.7 million receivable of its Mortgage and Realty Trust (MRT), which had been unable to make a principal payment, so shareholders can get that nagging problem off their minds. The company saw its individual retirement account sales rise 12.5 percent in 1994 to $18 billion.

T. Rowe Price was active in retirement accounts before they were a hot trend, being the first to offer mutual funds for Keogh plans for the self-employed and developing the first retirement plan record-keeping system to use mutual funds for defined contribution participants. Its defined contribution 401(k) retirement plan business has been a boon to its bottom line. It manages about $10 billion in retirement plan assets and has aggressively pushed to gain even more. Collins believes the nation's 401(k) market could double in size to $2 trillion by the year 2000 as employers increasingly emphasize profit-sharing-type plans over traditional pension plans. According to pension experts, T. Rowe Price is among the most-used providers and obviously in it for the long haul because of its significant investments in buildings, human resources, and technology dedicated to the 401(k) market.

In a Gallup study of intended uses of mutual fund investments, 72 percent of the individuals polled named "retirement."

"These days we see an older group of people with substantial assets who fear Social Security and pensions won't be there for them," said Collins, who points out that there is a lot of administrative work and accounting required in order to do the 401(k) business properly. "We made a bet on the 401(k) market, and it has turned out to be a fruitful opportunity."

Despite all the positives, investors must keep in mind that any company in this business will always be somewhat cyclical and at times profits will fall. There will be those pesky market corrections to deal with. "Some events, whether in the Middle East or in Washington, will be capable of knocking the market on its rear, but I think all that will happen is that we'll see a lot of funds switched into more conservative fund choices," predicted Collins, who expects the number of new competitors in the investment field to slow and some consolidations of firms to occur. "In the 1987 stock market crash, we found that some people were actually very aggressive because they felt there were bargains to be bought."

More than a few industry observers worry that, as the size of the mutual fund industry and its assets continue to grow, so will the possibility for massive movements of money whenever events become troublesome. Collins responds that, as far as the rest of this century and the 21st century are concerned, "mutual funds will become even more important, and, no matter how large this industry ever becomes, I see nothing in such large size that would ever give me pause."

T. Rowe Price Associates knows, just as Charles Schwab & Co. and Merrill Lynch & Co. do, that Americans have caught the investment bug in a big way.

Investment Close-Up: Charles Schwab Corporation

101 Montgomery Street, San Francisco, California 94104
(415) 627-7000

Charles Schwab is the largest discount brokerage firm in the United States, with more than 209 branch offices and 3.1 million customer accounts.

Chairman and CEO: Charles Schwab
Investor contact: Mark Thompson
Total employees: 6,500

Stock: Traded on the New York Stock Exchange under the symbol "SCH." Price of $36⅛ a share (5/16/95). Dividend of 24 cents a share, which has grown at a 46 percent annual rate over the past five years. Price-to-earnings ratio of 23.

Sales and Earnings: Sales of $1.26 billion in 1994, with earnings of $135 million. Five-year annual sales growth of 18 percent, with earnings growth of 56 percent.

Earnings per Share Growth: Five-year earnings per share annual growth rate of 65 percent. Five-year projected earnings per share growth rate (Institutional Brokers Estimate System) of 16 percent.

Data from Bridge Information Systems Inc.

Charles Schwab

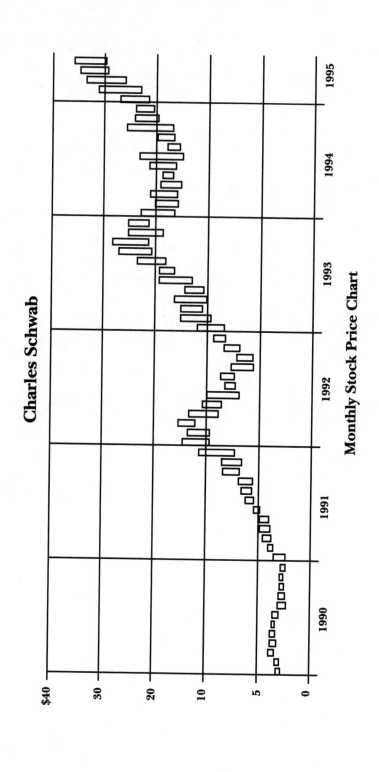

Monthly Stock Price Chart

Investment Close-Up: Merrill Lynch & Company Inc.

World Financial Center, North Tower, New York, New York 10281
(212) 449-1000

Merrill Lynch, whose principal subsidiary is one of the largest and most diversified securities firms in the world, provides investment, financing, insurance, and related services.

Chairman and CEO: Daniel Tully
Investor contact: Constance Melrose
Total employees: 43,800

Stock: Traded on the New York Stock Exchange under the symbol "MER." Price of $48 a share (5/16/95). Dividend of $1.04, which has grown at a 14 percent annual rate over the past five years. Price-to-earnings ratio of 12.

Sales and Earnings: Sales of $18.2 billion in 1994, with earnings of $1 billion. Five-year annual sales growth of 13 percent, with earnings growth of 315 percent.

Earnings per Share Growth: Five-year earnings per share annual growth rate of 54 percent. Projected (Institutional Brokers Estimate System) five-year earnings per share annual growth rate of 19 percent.

Data from Bridge Information Systems Inc.

Merrill Lynch and Company

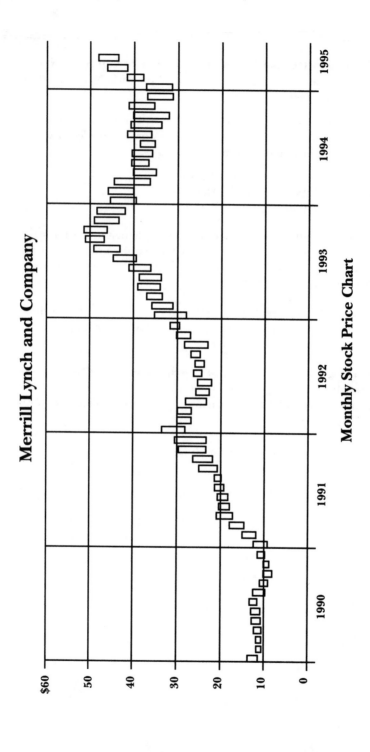

Monthly Stock Price Chart

Investment Close-Up: T. Rowe Price Associates Inc.
100 E. Pratt Street, Baltimore, Maryland 21202
(410) 547-2000

T. Rowe Price is investment adviser to a large family of no-load (no initial sales charge) mutual funds, as well as to institutional and individual investors.

President and CEO: George Collins
CFO and investor contact: George Roche
Total employees: 1,940

Stock: Traded on NASDAQ under the symbol "TROW." Price of $37⅝ a share (5/16/95). Dividend of 64 cents, which has grown at a 17 percent annual rate over the past five years. Price-to-earnings ratio of 18.

Sales and Earnings: Sales of $382 million in 1994, with earnings of $61 million. Five-year annual sales growth of 21 percent, with earnings growth of 26 percent.

Earnings per Share Growth: Five-year earnings per share annual growth rate of 23 percent. Projected (Institutional Brokers Estimate System) five-year earnings per share annual growth rate of 15 percent.

Data from Bridge Information Systems Inc.

T. Rowe Price Associates Inc.

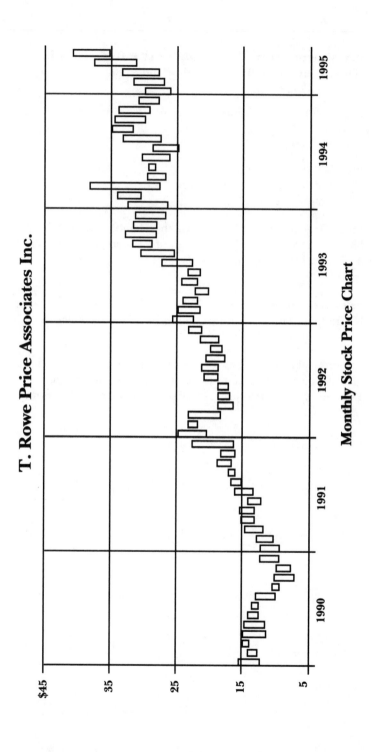

Monthly Stock Price Chart

6

Long-Term Health Care

A stroll through the 120-bed Heartland Health Care Center in Homewood, Illinois, where three-fourths of clients are more than 80 years old, demonstrates the aging of the U.S. population.

A couple who recently celebrated their 76th wedding anniversary, the husband and wife each a remarkable 101 years old, were sitting in a private room munching candy. Their wheelchairs facing each other, they chatted up the day's events at a high decibel level.

Down the hall, a slender, white-haired woman was being helped out of her wheelchair to obtain "gait training" that would enable her to walk with more confidence. A group of boisterous seniors in a large room happily sang along to the music from a phonograph recording.

Another half-dozen folks were engaged in rehabilitative exercises in a room that included a model kitchen designed so those recuperating could practice basic household chores before they return home. The overall facility is bright and clean, uses real china for dinner, has both a beauty shop and a massage therapist, and allows 24-hour visitation.

More and more Americans will be spending time in nursing homes, also called long-term health care facilities. In the next 15 years, the number of people in this country over the age of 85 is expected to double to six million. The Congressional Budget Office estimates that the number of nursing home residents will increase 24 percent by the 21st century to 2.1 million, which means that there will also be an accompanying 145 percent rise in national nursing home expenditures.

What's different about modern long-term health care facilities such as this one is that half of those in residence aren't there permanently, but rather are receiving subacute care that has traditionally been available only at hospitals. Subacute care provides highly skilled rehabilitative or medically intensive care for patients following a serious event or a significant change in condition. Such patients do not, however, require the intensity of diagnostic services or the aggressive procedures found in acute care. It's estimated that the total market for subacute care is more than $5 billion.

About 50 patients in the subacute area at this Heartland facility, owned and run by Health Care & Retirement Corp., are discharged each month after a typical stay of two weeks to two months. Subacute services include rehabilitation for stroke, neuromuscular disease, and postcardiac patients; therapeutics such as antibiotics, pain management, and cardiac support; complex wound care; treatment for infectious diseases such as HIV; complex respiratory care with ventilators at some facilities; dialysis; and care for tumors.

Sophisticated firms such as Health Care & Retirement, Genesis Health Ventures, and Living Centers of America are apt to grow 20 percent or more yearly, and their stock provides excellent investments for those looking to the future.

"Our business is no longer focused on traditional re-

tirement services, but on subacute care and medical specialty care in which we can provide a better quality of life for the individual while institutionalized," explained Paul Ormond, chairman, president, and chief executive officer of Health Care & Retirement, a Toledo, Ohio–based operator of 130 long-term care, skilled nursing, and rehabilitative services centers in 16 states. "The government is seeking to level the playing field so that people needn't be kept in hospitals, and we believe we fit in with the goal of finding the most appropriate lower-cost setting."

As we enter the 21st century, the highest quality companies in the $75 billion long-term care industry stand to benefit both from the aging of a population that will need greater care and from the industry and governmental push toward lower-cost medical care. Long-term health care firms are part of the solution to high health care costs, not part of the problem. In addition, moves to provide health insurance to the previously uninsured can open a new 38 million–person market for long-term health care.

They're taking advantage of opportunities such as on-premises pharmacy, rehabilitation, laboratory, and other services in order to gain market share and profits. Nursing home care currently accounts for only 8 percent of health care expenditures in this country, compared with 38 percent for hospital care and 19 percent for physician services.

This is a highly fragmented industry that has been dominated by small local companies. The number of nursing homes affiliated with chains still constitutes less than 20 percent of total beds in the industry. Acquisitions by the larger, stronger firms are expected to continue, though they'll pay lower prices than was the case in the late 1980s, when many overzealous industry players damaged balance sheets by getting too deeply in debt when they acquired. Lessons learned from that difficult period should encourage considerably more conservative growth strategies. Because of those pressures, however, companies found out where their costs lie and how to control them. That puts the industry at a distinct advantage when compared to other portions of the health care industry that are just now trying to track and cut their costs to meet the challenge of changes in the health care delivery system.

The long-term health care industry is poised for growth and consolidation. There are currently about 15,300 nursing homes in this country, containing 1.6 million beds. There are also 1,250 hospital-based nursing home units. The 20 largest nursing home chains operate 2,800 facilities, and all but one of them are for-profit organizations. Sixteen long-term care companies are publicly traded.

"For many years, the system gave encouragement not to send a person home, but that's changing," said Mike Walker, chairman and CEO of Kennett Square, Pennsylvania–based Genesis Health Ventures, which provides basic and specialty services through health care networks in 11 eastern U.S. states and the District of Columbia. "Also consider that the 1.6 million beds in the long-term health care industry are 95 percent utilized, versus the situation in which the 800,000 hospital beds nationwide are only 50 percent occupied."

His future competition, Walker believes, will be the health maintenance organizations (HMOs), the preferred provider organizations (PPOs), and the hospital-based HMOs. Acute care with surgery suites and 24-hour stays will become quite commonplace, he predicts. Once again, this fits in with the concept of managed care, placing a premium on high-quality and cost-effective alternatives to continued hospitalization.

"The average age of those in our nursing homes is 83 years, and advances in medical technology continue to increase life spans, so there is obvious potential," noted Edward Kuntz, chairman and CEO of Houston-based Living Centers of America, with 242 centers for either long-term care or the developmentally disabled, which operate primarily in Texas, Colorado, Florida, and Oklahoma. "Long-term care is a local business in which brand name means nothing and quality of care means everything, for the selection is made by family on the recommendation of doctors, friends, or hospitals."

Perhaps his firm's most innovative program has been one dealing with Alzheimer's disease through specialized units in 45 of its nursing homes, working in conjunction with consultants. This is an area of 25 percent annual revenue growth. In addition, the company has forged an alliance with Vencor Inc. to establish subacute ventilatory units in several centers and respiratory therapy in others.

The overall industry has a way to go in Alzheimer's treatment. The Agency for Health Care Policy and Research found that only 5.6 percent of all nursing facilities with such programs currently provide specialized training to their staff. Demand for services at facilities with high-quality programs will increase as we enter the 21st century. More than four million Americans are afflicted with Alzheimer's disease or a related dementia, and an estimated 12 million will be afflicted by the year 2020. Private-pay daily rates for these patients average 5 to 10 percent higher than typical nursing facility rates.

Health Care & Retirement is similarly expanding its number of beds for special care and operates 11 Alzheimer's units. It has another 25 medical specialty units that include 12 high-intensity rehabilitative care units, 7 transitional care units, 3 ventilator care units, 2 wound care units, and 1 coronary care unit. In addition, a new 120-bed state-of-the-art facility has been opened in Sarasota, Florida, but has not applied for a Medicaid license and is essentially designed to treat complex medical problems. This well-run, well-managed company has consistently posted double-digit earnings gains, and the likelihood of 20 to 25 percent future earnings growth seems to outweigh any investment risks on the horizon.

HCR initially entered the long-term care industry as a subsidiary of Owens-Illinois Corp., but in 1987 Kohlberg, Kravitz & Roberts completed a leveraged buyout of Owens-Illinois. So a new HCR was incorporated in August 1991 to acquire the health care businesses of Owens-Illinois, and an initial public offering was completed in October 1991. In November 1992 it acquired Heartland Rehabilitation Services Inc., which employs 70 therapists generating $5.5 million in revenue. More acquisitions are expected.

"The elderly are more affluent and more discerning these days, and they come to us because they appreciate a better quality of life while institutionalized, a more interactive, social environment," said Ormond. "We have shown our ability to improve the value of our assets and cash flow every year, our management team has been in place for years, and we have a broad number of avenues in which to grow."

The nursing home industry historically hasn't been managed all that professionally, and too many small operators cut corners, he noted. The concerns for HCR as it enters the 21st century, he believes, are making sure that its high standard of quality and service remains at the same level, that profit margins can be improved, and that any changes in reimbursement or the regulatory environment will be handled effectively.

Genesis Health Ventures, a strong regional operator of 58 nursing homes, in the past year acquired Meridian Healthcare, a privately held long-term care company in Towson, Maryland, that operates 36 long-term care facilities. In 1993, Genesis acquired Health Concepts and Services, which provides specialty medical supplies to more than 100 health care providers in the Baltimore area. Founded in May 1985 as a nursing home chain, since going public in June 1991 Genesis has greatly improved its financial condition. Twenty to 25 percent annual earnings growth is forecast. Walker, the founder as well as the chief executive, also cofounded two other nursing home chains in 1977 and 1981.

The strength of the Genesis network sets it apart. It consists of traditional nursing home care with specialty services such as rehabilitation therapy, subacute care, and pharmacy, but also includes physician clinics and home health care. This network approach allows Genesis to retain control of the patient flow and provides care both in and out of the institution over an extended period of time. It could also eventually lead to Genesis becoming a comprehensive geriatric prepaid health care plan. Expect other long-term health care firms to eventually include all of the components of the Genesis network. Another positive for Genesis is that it provides management, development, and marketing services to 15 retirement communities.

"Our margins are not excessive and our services are much in demand, but our real profit center for the future will be specialty medical services because its growth means our profit margins will pick up," said Walker of Genesis. "That in turn will have positive impact on our earnings and our share price."

Living Centers of America in 1993 bought Veri-Care Inc., an operator of 21 long-term care facilities in Alabama, Arizona, and Florida with 2,500 beds. This means Living Centers will have a total of 21,993 beds. The acquisition is a good fit, since Veri-Care will improve Living Center's occupancy rate and provide higher-paying patients. An oversupply of beds in the Texas and Colorado markets had been a problem for Living Centers, although moratoriums on construction are improving the situation. The company acquired Abbey Healthcare's 51 percent interest in Abbey Pharmaceutical Services in late 1994 and changed the name to American Pharmaceutical Services.

"For investors there are no 'home runs' in this business, no technological breakthroughs, but it's a good 'singles' game in which demographics and other trends point to solid long-term investment," explained Kuntz. As stated previously, the goals of the biggest companies are to grow through acquisition, expand the degree of health care offered, and thereby improve the modest 3.5 percent profit margin that's typical for the business.

It's likely for the near future that acute care hospitals will retain the highest-acuity subacute care patients, while long-term care facilities obtain lower-acuity subacute patients, according to a study of the industry by the Alex Brown & Sons Inc. investment firm. At the same time, competition is intensifying for subacute patients. Not only long-term health care chains are gearing up, but freestanding rehabilitation hospitals and psychiatric hospitals are also developing facilities to cater to the subacute. While this might provide some profit margin pressure, not every facility is well-positioned to enter the subacute field, and not all management teams have the ability to successfully develop a market for the services.

To enter the subacute market, renovation and equipment upgrades usually run $10,000 to $15,000 per bed. The biggest challenge, however, is recruitment and training of effective managers. Furthermore, marketing of a subacute program requires the building of relationships with a range of referral sources, such as physicians and insurance company case managers. It's also necessary to have sophisticated management information systems to keep tight controls.

To better understand subacute treatment, Dean Witter Reynolds health care industry analysts tracked the experience of patients in one subacute unit, half of them commercial insurance patients and the rest using Medicaid. Here are examples of the condition, treatment received, and likely length of stay:

• Patient No. 1: Recuperation from a coronary artery bypass graft. Patient was receiving intensive physical and occupational therapy two times daily, five days a week. Anticipated length of stay was three months.

- Patient No. 2: Degenerative disk disease. Patient was receiving intensive physical and occupational therapy two times daily, five days a week. Anticipated length of stay was 10 weeks.

- Patient No. 3: Small bowel obstruction related to cancer of the colon. Patient was receiving intensive physical and occupational therapy two times daily, five days a week. Anticipated length of stay was seven weeks.

- Patient No. 4: Failed total hip replacement. Patient was receiving intensive physical and occupational therapy two times daily, five days a week. Patient had been in the facility for more than two months.

- Patient No. 5: Cancer of the spinal cord. Patient was a paraplegic referred by an acute rehabilitation hospital. Patient was receiving intensive physical, occupational, and speech therapy two times daily, five days a week. Anticipated length of stay was 10 weeks.

Overall spending on long-term care continues to grow. The breakdown of estimated long-term care expenditures for 1995 includes $36.8 billion in out-of-pocket expenses, $28.4 billion in federal funds, $17.8 billion in state and local funds, and $2.7 billion in insurance, for a total of $85.8 billion. For the year 2000, it will grow to $58.8 billion in out-of-pocket expenses, $41.4 billion from federal funds, $25.7 billion from state and local funds, and $4.8 billion from insurance, bringing the total to $131 billion. Figures are from the Health Care Financing Administration.

One of the biggest challenges facing the industry involves conflicting incentives from reimbursement systems such as Medicaid and Medicare. The purpose of this chapter is not to delve into the intricacies of those programs. But by anyone's measure, government programs are difficult to understand, and, complicating matters further, they are undergoing change. The point worth keeping in mind is that only the most sophisticated providers will be able to function successfully in this increasingly complex environment. Others will simply throw up their hands at some point and get out of the business. That makes a strong case for chain-affiliated centers with proper systems in place to handle the job efficiently.

Federal Medicaid currently covers 29.4 percent, state Medicaid 22.5 percent, Medicare 4.1 percent, private insurance 2.8 percent, other government entities 1.8 percent, and the consumer 39.5 percent. The price paid for long-term care varies geographically, which makes it important for companies to be well located and diversified. The price can run between $20,000 and $50,000 annually for private-pay patients, with ranges from $55 to $65 per day in states such as Texas, up to $120 to $150 per day in northeastern states such as New Jersey. Medicaid per diem rates range from about $50 per day in low reimbursement states such as Kansas to $125 per day in New York. The reimbursement for subacute services ranges from $300 to $550 and higher per day.

Adding services to long-term care facilities provides a variety of advantages, according to Alex Brown & Sons.

For example, pharmacy services provide higher revenues than traditional nursing facility services. It's also a way to contain costs, since services provided to a company's own facilities are basically incurred at cost. In addition, having a sophisticated pharmacy program is attractive to both doctors and managed care providers as they seek placement alternatives for higher-acuity patients likely to consume a greater number of pharmaceuticals and supplies.

Rehabilitation, which includes physical, speech, and occupational therapies, also adds revenue and profits to a long-term care facility's operations and improves cost control.

Knowing how to price services will be increasingly important in the future. Another likely change will be that a greater number of facilities will be offering rehabilitation therapies directly, rather than through contracted services or therapists.

That the long-term health care industry will see incredible growth in the 21st century is just as certain as the reality that all of us are aging. Americans expect the best possible health care, especially in their senior years, and this industry knows it must provide it in a cost-effective manner. For shareholders, that can mean a profitable investment as well.

Investment Close-Up: Health Care & Retirement Corporation
One SeaGate, Toledo, Ohio 43604
(419) 247-5600

Heath Care & Retirement operates long-term care centers, provides rehabilitative services, and develops new specialty medical services.

Chairman, president, and CEO: Paul Ormond
CFO, treasurer, and investor contact: Geoffrey Meyers
Total employees: 18,000

Stock: Traded on the New York Stock Exchange under the symbol "HCR." Price of $27 a share (5/16/95). No dividend. Price-to-earnings ratio of 20.

Sales and Earnings: Sales of $615 million in 1994, with earnings of $42 million. Five-year annual sales growth of 13 percent, with earnings growth of 34 percent.

Earnings per Share Growth: Five-year earnings per share annual growth rate of 40 percent. Projected (Institutional Brokers Estimate System) five-year earnings per share annual growth rate of 19 percent.

Data from Bridge Information Systems Inc.

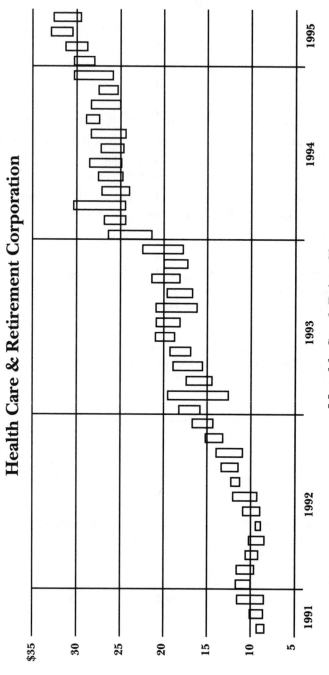

Health Care & Retirement Corporation

Monthly Stock Price Chart

Investment Close-Up: Genesis Health Ventures, Inc.

148 W. State Street, Kennett Square, Pennsylvania 19348

(215) 444-6350

Genesis Health Ventures provides basic and specialty health care services to the elderly through health care networks.

Chairman and CEO: Mike Walker

Investor contact: Cathy Adams

Total employees: 15,000

Stock: Traded on the New York Stock Exchange under the symbol "GHV." Price of $26⅛ a share (5/16/95). No dividend. Price-to-earnings ratio of 18.

Sales and Earnings: Sales of $389 million in 1994, with earnings of $17.7 million. Five-year annual sales growth of 25 percent, with earnings growth of 80 percent.

Earnings Per Share Growth: Five-year earnings per share annual growth rate of 11 percent. Projected (Institutional Brokers Estimate System) five-year earnings per share annual growth rate of 22 percent.

Data from Bridge Information Systems Inc.

Genesis Health Ventures, Inc.

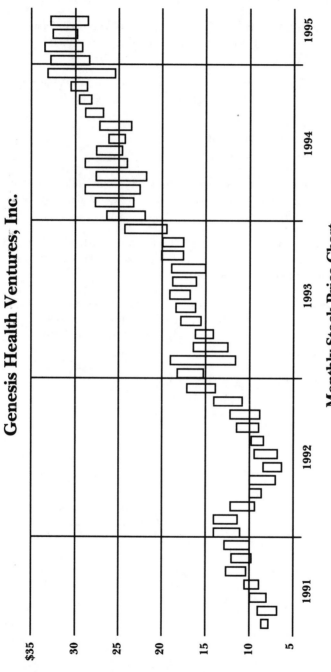

Monthly Stock Price Chart

Investment Close-Up: Living Centers of America Inc.
15415 Katy Freeway, Suite 800, Houston, Texas 77094
(713) 578-4600

Living Centers of America operates long-term health care facilities.

Chairman, president, and CEO: Edward Kuntz
Investor contact: Dorothy Wiley
Total employees: 17,800

Stock: Traded on the New York Stock Exchange under the symbol "LCA." Price of $28⅛ a share (5/16/95). No dividend. Price-to-earnings ratio of 15.

Sales and Earnings: Sales of $499 million in 1994, with earnings of $18.7 million. Five-year annual sales growth of 25 percent, with earnings growth of 44 percent.

Earnings per Share Growth: Five-year earnings per share annual growth rate of 15 percent. Projected (Institutional Brokers Estimate System) five-year earnings per share annual growth rate of 19 percent.

Data from Bridge Informations Systems Inc.

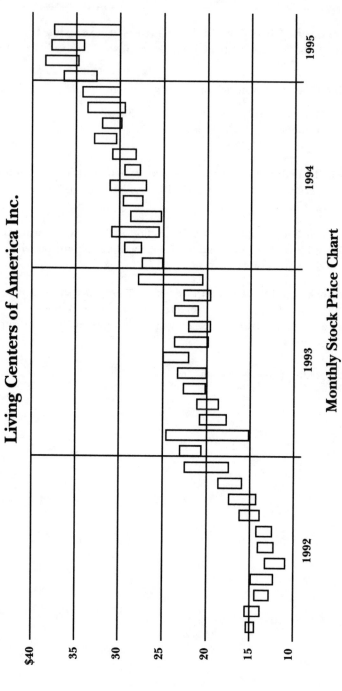

Living Centers of America Inc.

Monthly Stock Price Chart

$40
35
30
25
20
15
10

1992   1993   1994   1995

7

Motorola

The wide white hallway of Motorola Inc.'s world cellular group headquarters in Libertyville, Illinois, where four separate production lines make 100 different models of flip phones, leads directly to the 21st century.

The company isn't content with just its profitable cellular telephones, two-way radios, and pagers, which are succeeding around the world—making inroads even in the tough Japanese market. Pushing much further, it is part of an alliance to offer a nationwide digital cellular network. It also has an ambitious global satellite communications system in the works to make sure you can make and receive calls no matter where you are on this planet.

Motorola's reputation for quality and its image as a major beneficiary of the wireless revolution are propelling both its profits and its stock.

A blue "static-dissipating" smock and safety goggles must be donned before you enter the manufacturing area. There you encounter a computerized conveyer where 200 workers and state-of-the-art machines create and test world-class products of modern chip technology. The chips are first put on the PC board, with photographs taken and projected onto a computer screen to find the best point of "solderability." Numerous operators monitor machines while the board is gradually completed and tested. As assembly continues, workers add keypads, microphones, and speakers to the phone. There's a three-foot "drop test" of the receiver, as well as 120 different electrical tests.

After many other tests, such as placing the phone in cold and hot chambers, the two-hour assembly is finally complete. The small flip phone, so named because you flip it open to use it, is now ready. Motorola has designed, assembled, and shipped more cellular telephones than any other manufacturer. Both improvement and reduction in number of parts are goals with each successive model. For example, the MicroTAC Ultra Lite weighs 5.9 ounces, the first cellular phone to break the six-ounce weight barrier, and is 20 percent lighter than the previous model. It lets the owner choose between a silent vibrator alert or a conventional ringer, and new nickel metal hydride batteries provide extended talk times.

This exacting process hasn't gone unnoticed. Not only did Motorola win the U.S. government's first Malcolm Baldrige National Quality Award, but MicroTAC was awarded Japan's coveted Nikkei Award for creative excellence and Germany's Baden-Wurttemberg Design Prize. These phones will be shipped out promptly because they're a hot consumer item, with especially rapid sales growth in the Asia-Pacific and Latin American markets. Motorola makes products compatible with all major cellular system formats and sells them in more than 50 countries worldwide. Up to 80 percent of future phone demand in many markets will be for handhelds, and the number of cellular phones made by Motorola is expected to double by the year 2000. Gains in cellular orders of 50 percent or more have been common in recent quarters.

"We're well positioned for the 21st century because our semiconductor and wireless businesses will provide consistent growth on a global basis," said Gary Tooker, a 32-year veteran with Motorola who became vice chairman and chief executive in December 1993 after previous boss George Fisher left to run Eastman Kodak. "In addition, the fact that we put 10 percent of our money into research and development lets us invest in projects such as Iridium Inc. and create new products."

Because Motorola pioneered technological advances such as two-way radios, cellular telephones, and pagers, its name is known worldwide, Tooker noted. That gives it not only clout in expanding overseas sales but also confidence to try the new and daring.

The Iridium global satellite communications system puts Motorola into the futuristic realm. A worldwide satellite-based cellular phone system that Motorola believes has technological superiority, Iridium is based on 66 small low-flying satellites and earth stations interconnected with the public telephone network. It's designed to allow users to communicate anywhere in the world through a portable handset and is expected to be operational in 1998. In addition to voice services, Iridium telephones will be designed to transmit or receive wireless digital data and fax and paging signals, thereby bringing telecommunications capabilities to remote and unserved areas.

The project is already paying dividends. Partners and lenders through Iridium are funding a market opportunity for Motorola that rivals its present annual worldwide cellular phone sales. Investors in Iridium Inc., the new company that will establish the system, include telecommunications operators and industrial companies in the United States,

Canada, Venezuela, Italy, Saudi Arabia, Russia, Japan, China, and Thailand. For its initial equity commitment of about $270 million, Motorola has received contracts to deliver about $6 billion in products and services to Iridium over 10 years. Design, construction, and launch of the satellite network and ground control system are included, along with ongoing operation and maintenance.

The long-term viability of Iridium is not a sure thing, however, and some industry analysts caution that it remains to be seen if it can handle competition from conventional wired communications and less expensive satellite systems. That's a valid point. However, Motorola executives point out that two decades ago critics similarly scoffed at the $200 million it spent to develop the cellular phone business. Go back three decades and its ambitious move into semiconductors was also criticized.

Semiconductors now constitute about 28 percent of total Motorola sales of more than $22.2 billion, with its communications segment of two-way radios and pagers providing slightly less than that. General systems, which includes the fast-growing cellular phones and also computers, ranks first, followed by government electronics and information systems. Within Motorola's broad product lines are automotive and industrial electronics, defense and aerospace electronics, data communications, and information processing.

Renowned for visionary long-range planning, a tireless battle to get its products into Japan, where they now comprise 25 percent of that country's cellular market, and a corporate emphasis on quality, Motorola is a huge American company that has traveled to the beat of a different drummer. It is a company used as important leverage by the U.S. government in trade talks. President Clinton in discussions with the Japanese government in 1994 pointed out Motorola's success since the mid-1980s, when it was granted access to several outlying areas of Japan, but sharply criticized the Japanese for effectively shutting it out of the larger Tokyo cellular market. This argument apparently rang true, for Motorola and the Japanese company I.D.O. were able to make a significant deal in which I.D.O. will build cellular base stations that work with Motorola technology. Making Motorola a more viable competitor in Japan undoubtedly played a role in cooling tempers and headed off serious trade sanctions against Japan by the United States.

No one knows more about radio transmission than Motorola, and no one has a broader portfolio of semiconductors than Motorola.

Motorola's digital technology lets users send six times as much information over a channel that now carries one analog voice signal. Analog signals use electrical waves to duplicate the sound waves of the human voice, while digital signals use electronic bits designated as ones and zeroes to communicate in the same manner as computers. The goal of the proposed network is the ability to offer one telephone number to a consumer at which he or she can be reached no matter what the location on any day. Two-way paging services, voice mail, and other features would all be delivered in a small radio phone.

Motorola supplies the chip that drives Apple's Macintosh computers and makes the PowerPC, a new computer chip jointly developed by Apple and IBM that has been the subject of a multimillion-dollar advertising blitz in 1994. It's holding its market position as the fourth largest semiconductor manufacturer during this latest period of growth for the industry. Products like the MicroTAC phone and the Wrist Watch pager are filled with Motorola semiconductors, as are traffic lights, facsimile machines, and factory automation. If slowing demand for personal computers becomes a factor, it's less of a concern for Motorola than for others. Only 15 percent of its chip demand is for PCs.

A major player in the growing market for personal digital assistants, Motorola in 1994 introduced the $1,500 Envoy, a powerful pen-based PDA that provides two-way wireless data communications and an operating system that automatically finds and filters information even when the device is turned off. It is, in the opinion of some industry experts, the first PDA that actually does what its manufacturer says it would do. The Envoy squeezes most of its working parts onto two microchips. It weighs 1.7 pounds and is 7.5 inches wide, 5.7 inches high, and 1.2 inches thick, with a 3-by-4.5-inch touch-sensitive screen. Software links the user to both wireless and telephone networks, as well as on-line information services.

Two important products scheduled to debut in 1995, CableComm and VoiceNow, underscore Motorola's ability to innovate through partnerships. Motorola has joined with Hewlett-Packard to produce a new generation of set-top cable television converter boxes. This CableComm system will not only receive standard TV pictures, but computer data, telephone communications, video telephone signals, and interactive personal communications services. It's also teaming with Paging Network, Inc., the nation's largest paging company, to introduce the new VoiceNow personal communication service that features a palm-size portable wireless answering machine. In a bid to dominate the next generation of computer-chip manufacturing, Motorola has joined forces with AT&T, IBM, and Loral to develop a process that uses x-rays rather than ultraviolet light to create semiconductors more advanced, more powerful, and considerably smaller than those in use today.

"We've targeted 13 to 15 percent growth for Motorola in the future, which allows us to double every five years," said Tooker, who spent his first 25 years at the company in the semiconductor business. "But we could have growth rates higher than that, when you consider that two-thirds of the world's population is just now starting to get exposed to all of this."

Tooker's expectations are generally considered to be quite reasonable, with consistent mid- to high-teen percentage growth perhaps even more likely.

Worldwide, the United States recently represented 44 percent of Motorola sales, Europe 21 percent, the Asia-Pacific region 19 percent, Japan 7 percent, and the rest of the world 9 percent. As a nationwide zeal for American know-how to compete effectively internationally grows, the three-year-old Libertyville plant is much studied. Around election time, it's sometimes difficult to find room for all the politicians wanting to have their pictures taken here as they spout off about the future of U.S. industry.

"We're the American statement, with 85 percent of the cellular product worldwide made right here, as we take on 30 competitors and beat them," smiled Robert Weisshappel, senior vice president in charge of the operation, whose biggest competitors are Japanese and Scandinavian firms. "I actually see the Japanese doing these days what American companies used to always do when they were falling behind, that is, talk about new and improved products all the time and use it as a reason to raise prices, even though the new products may not be all that different from the old ones."

As advances are made in the new communications, at some point it will all become so commonplace that average folks will probably act as though it's always been here. "Making cellular more a part of the regular phone is the next step, leading to one day when there'll be a big channel in the home and people will simply feel that they have a phone that does more," said Weisshappel, a 24-year veteran of the company. With a day-care center currently handling 125 youngsters, dry cleaning, two convenience stores, and a first-rate cafeteria, the Libertyville facility is a model in other ways as well. And, whenever possible, workers are rotated into different positions so that they keep sharp in their work and avoid boredom.

Motorola says things that other companies might feel somewhat sheepish about saying, such as its frequently stated goal to be the finest corporation in the world, its motto of "total customer satisfaction," and talk of employee empowerment. Yet it doesn't just give lip service to these maxims, but rather injects them into an atmosphere that's often marked by conflict.

Open dissent is encouraged among managers and employees as the company actively seeks to detect flaws in any of its logic, goals, or products. The filing of a "minority report" by those who disagree with the way things are being done or have original ideas is an accepted part of the process. It's a demanding work atmosphere, to say the least, but innovative, dependable products are the result. For example, the concept that became Iridium was initially rejected by division managers, but the researcher who originated it was later able to present it as a minority report. Top management went for the idea in a big way, and Iridium will soon be a reality. Of course, Motorola is also quite happy to get as much public relations mileage out of its quality image as possible, mentioning all of its awards and programs prominently in literature for customers, the public, the media, or employees. Pride and self-confidence are big parts of the Motorola corporate persona.

Founded by entrepreneur Paul V. Galvin as the Galvin Manufacturing Corp. in Chicago with five employees in 1928, it led its first initiative into the fledgling automobile radio market—another concept that many people thought was downright frivolous—under the brand name *Motorola,* a new word that suggested sound in motion. Its two-way radio "Handie-Talkie" business in World War II was a big success. Galvin had authorized the development of that portable military radio without a government contract after he toured Europe in the mid-1930s and decided that war was imminent. The firm's name was changed to Motorola Inc. in 1947, and the brand-new semiconductor business was the next emphasis in 1949. After the elder Galvin's death, his son Robert Galvin provided leadership as the company expanded into international markets in the 1960s. It phased out of consumer electronics, selling its Quasar color television business to Matsushita Electrical Industrial Co. of Japan in the mid-1970s, to focus on microchips and wireless devices. But it came back to woo consumers in a big way as a major supplier of cellular telephones and pagers in the 1980s.

The emphasis upon quality was spawned at a 1979 Motorola corporate officers meeting in downtown Chicago, when Arthur Sundry, then the manager of the company's two-way radio operations, spoke up at this largely upbeat, social session with the comment: "I think our quality stinks. Some of our competitors are much better, and we ought to do something about it."

That stunning comment marked a critical juncture for company management, which took the comment to heart and set about installing the type of world-class quality control that the Japanese were already using to dominate numerous businesses. If only other American companies had caught this same passion for getting the job done right! The company now estimates that it saves more than $2 billion annually from quality programs that emphasize teamwork. Several programs are noteworthy.

What's known as the Six Sigma initiative was begun in early 1987. Six Sigma is a statistical term for 99.99966 percent perfection, which translates to a defect rate of 3.4 parts per million in each step of a process. The company committed to a quality goal of 10× improvement in number of defects by 1989; 100× improvement by 1991; and Six Sigma capability by 1992. Under the program, managers learned to break down their manufacturing operations to find the basic causes of mistakes, and engineers altered product design to permit more variation in the size of parts and more leeway in the manufacturing process. For the most part, the 1989 and 1991 goals were met, although the 40 defects per million logged in 1992 did fall short of the bold Six Sigma goal. However, the program has resulted in significant improvements in quality of products and services. The current range of 20 to 30 defects per million shows further progress. The company now has a goal of a 10× reduction in defects every two years. Pushing toward Six Sigma—and perhaps one day even advancing beyond it—continues.

The company also requires that each of its businesses develop a customer satisfaction index, carefully based on the desires of the particular types of customers they deal with, and then set aggressive improvement goals.

Motorola University, which is what the company's training and education institution is now called, began in 1980 as a five-year plan with a $35 million budget. More than a few executives questioned the concept at that time, but it has proven to be more than worth the effort since its opening in 1986. The program has included management education as well as training in sales and marketing, manufacturing, and technology. The goal is five days of training for each Motorola employee. For example, it provides a training program with a typical Motorola title of "Envisioning, Energizing, and Enabling" in its management institute to stimulate those in middle management.

The annual Motorola total customer satisfaction team competition, sort of an Olympics dedicated to quality, efficiency, and cost savings, is a worldwide corporate event in which the firm's top managers act as judges of the finalists. Twenty-four final teams from Europe, Asia, and North America are the survivors of a year-long process. They're brought together to make presentations about why their ability to solve an important corporate problem in their area was noteworthy. These can run the gamut from developing a new computer chip to streamlining an order process to improving the efficiency of boiler operations. The competition is followed by an awards banquet at which gold and silver medals are given out.

The planet is getting smaller. At the main Motorola corporate campus in Schaumburg, Illinois, Keith Bane, chief corporate staff officer, pointed to a map of the world as he noted the amazing economic potential of China for paging and cellular products. He considers the $1 billion in revenues the company derived from China in 1993 to be the "tip of the iceberg" for this nation with 22 percent of the world's population.

In the spring of 1994, Motorola landed the first cellular telephone contract to be awarded by one of the former Soviet States—a $33 million system in Kazakhstan. Large cellular contracts in Jordan and Mexico have followed. "I can certainly envision Motorola at some point having multiple headquarters around the world, with vice chairmen in various locations," said Bane. "Our aggressive view of globalization means that the 56 percent of our business that's outside the United States today will grow to 75 percent by the year 2000."

If Motorola can blanket the wireless media here, it can similarly blanket a foreign country, he reasons. Motorola has always had a knack for making the "right" moves, such as getting out of the color television business and emphasizing high tech. However, the biggest concern in some circles is that widely praised Motorola could fall prey to "IBM disease," that is, so believing its positive clippings and corporate philosophy that it considers itself invincible and incapable of error. Such an attitude always spells trouble.

"It's true that any company can get complacent, and everything is cyclical," said Bane, vividly recalling some significant semiconductor downturns of past years. "However, our fundamentals are that we don't run on a maximum annual profit basis and aren't a dividend stock, but instead actively spend money to develop new products and enter new markets."

Motorola management in its letter to shareholders in a recent annual report outlined the following basic elements of its long-term corporate strategy:

- Quality improvement to achieve total customer satisfaction and market leadership through the empowerment of our people.
- Cycle time reduction, both in customer service and product development, to reduce costs and lead new markets, as well as serving customers with products that help them manage time and become more productive.
- Technology leadership, leveraging strength in software, manufacturing, microelectronics, and radio communications.
- Investment in the future, in training, in research and development, in production tools and facilities, and in technology.
- Partnerships, with other companies, with customers, and within Motorola, to leverage available resources and enter exciting growth markets while making efficient use of our financial resources.

That sums up the personality and strength of this company poised to continue its success into the 21st century. Expectations are extremely high, and progress will be closely watched. There was some surprise and consternation at the company when high-visibility chairman George Fisher bolted to join Eastman Kodak in late 1993. However, few companies have so strong a management team, philosophy, and goals as Motorola. In addition, no others are so well positioned with products in global demand.

Investment Close-Up: Motorola Inc.

1303 E. Algonquin Road, Schaumburg, Illinois 60196
(708) 576-5000

Motorola is a leading worldwide supplier of wireless communications, semiconductors, and advanced electronic systems and services.

Chairman: William Weisz
Vice Chairman and CEO: Gary Tooker
Investor contact: Tom Schultz
Total employees: 132,000

Stock: Traded on the New York Stock Exchange under the symbol "MOT." Price of $61 a share (5/16/95). Dividend of 40 cents a share, which has grown at a 15 percent annual rate over the past five years. Price-to-earnings ratio of 22.

Sales and Earnings: Sales of $22.2 billion in 1994, with earnings of $1.56 billion. Five-year annual sales growth rate of 19 percent, with earnings growth of 3 percent.

Earnings per Share Growth: Five-year earnings per share annual growth of 25 percent. Projected (Institutional Brokers Estimate System) five-year earnings per share annual growth rate of 19 percent.

Data from Bridge Information Systems Inc.

Motorola Inc.

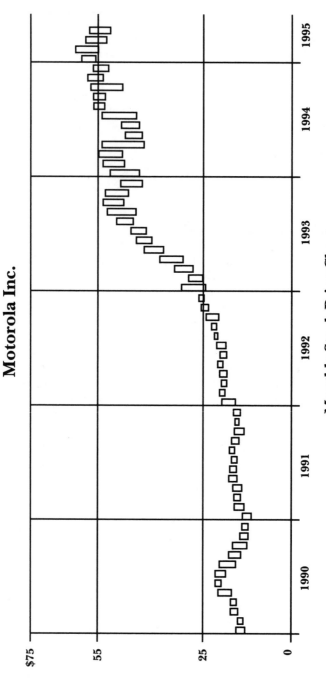

Monthly Stock Price Chart

8

Variable Annuities

Mention retirement to many Americans and they get very nervous.

Fewer people have real confidence about the long-term viability of Social Security, their pensions, or their jobs. Longer lifespans of modern Americans also means savings and retirement income must stretch a long time through different economic periods. In addition, the fact that many couples have waited longer before having children means educational expenses are coming later in life and bumping into retirement plans.

They do know that something has to be done. It will be necessary to pilot your own retirement investments in order to succeed in the future, and that means avoiding the tax bite and putting money in growth vehicles. Some instruments are well suited to do both.

Variable annuities are a hot investment that now totals more than $175 billion in assets, growing at a 17 percent annual clip that should accelerate in the next century. Whenever Congress turns to raising taxes, American investors turn to variable annuities. The Tax Reform Act of 1986 that eliminated so many tax-saving opportunities provided the initial stimulus, and further reform in 1993 that boosted the top marginal tax rate gave yet another big push. It hardly comes as a surprise that most experts believe tax boosts are likely in the future as well.

A variable annuity is a product offered by insurance companies, brokerage firms, and banks that permits you to invest in a wide range of mutual funds and defer accumulated earnings until you begin to withdraw your money. That's likely to be when you're retired and in a lower tax bracket.

It is an opportunity to invest your money with some of the investment world's most successful mutual fund families. The number of variable annuity mutual funds grew by 21 percent to 936 in 1994, indication that investors demand choice in their long-term goals. Twenty percent of all stock funds sold by brokers and insurance agents these days are in variable annuities.

In terms of performance, the variable annuities of Phoenix Home Mutual Insurance, Fidelity Investments Life Insurance Co., and Aetna Life Insurance and Annuity Co. offer a wide range of investment choices that include some subaccounts ranking among the very best.

Because you can direct your assets among variable annuity portfolios, your return varies depending on how those you select perform. The size of your account at retirement similarly depends on your investment acumen. That makes variable annuities different from traditional fixed annuities, in which your account grows at a fixed rate of interest until you begin to withdraw your money. In addition, unlike fixed annuities, variable annuity subaccounts are legally separate from the insurance company's general accounts, and your funds therefore won't be lost or frozen if the company fails.

All annuities are basically contracts with an insurance company. In return for paying a lump-sum premium today or making several subsequent premium payments, you'll receive a stream of payments from the company in the future. There's also a death benefit that protects against investment loss at the time of death. Over time, a well-managed variable annuity should handily outperform a fixed annuity. Selection of a variable annuity involves the selection of a subaccount with a proven track record and good prospects for the future. The annuity owner follows the accumulation unit value (A.U.V.), which is calculated by measuring the change in value of the investment, adding the portfolio's income and realized capital gains, and subtracting the management and insurance expenses. It's similar to the net asset value of a mutual fund.

If you can't stomach the vagaries of the stock market, don't choose a variable annuity. The conservative investor who just cashed out of a certificate of deposit may not be ready to add to his or her risk tolerance. The fixed accounts within variable annuities that offer a guaranteed rate for one to three years won't make sense either, since their average rate lately has been only around 4.5 percent. You'll still have to face the drain from the average annual insurance expense of 1.25 percent, plus annual fund expenses, which can bring total costs to around 2 percent a year. Those insurance expenses pay for the guaranteed death benefit, ensuring that if you die during the annuity's accumulation years, the value of the annuity to your beneficiary will be at least as much as you put into it. In addition, variable annuities have annual contract charges of $25 to $30.

When investing in an annuity, be sure you can afford to leave your money in until age 59½, because early withdrawals can be expensive. The Internal Revenue Service exacts taxes and a 10 percent penalty on the accumulated earnings. There's generally also a surrender charge if you cancel your annuity within a certain period of time, that charge typically starting at 8 percent and declining each year until it disappears.

Due to all the costs involved, it's best to be in at least the 28 percent bracket in order for variable annuities to be worthwhile. They're for investors with a substantial sum (at least $25,000) on hand, who intend to stick with the annuity for at least 15 years. Investing in a stock subaccount makes the most sense because it should provide enough growth to cover fees and still return a significant profit. Of course, going with an annuity product whose value can fluctuate is much different from the past. Economic circumstances are different as well.

"Today's consumer is looking at a period of low rates and an environment in which people feel they can depend less on Social Security and have less job security," said Robert Fiondella, chairman and chief executive of Phoenix Home Mutual Insurance Co., Hartford, Connecticut. "They also realize the historical return on equities is 4 percent higher than fixed-rate choices, so as they increasingly focus on returns, the variable annuity looks good."

The Phoenix Home Life Big Edge Plus Growth subaccount has a three-year average return of 14 percent. It offers balanced, bond, international, money market, total return, and guaranteed interest portfolios. The Big Edge permits unlimited free transfers between its investment options as your needs and objectives change. When you consider a variable annuity, look at who's managing the money and their experience over a long period of time, said Fiondella. Expect to do well in down markets and participate in up markets, for growth investing has never lost money over the long run.

From Fidelity Investments Life Insurance Co., Boston, the Fidelity Retirement Reserves variable annuities offering the Fidelity Asset Manager and Fidelity Growth portfolios have three-year returns of 10 percent and 12 percent, respectively. Other choices include the Fidelity Equity Income, High Income, Index 500, Investment Grade Bond, Overseas, Contrafund, Asset Manager Growth, and money market portfolios. Many new annuity investors in the Fidelity product already have money with this mutual fund giant in other accounts. The annuity portfolios "clone" the larger funds available to general investors. You are limited annually to 18 separate telephone switches, each with a minimum of $250. After that point, switch requests must be made in writing.

A variable annuity is just a part of a complete plan for your retirement. Look into choices that offer the greatest tax advantages.

"Our philosophy would be to maximize contributions to your company 401(k) plan and your individual retirement account first, but, over and above that, focus on variable annuities," said Richard Jameison, president of Fidelity Investments Life Insurance. "The deferral aspect is obviously an advantage, though keep in mind that it's not a tax dodge, for eventually you'll be taxed on it."

The 401(k) and the IRA both require that you start withdrawing money by age 70½, while annuities will usually permit you to delay withdrawals until age 85. Both of the others also have maximum contributions, while annuities have no cap on how much you can put away. In addition, the 401(k) from your employer may not have the variety of investments available in an annuity.

Variable annuities these days range from those with a few subaccount choices to those with a wide spectrum of selections. More and more Americans are coming around to the concept of variable returns for their retirement investments. In the past 25 years the whole concept of annuities has changed from lifetime guarantee to that of an accumulation product, Jameison noted. Because of the surrender charge, he advises that a variable annuity investment must be long-term money. Make sure you know what you're buying, and definitely don't use the money to fund a kid's education or as an emergency fund.

Aetna Life Insurance and Annuity Co., Hartford, Connecticut, whose Account B Variable Fund emphasizes growth and income, has turned in a three-year average annual return of 6 percent. It hasn't had a negative return in 10 years. Other selections it offers are Aetna's Income Shares, Investment Advisers Fund, and money market funds, as well as additional portfolios from the Neuberger & Berman, Scudder, Twentieth Century, and Alger fund families. A dozen transfers of $500 or more are permitted annually. After that, there's a $10 fee for each additional transfer.

"The variable annuity is growing in popularity because it's an ideal packaged retirement product with investment options, the ability to make regular deposits, and an 800 number in the case of most companies," said Thomas West, former senior vice president of Aetna Life. "Our buyers vary considerably, with the bank CD rollover buyer usually 50 and older and more conservative, while the customer going through a broker is in his or her 40s and much more receptive to equities."

Not only do the profiles of investors vary, so do the amounts put into these products. Older investors may bring lump sums transferred from other investments, while younger investors add gradually to their holdings, West has found. A lump sum contribution from an older investor averages about $38,000 at Aetna, with $25,000 being the lower end and one in 10 contributions being more than $100,000.

Always shop around for a variable annuity and get literature from several, as well as total return figures for one and three years after all fund and insurance expenses have been deducted. There are some other excellent choices based upon number of funds offered and quality of performance.

The Best of America IV/Nationwide variable annuities from Nationwide Life Insurance Co., Columbus, Ohio, have provided good returns using portfolios run by outside managers. One subaccount holding the Fidelity Growth portfolio has a three-year average return of 12 percent, while one investing in the balanced Fidelity Asset Manager has a three-year annual return of 10 percent. Among many other choices are funds from the Dreyfus, Neuberger & Berman, Oppenheimer, and Van Eck groups. There's an unlimited ability to transfer among variable investments at no charge.

Meanwhile, the Franklin Valuemark III variable annuities from Allianz Life Insurance Co. of North America, Berwyn, Pennsylvania, offers an Income Securities balanced portfolio with a three-year return of 12 percent. Among other portfolio choices are adjustable U.S. government securities, equity growth, global income, high income, international equity, precious metals, real estate securities, utility equity, money market, and zero-coupon bonds. Twelve transfers among funds of $1,000 or more each are permitted. After that, the fee is $25 or 2 percent of the transferred amount, whichever is less.

Remember that, even if the very same mutual fund is involved, the costs associated with the variable annuity will differ because the sponsoring insurance firms differ in their charges. For example, according to the Morningstar Mutual Funds investment advisory, the cheapest way to buy Fidelity funds is straight from Fidelity itself for its 1 percent annual contract charge, rather than the slightly higher amount charged elsewhere. Some of the other mutual fund families selling variable annuities include Scudder Horizon Plan and Vanguard Variable Annuity Plan. Since they're sold directly to buyers, rather than through brokers, their costs are lower. The average insurance expense for variable annuities is 1.27

percent annually, according to Morningstar. However, Scudder Horizon costs 0.63 percent, and the Vanguard Variable Annuity Plan costs just 0.55 percent. Vanguard and Scudder also have unusually low fund expenses and no surrender charges.

Annuities can definitely maximize the income you'll receive at retirement. Consider the hypothetical case of a 50-year-old individual in the 33 percent tax bracket who puts $25,000 into a taxable investment and into a tax-deferred annuity. Both investments earn an 8 percent rate of return, and withdrawals are delayed until age 70. The taxable investment with systematic withdrawals from age 70 to age 90 would be $476 a month for 20 years. The annuity starting at age 70 would pay $655 a month for life.

Selecting stocks over fixed returns can also make a significant difference. Fidelity offers what it calls the "Tale of Two Brothers" to dramatize that point.

In its hypothetical case, twin brothers turned 65 and retired on January 1, 1974, when Richard Nixon was president and interest rates were at a historic high. Charles, the conservative brother, bought a $50,000 annuity and was guaranteed $375 each month for the rest of his life. Robert, the more aggressive brother, put his money into a self-directed annuity and selected a Standard & Poor's 500–based stock portfolio. His first check was $330, $45 less than Charles received. That year the stock market tumbled 25 percent and Robert received a check of $236, a decrease of more than 28 percent.

At a family reunion five years after their initial investment, Charles was still receiving his $375 a month and Robert's monthly income was $304. In 1984, the two brothers celebrated their 75th birthdays together. Charles was still receiving his $375 per month, although he did admit to Robert that the money just didn't go as far as it used to go. Charles was surprised to hear that Robert's checks were up to $497. After the stock market crash in 1987, Charles was sure his brother's income investments would go down. They did go down. But while he received just $695 in November of 1987, that was still $320 more than his brother.

Take time to figure out what you believe your retirement would really require. Find out the value of your employer pension plan, your retirement benefits, and your Social Security status. Inflation, the rates of return expected, and a realistic expense budget are crucial considerations. Eighty percent of your last high year of income will probably be necessary in order to maintain the same lifestyle. Remember that your needs won't be static in retirement. Greater leisure time often results in more travel and entertainment spending, and you likely won't have the same car for 25 years of retirement. Housing and food costs are important. Assume the worst and hope for the best in your planning. We all know stories of individuals who didn't put enough money aside when they were younger and therefore had to live as paupers in their final years or depend entirely on the financial generosity of their children. It's a position no one wants to wind up in.

There are other considerations about variable annuities, such as a number of options available to you in deciding how you want your variable annuity's income and principal paid back to you. Here are examples:

• The lifetime income option doesn't stop payouts to you no matter how old you live to be. However, if you die immediately after you select this choice, your heirs don't receive a refund of any of the money you paid into the policy. The insurance company is betting, based on actuarial tables, that you won't live as long as you think you will.

• Lifetime income with a minimum number of payments guaranteed is an option that will ensure a payout for as long as you live. However, if you die before a set time period, the income payments will continue to be paid to your designated beneficiary until the end of the fixed period.

- Joint and survivor income, which gives you and your annuity income partner income for the rest of your lives. Upon the death of either person, the income continues for the survivor as a percentage of the original amount.

- Joint and survivor income with a guarantee period, which is like joint and survivor except that if you and your partner die before a specific number of payments, your beneficiary will receive income for the balance of the guarantee period.

All of this is somewhat complicated, but your long-term financial future and retirement are worth taking the time to comparison shop and run all the numbers. Variable annuities are costly and should be entered into only as a long-term investment. Many critics say a shrewd investor could do better investing outside of these tax-deferred vehicles using tax-exempt choices and aggressive growth vehicles. That, however, requires some discipline and perhaps even greater investment savvy. The variable annuity provides a strong component in a comprehensive retirement plan that also includes 401(k) plans, IRAs, and conventional investments.

The variable annuity's popularity will grow stronger in the 21st century as more members of the baby boom generation become older and get serious about their retirement. The number of portfolios available will also become much more impressive. Learn about this product now so you can make intelligent choices later, rather than waiting too long to commit your dollars or responding to a sales pitch without full comprehension of what you're doing. Someday in the coming century you'll thank yourself.

Investment Close-Up: Top Variable Annuities

"Big Edge Plus"
Phoenix Home Life Mutual Insurance Company
100 Bright Meadow Boulevard, Enfield, Connecticut 06083
(800) 447-4312

Its $471-million-asset Phoenix Big Edge Plus Growth subaccount had a three-year average annual return of 10.72 percent (through 3/95) and five-year average annual return of 15.04 percent.

"Fidelity Retirement Reserves"
Fidelity Investments Life Insurance Company
82 Devonshire Street, Boston, Massachusetts 02109
(800) 634-9361

Its $997-million-asset Fidelity Asset Manager subaccount had a three-year average annual return of 7.02 percent (through 3/95) and five-year average annual return of 10.19 percent.

Its $438-million-asset Fidelity Growth subaccount had a three-year average annual return of 9.65 percent and five-year average annual return of 11.88 percent.

"Aetna Variable Annuity"
Aetna Life Insurance and Annuity Company
151 Farmington Avenue, Hartford, Connecticut 06156
(800) 262-3862

Its $73.2-million-asset Aetna B Variable Annuity emphasizing growth and income had a three-year average annual return of 5.54 percent (through 3/95), a five-year average annual return of 8.38 percent, and a 10-year average annual return of 12.54 percent.

"Best of America IV/Nationwide"
Nationwide Life Insurance Company
One Nationwide Plaza, Columbus, Ohio 43216
(800) 243-6295

Its offerings include the strong-performing Fidelity Asset Manager and Fidelity Growth subaccounts also offered by Fidelity Retirement Reserves.

"Franklin Valuemark"
Allianz Life Insurance Company of North America
10 Valley Stream Parkway, Berwyn, Pennsylvania 19355
(800) 342-3863

Its $1-billion-asset Income Securities balanced portfolio
subaccount had a three-year average annual return of 5.93 percent
(through 3/95).

Data from Morningstar Inc.

9

Pfizer

The 50-foot-long display windows of the giant pharmaceutical company's headquarters on midtown New York's 42nd Street extol the virtues of "Pfizer: Bringing Science to Life."

One large expanse of window traces the creation of new medicines from the research stage through Food and Drug Administration approval, then on to general availability. Another explains the history of the company since its founding in 1849 by Charles Pfizer and Charles Erhart, German immigrant cousins.

In the hospital product window is a display that includes an artificial hip and knee that move. (Pfizer made the artificial hip replacement of professional baseball player Bo Jackson, though it doesn't publicize the fact, since rough-and-tumble Bo obviously doesn't use it as generally recommended by the company.)

Inside the black-and-steel headquarters building, the

lobby features a modern mural and mosaic depicting test tubes and other assorted research instruments.

Such history and imagery give a different spin to a $75 billion drug industry that's lately been represented as one of the villains of corporate America. Overpriced pharmaceuticals, enormous profits, and bloated sales forces have been the public perception. Perhaps one day another window or mural may depict the late-20th-century health care move toward a managed care system in response to the outcry for lower-priced drugs and services.

Pfizer, an enormous $8 billion-in-sales company with nearly half its sales and profits outside the United States, is a research-oriented company that's in the picture for the 21st century. Getting its act together after some lackluster years in the 1980s, it has moved from a return on capital lower than industry rivals to one that leads the pack. Not only is it expected to survive the changing health care environment undamaged, but there could be pluses. There may be a shakeout of weaker rivals, and a move toward universal prescription coverage could increase demand and sales.

"We have an aging, wealthier population with high expectations for quality of life and health care, and this is occurring during a whole new golden age of drug discovery," explained Henry McKinnell, Ph.D., executive vice president and chief financial officer of Pfizer Inc. and president of its hospital products group. "But these will also be turbulent times, and the successful companies will be those with research capability and short-term financial capability."

Health care spending in the United States will reach $1 trillion for the first time in 1994, representing a record 15 percent of the nation's gross domestic product. Expensive medical advances and a longer life span for most Americans are some reasons for higher expenditures. But change is under way, with 35,000 pharmaceutical industry jobs eliminated in a recent 15-month stretch. In addition, the number of individuals enrolled in health maintenance organizations over the past five years has risen from 29 million to more than 41 million. Prices increasingly are being set by cost-conscious large-scale buying cooperatives such as HMOs, a trend likely to accelerate under the prospects of managed care.

Pfizer has a portfolio of products "second to none" that can contribute to lowering the overall cost of health care, McKinnell believes. His logic is that drug costs make up only 6 to 7 percent of overall health care costs, and, most important of all, they also help keep people out of hospitals. The period in which companies sold drugs to physicians solely on the basis of their efficacy and safety are over. The cost of prescription drugs, after all, had increased at six times the rate of inflation between 1980 and 1992, with some widely used drugs increasing by 100 to 150 percent in that period. The double-digit growth of drug prices nationwide in the late 1980s has now slowed to 3 percent or less. Another period in which the $75 billion pharmaceutical industry "overearns" just isn't going to happen again.

Still, Pfizer doesn't believe sales and marketing should be drastically reduced even in this environment of change.

"Some think that if you're going to be selling to large managed care organizations, you don't need to visit physicians anymore, but this overlooks the fact that it's the physicians that have to use the drugs," said McKinnell, who emphasized that, without a doubt, pharmaceuticals will continue to be the company's major profit center in the coming century. "If you have an array of new products, you must visit both the managed care organizations and the physicians, so we see increased need for a sales force."

Selling the financial savings of a product requires more skill than simply selling a product, so a coordinated and sophisticated sales force with laptop computers is already in place. "It takes $350 million and eight years to develop a new drug these days, and for every new drug, another 20 don't make it through," he said, pointing out that alliances between companies to cure certain diseases will become common. "This is an innovative business that's subject to product cycles and always has risk, for all it takes is one dead rat and you've lost a major project."

Pfizer's commitment to research and development is so strong that it spent more than $1.5 billion on it in 1994. It has doubled the number of research scientists on board since the early 1980s. The company boasts the most impressive pipeline of new products in its history, with half of its earnings coming from products introduced since 1990. Industry analysts expect that strong current earnings growth in the high teens will likely settle into the mid-teens or slightly lower for the long haul.

Among the standout drugs fueling its growth and profitability are:

- Procardia XL, the leading cardiovascular drug in this country, the third largest selling pharmaceutical of any kind in this country and Pfizer's first billion-dollar product. This calcium channel blocker for treatment of angina and hypertension, with which one daily dose provides essentially even 24-hour blood levels with few side effects, is available only through Pfizer in this country. Many industry experts had expected that Pfizer would be in deep trouble when its original heart drug, Procardia, went off patent in 1991, but a strong campaign was launched to switch users to the newly approved Procardia XL. The difference is a handy single daily dose rather than Procardia's four-times-a-day dosage.

- Diflucan, discovered by company researchers, is the leading systemic antifungal worldwide. Sales and market share continue to grow as a result of a continued increase in the number of people treated for fungal infections. People with suppressed immune systems, such as those with AIDS, cancer patients undergoing chemotherapy, organ transplant patients, and burn victims are susceptible to life-threatening fungal infections. Before this product was introduced, the only drugs available often caused severe side effects and usually had to be administered intravenously. Diflucan's side effects are modest, and it's available in both oral and intravenous forms. This simplifies treatment and often reduces total cost. Safety and ease of use has led to rapid growth in its selection for less severe fungal infections.

- Zithromax is the first of a new class of antibiotics that targets delivery directly to the site of infection. It achieves high and sustained tissue levels and is carried by white blood cells to the site of the infection, providing a high concentration of the drug where it is needed most. A shorter dosage regimen is the result. A broad range of respiratory tract and skin infections that formerly required several daily doses of treatment for 7 to 14 days can now be treated effectively just once a day for 5 days. Chlamydia, a common sexually transmitted disease, can generally be cured by a single dose.

- Zoloft, a new-generation antidepressant, provides relief from depression with few of the side effects of earlier classes of such drugs. Its percentage of the antidepressant drug market continues to grow. This new class of selective serotonin reuptake inhibitors is effective in treating the debilitating symptoms of depression and is much less likely to cause cardiovascular and other side effects.

- Norvasc, a new one-a-day calcium channel blocker for treatment of angina and hypertension. It is the leading calcium channel blocker in a number of countries in which it was introduced in the early 1990s. The drug has a smooth onset of action and mild side effects. In clinical studies, Norvasc has been safely administered to patients with mild to moderate congestive heart failure, unlike most calcium channel blockers.

- Cardura, an alpha blocker for the treatment of hypertension. Alpha blockers are now included by the Joint National Committee on Detection, Evaluation and Treatment of High Blood Pressure as first-line therapy for hypertension. The FDA approved the use of Cardura in benign prostatic hypertrophy, which can otherwise require expensive surgery.

How hot are Pfizer's newest products? In a recent quarter, the four drugs Zithromax, Zoloft, Norvasc, and Cardura generated an aggregate sales increase of 71 percent.

The company has also gone to the FDA for approval of another possible billion-dollar product called Tenidap, an antiarthritis drug that may drive that disease into remission. What's most important to the long-term future is the replenishing of this impressive product mix. In the modern health care environment, it's becoming clear which companies have new products and which have simply relied on their marketing and sales efforts to carry them through. Some companies that didn't have a strong future stream of drugs are now part of consolidated companies, among them SmithKline Beecham, Marion Merrell Dow, Rhone-Poulenc Rorer, and Bristol-Myers Squib. While such mergers end some duplication of efforts, particularly in marketing, even with greater size they won't be successful without popular new drugs. At the same time, smaller firms are not necessarily more adept at finding breakthroughs, for financial strength is becoming increasingly important in research.

Pfizer management anticipates a short-term climate in which weaker pharmaceutical companies merge to end duplication and improve efficiency, but, further along, increased mergers of large successful drug companies will occur as well. At the same time, some biotechnology firms are near meltdown stage because they have little cash left and are finding it increasingly difficult to obtain funding.

William Steere Jr., chairman and chief executive of Pfizer, in his presentation "Pfizer 2000: The Vision of Our Future," gave this vision of his company's future:

"We at Pfizer are absolutely committed to succeeding and truly prospering in the fiercely competitive environment in which we're going to have to operate. Our vision for the future is a simple but powerful one: to remain a research-based, diversified health care company operating globally; to become a company whose culture of enterprise fosters competitiveness, productivity, and continuous improvement; and to realize our destiny—a permanent place in the very top tier of health care companies worldwide."

As president of the Pharmaceutical Manufacturers Association during reform discussions in Washington, the intense, deliberate Steere has been the key spokesman for the industry. In a side issue, he had to defend Pfizer's 1993 net income report against accusations that he's been spending heavily and delaying sales in order to deliberately dampen its profit growth and thereby take heat off the drug industry at a time of scrutiny by Washington. In addition, the company's reported 15 percent gain from continuing operations for 1993 was poorly received by analysts who had expected a more impressive 24 percent rise in earnings. Steere responded that Pfizer is feeling considerable heat from the move toward cost containment, having had to cut 1,000 jobs since 1992, trim 3,000 more in the next three to five years, and write off some assets. Such moves cost it more than $750 million in charges to earnings in 1993 but are expected to result in an annual cost savings of about $130 million. The company claims it simply didn't want to delay the inevitable.

Coming to Pfizer as a salesman after his graduation from Stanford University in 1959, Steere held nearly every marketing job, in addition to roles in product management and strategic planning. The recordbreaking Procardia XL launch in 1990 was one of his finest hours. The trim, athletic Steere is a fitness buff whose desire for leanness extends to his company. When he became top executive in 1992, he immediately sold off noncore business Coty Cosmetics and Pfizer's specialty minerals and chemicals operations because he believed they didn't fit his focus for the company's future.

Steere's basic blueprint for long-term Pfizer success is as follows:

- Maximizing sales and profits of innovative, timely, cost-effective products that can generate sales and profits needed to support future research and development projects.

- Continually increasing the productivity of the research process from the idea to the lab, the clinical development stage, the regulatory review stage, and, ultimately, the approval stage.

- Anticipating changing dynamics and trends, such as purchase and payment for drugs by concentrated, powerful entities such as government health authorities, hospitals, and managed care organizations with continually increasing demands for discounts and services. There will also be a growing demand for cost/benefit analysis of competing therapies to find which products work best and at what comparative cost.

- Keeping the business properly focused, properly structured, and productive so it can deliver maximum value to customers and shareholders. That means increasing productivity and profitability of the pharmaceutical business, as well as hospital products, consumer health care, food science, and animal health.

Well positioned for the 21st century, Pfizer is a company with its origins in the mid-19th century. Its long corporate history began in 1849 when founders Pfizer and Erhart, whose photographs are featured in the headquarters window, set up a small fine chemicals factory in Brooklyn. "Pfizer Quality" was the corporate motto, which by 1915 was cut into steel dies and pressed into the wax that sealed the bottles of its products. The earliest medicinal products included santonin, a preparation used to combat parasitic worms. By the turn of the century, Pfizer's main product was citric acid, used to flavor foods, soft drinks, and medicines. In the 1940s, Pfizer introduced mass production of penicillin. Ninety percent of the penicillin that went ashore with the Allied forces on the beaches of Normandy in June 1944 was produced by the company.

Then, in the late 1940s, Pfizer isolated a new antibiotic known as oxytetracycline, effective against a range of bacteria that caused more than 100 diseases. The resulting product, named Terramycin, was one of the firm's most important, its tremendous commercial demand leading Pfizer into international markets. The antidiabetes medication Diabinese, launched in 1958, for decades was the leading therapy in its field. Pfizer was also active in development and distribution of the Salk and Sabin vaccines that eliminated the threat of polio in the 1950s and early 1960s. In August 1961, it was first to receive approval to market the more convenient Sabin oral vaccine. Developed in the company's research labs in the 1960s were the diuretic Renese, the antibiotic Vibramycin, the antipsychotic Navane, and the depression treatment Sinequan.

The 1970s brought the introduction of Minipress, first of a Pfizer-discovered class of antihypertensive agents. The drug Mansil for the treatment of tropical diseases, developed at Pfizer laboratories in Sandwich, England, won the Queen's Award for Technological Achievement. Leading products of the 1980s included Feldene for arthritis, Cefobid for serious infection, and the previously mentioned Procardia for angina.

"We've been a growth stock forever, and now, with more than $8 billion in sales, we have the greatest global strength of our competitors," said McKinnell. "We've increased our focus on health care and over the last four years have divested any businesses that don't fit in with that focus."

Pfizer's health care division, which includes pharmaceuticals and the medical devices group, recently represented 78 percent of the company's revenues, while the food science group accounted for 9 percent, the animal health division 8 percent, and consumer health care 5 percent. Pharmaceuticals will always be Pfizer's big gun, providing the strongest earnings gains as well. The additional weapons in the company's arsenal, while not currently showing earnings momentum, offer promise for the future, and the company is prepared to sell off any businesses that don't fit in with overall goals or don't deliver enough profits.

The hospital products group includes orthopedic implants and bone cement, electrosurgical devices and disposables, angioplasty and angiography devices, and impotence and incontinence implants.

The food science group includes specialty products such as Litesse, a one-calorie bulking agent that replaces sugar and fat. Litesse and polydextrose are used in low-fat candy products such as Mars Milky Way II and Cadbury's Lite Milk Chocolate. The animal health products division is a leader in animal health products used in the worldwide cattle, swine, and poultry industries.

Visine, Ben-Gay, Desitin, Unisom, Plax, Barbasol, and Rid are among popular consumer health care products made by the company. Vanishing Scent Daytime Ben-Gay and Visine Extra with moisturizing relief are prime examples of the updating of older products, which Pfizer has used to good advantage in pharmaceuticals. While over-the-counter products make up only 5 percent of ongoing sales, they fit the company's long-term goals.

Of course, Pfizer won't be the sole survivor among 21st century pharmaceutical firms, even if it is the best-situated investment opportunity. Three other companies in particular stand out as capable of outperforming their peers and handling change. For them, the future may even be better than the "good old days."

Merck & Co., the drug industry titan of the 1980s, has made a bold move that should generate superior total returns for a long time. For $6 billion in cash and Merck stock, it bought Medco Containment, which sells prescription drugs by mail. This should allow this Whitehouse Station, New Jersey–based firm to cut its sales force, thereby reducing costs, and will be a big boost in the marketing of its most popular drugs. Its Proscar for prostate enlargement and Fosamax for osteoporosis are significant due to the aging population and a growing emphasis on preventive care.

Schering-Plough Corp., a medium-sized pharmaceutical company based in Madison, New Jersey, should be able to continue its impressive earnings growth of 15 percent a share. It features a strong product pipeline, with its popular new antihistamine Claritin rapidly gaining market share. Anticancer and antiviral drug Intron A is also doing well. More than one-half of its drug business is overseas, which provides some protection from the effects of U.S. health care reform. Consumers are familiar with its market-leading Afrin, Coppertone, and Scholl's brands as well.

Warner-Lambert Co. of Morris Plains, New Jersey, has signed deals with Burroughs Wellcome and Glaxo Holdings to expand its over-the-counter business to include Wellcome's antiviral agent Zovirax. This joint venture will also help develop and promote a version of Glaxo's Zantac, the world's largest selling drug for ulcers. In addition, Warner-Lambert is launching its own Cognex drug for treating Alzheimer's disease. In January 1994, the firm received FDA approval to sell its anticonvulsant, Neurontin, as a treatment for epilepsy. Familiar brand names in other products are Halls, Listerine, Benadryl, Schick, Trident, Chiclets, Dentyne, and Junior Mints. Profits should grow at a double-digit annual rate.

Investment Close-Up: Pfizer Inc.

235 E. 42nd St., New York, New York 10017
(212) 573-2323

Pfizer is a leading ethical pharmaceutical producer that also holds important positions in hospital products, animal health items, nonprescription medications, and food ingredients.

Chairman and CEO: William Steere Jr.
Executive vice president and CFO: Henry McKinnell
Investor contact: James Gardner
Total employees: 39,000

Stock: Traded on the New York Stock Exchange under the symbol "PFE." Price of $81¼ a share (5/16/95). Dividend of $2.08 a share, which has grown at a five-year average annual rate of 12 percent. Price-to-earnings ratio of 19.

Sales and Earnings: Sales of $8.3 billion in 1994, with earnings of $1.3 billion. Five-year annual sales growth of 6 percent, with earnings growth of 9 percent.

Earnings per Share Growth: Five-year earnings per share growth rate of 16 percent. Projected (Institutional Brokers Estimate System) five-year earnings per share annual growth rate of 14 percent.

Data from Bridge Information Systems Inc.

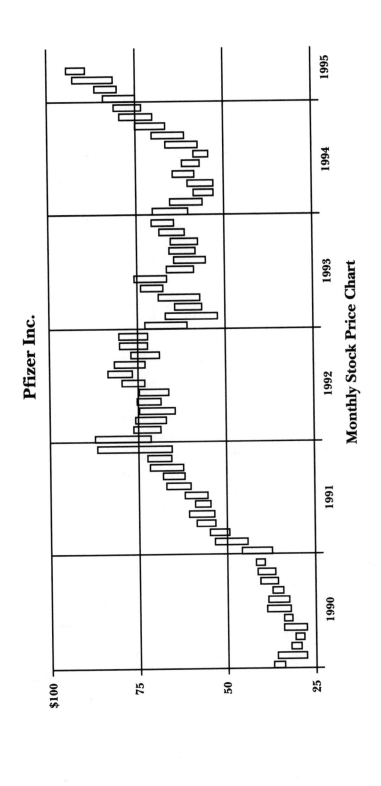

Pfizer Inc.

Monthly Stock Price Chart

10

Rebuilding America

The early morning earthquake on Monday, January 18, 1994, jolted the Los Angeles basin with a severe shock registering 6.6 on the Richter scale, quickly crumbling sections of several of the nation's most-traveled freeways.

The buckling or collapse of parts of five major freeways, including the busy Santa Monica and Golden State, spelled long-term chaos for commuters dependent on their cars. Nearly three million vehicles typically use the Los Angeles freeway system during rush hour. Making matters worse, what little mass transit exists in that car-obsessed city is also centered on freeways, in the form of buses and car pools. An estimated 100 million pounds of freight travels along the corridor each day.

Suddenly everyone was talking infrastructure.

But that's how infrastructure always comes up—when disaster hits. Otherwise it's out of sight, out of mind. The heavy construction firms that did the cleanup and received the contracts to rebuild the freeways just wish there'd be as much interest year-round on the more gradual deterioration of the nation's aging roads, bridges, tunnels, and waterways.

"Everything's just wearing out," explained Jack Feller, the recently retired chairman and chief executive of Kasler Holding Co., a heavy construction firm headquartered in Highland, California. "Highways and bridges, particularly those in the East and California, are carrying far more traffic than they were designed for."

Seismic upgrading of bridges in California for some time has been a big growth area for contractors, with many bridges needing to be rebuilt altogether. Since its 1989 earthquake, the San Francisco Bay Area has begun a 10-year program of repairing, widening, and replacing bridges.

"Dams, aqueducts, and sewers need to be fixed, maintained, and made capable of handling larger amounts of water than they were originally designed for years ago," added Bill Barton, chief financial officer of Granite Construction Inc. of Watsonville, California.

There's a dire need for infrastructure repair throughout the country as we enter the 21st century. Even the most casual observer can see that America's deteriorating highways, bridges, airports, water storage systems, and sewage treatment facilities need some serious fixing up.

Kasler Holding and Granite Construction are two good bets to do a lot of that necessary work. The trend toward privately developed toll road projects also looks promising for these large construction firms, for it will improve their profit margins. Each has a backlog of orders, little debt, and conservative management that knows how to make low bids but still turn a profit. Their stocks represent solid 10- to 20-year plays on the long-overdue repair of the American infrastructure. The investor will, however, have to be patient and put up with some volatility tied to the vagaries of economic cycles and government funding along the way.

So forget the information superhighway for a moment, since it seems we can barely drive our cars down a conventional superhighway these days. The deteriorating conditions are the type we used to mock in the old Soviet Union. It's not as though we were never warned, either. Studies by the Congressionally mandated National Council on Public Works Improvement in the 1980s concluded that "the quality of America's infrastructure is barely adequate to fulfill current requirements, and insufficient to meet the demands of future economic growth and development."

As a motorist, I find myself spending considerable time eluding potholes on the expressway. Sometimes they're so enormous and deep that sections of the roadway must be closed to traffic. Many other Americans maneuver through a similar slalom course each day. Eighty-five percent of workers get to their jobs in private vehicles, and the portion who carpool or use public transportation has been in decline. More than one million miles of highways need to be resurfaced in the next decade. Sitting in your car in bumper-to-bumper traffic on the expressway during a variety of even "off-peak" drive times is becoming more common. In fact, Americans now spend two billion hours in traffic jams each year. The Infrastructure Institute at Cooper Union in New York estimates that, by the year 2005, traffic delays due to inadequate roads may cost the nation $50 billion annually in wasted fuel and lost wages.

The queasy feeling you may get in the pit of your stomach when driving over an old bridge is probably nature's way of giving a warning. About 40 percent of U.S. bridges are rated deficient, with an average of 120 collapses each year. Furthermore, 28 million Americans are being served by inadequate sewage treatment plants. The number of Americans fleeing the central cities for the suburbs makes it difficult for older cities to maintain their decaying public works and also puts new stress on the infrastructure of rapidly expanding suburbs due to so many new homes, automobiles, and shopping malls. The aging of the baby boom generation particularly means steady demand for up-scale homes. Since 1960, growth in the number of both autos and households has been significantly higher than the general growth of the population, putting more stress on public works.

As if all that's not bad enough, the Federal Aviation Administration estimates that 58 airports will be seriously congested by the year 2000, causing significant delays for three-fourths of the nation's air passengers.

The price tag to fix things up is enormous. Repairing the nation's infrastructure could cost as much as $3.3 trillion, or about three-fourths of the nation's gross national product. That estimate includes $1.6 trillion for highways, $53 billion for bridges, and $142 billion for water supplies.

The 1991 Federal Intermodal Surface Transportation Efficiency Act authorized expenditure of $151 billion over five years on infrastructure, and this legislation is only now beginning to benefit the construction industry. It's a start, but no panacea for the long run. The planned spending level represents an average increase of $7.3 billion annually, or 41 percent, over the previous five-year transportation program. Besides the spending increases, the act established a 155,000-mile national highway with plans to widen some existing highways, connect heavily traveled arteries, and re-design others. Individual states now have greater flexibility in how they spend their funds, and a greater amount of money is also dedicated to mass transit.

"We're seeing mass transit programs grow as cities such as Los Angeles attempt to tie everything together, and we're also seeing airports expand and rural areas upgrade existing roads," said Granite Construction's Barton. "The road-block at the state and local level is how much money is appropriated, with some states such as California, Texas, and Florida using gas tax to improve roads and mass transit."

In existence since 1922, Granite Construction is the nation's fourth largest heavy construction contractor. It has built mass transit systems in San Francisco and Washington, D.C., as well as numerous highways, bridges, dams, tunnels, canals, and airports. Its ownership of substantial gravel, rock, and sand reserves, and one of the largest heavy construction equipment fleets in the country, attest to its power in the industry.

Privatized toll road operations are expected to play a significant role in the future of American roadways. Private highway ownership has already been successful in many parts of Europe, and in this country California has become the leader. While not a perfect solution, it can take up some of the slack in infrastructure funding. A large share of the solid and hazardous waste facilities in this country is already in private hands.

Barton points to two new Granite Construction projects in California's Orange County. The San Joaquin Toll Road, a joint venture with Kiewit Pacific Co., is funded from the municipal bond market and will ultimately be repaid through tolls. Another example is a privately financed express-lane toll road within the median of the Riverside Freeway that extends for 10 miles.

Kasler Holding, operating primarily in the western United States, is the new name for the combination of Kasler Corp. and the Montana contracting firm WCG Holdings Inc. The Kasler emphasis has traditionally been concrete highways, bridges, airport runways, flood control channel projects, and water distribution facilities. WCG targeted infrastructure projects, contract mining, and environmental cleanups. The addition of WCG lets Kasler add more states to its prospective business list and include dirt moving and other services in its bids.

The demolition and reconstruction of the multilane, two-span Valley Circle Bridge located on Highway 101 in Calabasas, California, is a recent Kasler project. So is the widening of a 2.7-mile stretch of the existing median on Interstate 580 in Pleasanton to accommodate Bay Area Rapid Transit facilities. Yet another project involves construction of a two-mile section of a light rail system in Denver, including two transit stations.

"We want to be a billion-dollar company in five years, so we're actively looking at other potential acquisitions," said Feller. "We want to be a large construction company, not just a company in the management of construction."

Kasler Holding has set up a subsidiary in Mexico and intends to work with Mexican subcontractors there on projects to improve that nation's infrastructure as well. Discussions held several years before the North American Free Trade Agreement had exposed the insufficiency of Mexico's transportation in terms of traffic capacity, number of transportation options, and quality of roads and systems. It didn't meet the requirements of an open, competitive economy that depends on efficient handling of merchandise. In light of this, the Mexican government has put into effect extensive road-building programs, many of them opened to private investment and management.

It's clearly catch-up time for this country's infrastructure. Improper maintenance of existing older structures coupled with a general tightening of federal purse strings in recent years are to blame.

U.S. Labor Secretary Robert Reich is one of many Americans who would argue that good infrastructure is one of the basics that a nation owes to its citizens. In his book *The Work of Nations: Preparing Ourselves for 21st Century Capitalism* (Alfred A. Knopf, New York: 1991), he uses infrastructure as an example of a general decline of public investment that also carries through to education, training, and other public improvements. In the 1950s, Reich notes, the nation made a commitment to building a modern transportation system, but its gradual withdrawal of funds that began in the 1970s and accelerated in the 1980s has resulted in today's specter of collapsing bridges and crumbling highways. Much of what the federal government has actually underwritten in recent years has been dedicated to downtown convention centers, office parks, and research parks used by society's elite rather than the highways used by the majority of U.S. workers, he believes. Positive national economic policy should enhance the capacities of citizens to lead full and productive lives that include, among a great many other things, good infrastructure.

The numbers explain the story of decay. In 1965, about 5.5 percent of all federal outlays went for infrastructure, but by the 1990s that share had fallen to 2.5 percent. The amount spent has dropped from 3 percent of U.S. gross domestic product in the 1950s to less than 0.5 percent today.

Countries such as Germany, Japan, and France spend a much higher percentage of their gross domestic product on infrastructure than the United States does. Cooper Union's Infrastructure Institute points out that Japan is undertaking an $11 trillion, 10-year capital reconstruction program and commits 15 percent of its gross national product to infrastructure investment from both public and private sources. Taiwan has embarked on an ambitious six-year, $300 billion plan to build new highways, railroads, subway systems, water treatment plants, and sewage systems. Of course, all is not perfect overseas either, especially when it comes to building new airport facilities. It took two decades to receive the go-ahead for the construction of the new airport in Munich, Germany, and the unsatisfying result is an airport that will be operating at full capacity in five years. That's hardly a long-term solution.

While the heavy use of public transportation in Europe

is sometimes presented as a model for the United States, there are considerable differences. European cities tend to have much greater population density and more concentrated work centers that conform better to mass transit. Their ancient narrow streets discourage automobile travel. Gasoline prices are also much higher than in the United States. In the 1980s, U.S. metropolitan areas such as Miami, Washington, D.C., Atlanta, and Portland, Oregon, invested heavily in mass transit systems. However, ridership has been disappointing and automobile traffic congestion hasn't declined significantly. The percentage of commuters using public transportation for work continues to decline steadily despite such well-meaning efforts. The automobile remains king as we enter the 21st century.

Although Kasler Holding and Granite Construction are strong firms that have their wagons hitched to the right trend at the right time, an investor in their stock must always be realistic.

"Kasler Holding stock is a good long-range investment, not a short-range one," said Feller, adding that he's proud the company is cash-conscious and has no debt. "It's also a cyclical stock, for construction firms are generally the last to pull out of recession and the last to go into recession."

Strength for the long haul is important. "The investor should view Granite Construction stock as a value, based on the resources we can bring to the marketplace and the fact that 40 percent of our assets are in revenue-producing plants or equipment," said Barton, who notes that the large number of pit sites the company owns translates into shorter distances to transport materials and equipment and therefore lower bids on jobs. "The concern is to not expand faster than your resources and to keep in mind that fields such as environmental cleanup can present not only great opportunities, but potential penalties as well."

It's going to be tougher for smaller heavy construction

firms to survive in the 21st century, and they most likely will be bought up by firms like Kasler Holding or Granite Construction. Greater sophistication and strong finances will be important in this industry, for it now takes more time and effort to find land, go through environmental impact studies, and come up with the lowest bid in order to get the job.

The economy and the government will always be a concern. "I sincerely hope that the government doesn't continue massive deficit spending," Feller said with a sigh. "It must be curtailed if we're to get things moving." Getting things moving makes a big difference in terms of employment, for each $1 billion spent on infrastructure translates into an estimated 50,000 additional public and private jobs.

The construction industry is a much more efficient one than it was 50 years ago when Feller got his start in the business. "Technology has been a tremendous boon to our business, especially with the type of equipment that's able to push concrete 2,000 feet in the air or survey large areas on land and air with just one instrument," Feller mused. "Unfortunately, another more unfortunate change is that no one ever does business on just a handshake anymore like they did in the old days."

In the new construction environment, the computer is used for analysis, while rehabilitation and maintenance are emphasized over new construction. Both Kasler Holding and Granite Construction are actively involved in scholarship programs for people at the high school and college level who exhibit an interest in the construction field. That's an important step, for the annual number of individuals receiving undergraduate degrees in civil engineering tumbled by 27 percent during the 1980s and remains a big problem. This unfortunately is occurring just as many senior engineers are reaching retirement age. Articulate, quality engineers have never been more needed, and with the increasing importance of working directly with government and the public in order to see projects through, the abilities to speak effectively and write well are vital to success.

Another industry problem is that, due to the extremely low number of births in this country in the 1970s, there will be far fewer young people who can handle physically demanding construction and public works jobs. A report by the Population Reference Bureau recommends that, because of this situation, more capital and technology may be necessary to make work less physically demanding and workers more productive. It also speculates that the competition for scarce labor will probably push wages up and also encourage cities to turn to overseas labor markets to obtain workers. That could even result in moves to change U.S. immigration policies to fit labor needs, it predicts.

"America's Crumbling Infrastructure: Confronting the Crisis," a report by Samuel Schwartz and Clark Wieman of the Infrastructure Institute at Cooper Union, offers the following transportation initiatives, which could make a significant difference in dealing with our current problems:

- Using public transit to link rural areas to services and marketplaces.

- Maximizing the mix of options by providing infrastructure for each, such as bicycle paths, lockers, and new street designs to better accommodate and protect pedestrians.

- Linking transportation to growth management plans and reducing car travel by penalizing parking rather than subsidizing it, boosting transit subsidies, and actually paying employees to walk or bicycle to work instead of driving their cars.

- Preserving existing unused transportation corridors, such as abandoned rail lines, for bicycling, walking, and future transit.

- Regulating shopping mall size to encourage transportation efficiency and preserve neighborhoods.

As we enter the 21st century, bold steps must be taken to shore up the nation's crumbling infrastructure. On the positive side, it no longer is a hidden issue. Federal, state, and local governments know exactly what needs to be done. Whether it's accomplished through public or private funding, and whether it's accomplished sooner than later, heavy construction companies Kasler Holding and Granite Construction will be among those ready to do the job.

Investment Close-Up: Kasler Holding Co.
27400 East 5th Street, Highland, California 92346
(909) 884-4811

Kasler Holding Co. performs general contracting work, specializing in the construction of concrete roadways, bridges, and other public works projects such as airport runways.

President and CEO: John Wimberly
CFO and investor contact: Gregory Rutherford
Total employees: 1,075

Stock: Traded on the New York Stock Exchange under the symbol "KAS." Price of $5½ a share (5/16/95). No dividend.

Sales and Earnings: Sales of $259 million in 1994, with earnings of $700,000. Five-year annual sales growth of 12 percent, with earnings decline of 19 percent.

Earnings per Share Growth: Five-year earnings per share decline of 36 percent.

Data from Bridge Information Systems Inc.

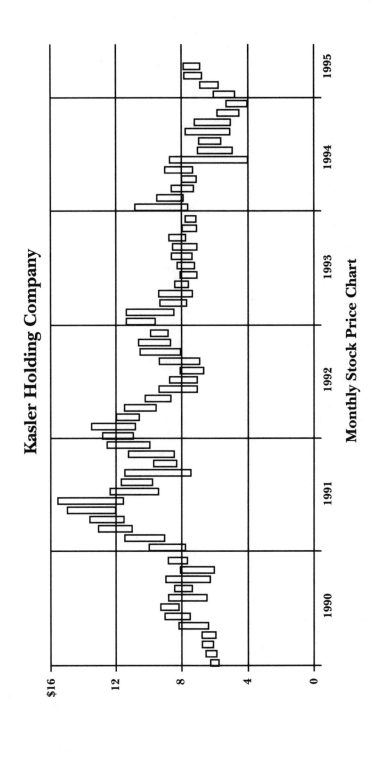

Kasler Holding Company

Monthly Stock Price Chart

Investment Close-Up: Granite Construction Inc.

585 W. Beach St., Watsonville, California 95076
(408) 724-1011

President and CEO: David Watts
CFO: Bill Barton
Investor contact: Michael Lawson
Total employees: 3,000

Granite Construction Inc. is a heavy construction contractor primarily serving the public sector as well as private industry. It is also a manufacturer of asphalt and other construction materials. Earnings are expected to improve from depressed levels.

Stock: Traded on NASDAQ under the symbol "GCCO." Price of $21⅜ a share (5/16/95). Dividend of 20 cents a share, which has grown at a 7 percent rate over five years. Price-to-earnings ratio of 11.

Sales and Earnings: Sales of $693 million in 1994, with earnings of $19.5 million. Five-year annual sales growth of 4 percent, with earnings decline of 16 percent.

Earnings per Share Growth: Five-year earnings per share annual decline of 24 percent. Projected (Institutional Brokers Estimate System) five-year earnings per share growth rate of 13 percent.

Data from Bridge Information Systems Inc.

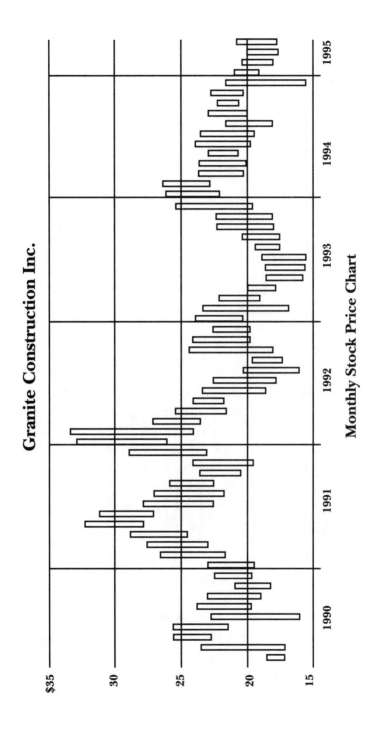

Granite Construction Inc.

Monthly Stock Price Chart

11

Toys "R" Us

A little girl wearing bright pink snowboots was pushing buttons on several "sound" books, alternating "woofs" with "meows" and an occasional loud "oink."

"This one's a fun book because it glows in the dark," the sales representative was telling a young mother with two small children as she held up the book and motioned with it toward several others. "These three are also good selections the children should enjoy."

On a cardboard placard, the children's bestseller list included *My First Word Book* by Angela Wilkes, for babies and toddlers; *Fireman Bear*, illustrated by Carole Etow, for preschoolers; *Giving Tree* by Shel Silverstein, for young readers; and *Goosebumps* by R. L. Stine, for young adults.

There are tables and chairs for small children to page through books, and the display racks go all the way to the floor so youngsters can reach them. There is carpeting in a multicolor dot pattern of blues, greens, and reds.

Welcome to Books "R" Us. This brightly lit, 600-square-foot bookstore within a Toys "R" Us store that stocks 1,200 titles is just one of the reasons why this international toy retailer has bright prospects for the 21st century. It marks a departure from the past, when the company had a limited selection of titles stuck in the back of the store and there wasn't a knowledgeable sales representative assigned to the area to answer any questions from kids and parents.

The 317 new Books "R" Us locations communicate the worthy concept that books are fun, just like toys, and bring in new profit for the company. Research had found that parents were frustrated that their children weren't reading, and that kids often didn't like the adult librarylike feel of many conventional bookstores.

Toys "R" Us is more than just fun. It represents a stock investment that should grow right along with the company.

There's more that's new at Toys "R" Us these days. The Barbie Shop, an aisle featuring every possible doll and accessory of the beloved Mattel star, is near the front of the store. There's the Parties "R" Us section, with two long, colorful aisles of kids' wrapping paper, balloons, noisemakers, and paper plates. That one-stop shopping idea for children's parties hasn't quite taken off yet. A few stores are also testing a Lego shop, where kids can examine those popular build-it toys in one place, and a Little Tikes shop, where that manufacturer's large indoor/outdoor castles, playhouses, and slides can be enjoyed. A plush toy shop is likely next as the company continues to expand its new boutique concept.

If these ideas play here, they'll play all over the world.

"We're trying to make our stores more interesting and consumer-friendly," said Michael Goldstein, chief executive of Toys "R" Us Inc. and a driving force behind the new boutique approach. "It's great to be number one in your business, and a positive for us going into the 21st century is the fact the toy business is similar all over the world with the same product lines from multinational toy companies."

For example, 70 to 80 percent of its European toy sales are the same toys sold in America. The only market that's significantly different is Japan, because of restrictions placed on foreign retailers there. Only 30 to 40 percent of the items are from multinational toymakers, though that situation is expected to gradually change.

"We're not worried about the information highway and interactive home shopping having a negative impact on our business in the future," Goldstein added. "Toys are either too low priced to make them worth selling that way, or else so bulky that they'd require heavy shipping charges if you ordered them."

With nearly $9 billion in sales, Toys "R" Us has captured 25 percent of the U.S. toy market to easily rank first in sales in its industry. It has vanquished several competing toy chains that were what the company refers to as Toys "R" Us "clones." Those imitators simply couldn't cut costs as effectively as the real thing.

The scope of this Paramus, New Jersey–based company is far-reaching, fueled by a cash-rich financial policy of owning its own real estate and carrying little debt. It already has 618 U.S. Toys "R" Us stores, with another 70 to open annually on the way to its goal of at least 900 stores here. Internationally, it has 298 stores in 20 countries. That compares with just five international stores a decade ago. There are also 211 Kids "R" Us clothing stores, whose once-sagging profitability has been improved in the past two years. The company still hasn't quite figured out what to do with Kids "R" Us, whose size and earnings pale in comparison to the Toys "R" Us outlets. It could, for example, conceivably be spun off to shareholders as a stand-alone business at some point.

Using mass media advertising to gain consumer recognition of its wide merchandise selection and everyday low prices, Toys "R" Us sells children's and adult toys, games, bicycles, sporting goods, electronic and video games, home computers, small pools, recordings, and children's furniture. Most of its 46,000-square-foot stores are freestanding or located in strip shopping centers. It has 19 enormous warehouse/distribution centers around the country and the world that benefit from extensive computerization, just as the stores do.

Goldstein, who will steer Toys "R" Us into the 21st century, was named chief executive officer in January 1994 when founder and long-time chairman Charles Lazarus relinquished day-to-day responsibilities to concentrate on international development and new merchandising concepts. Before joining Toys "R" Us, Goldstein, a C.P.A. by trade, was a partner of Ernst & Young and an executive with Lerner Stores Corp. He also holds the title of executive vice president and is in line for the chairmanship whenever the 70-year-old Lazarus eventually decides to retire.

Just as company mascot Geoffrey, a stuffed giraffe, is irrevocably tied to the company image, so is Lazarus. In fact, he bought the original (then unnamed) Geoffrey toy for $50 in the early 1950s on a trip to Italy. He decided it was just what the company needed to give it some personality. Geoffrey appears in all advertising and usually on the cover of the Toys "R" Us annual report as well. In graphics showing company sales, earnings, and stockholder equity over the years, several illustrations are prominently displayed in which Geoffrey's neck becomes longer and longer as the numbers get larger. That neck really stretches in the graphic depicting annual sales increases from $1 billion to $8 billion over the past decade. The forerunner of Toys "R" Us was called Children's Supermarket. Lazarus started out selling baby furniture in Washington, D.C., after serving as an army cryptographer in World War II. He later moved on to toys, employing a self-service, everyday-low-prices approach that eventually wiped out the toy departments of most big department stores.

Lazarus has boldly predicted that by the 21st century Toys "R" Us will have nearly $20 billion in sales and will open outlets in China.

The claim to fame of Goldstein, Lazarus's handpicked successor, has been his ability to squeeze profits from the mature U.S. toy market by utilizing advanced computer control of inventory and product orders, as well as by shaping up Kids "R" Us finances. He's one of a number of key executives that Lazarus has pulled together from a variety of fields, ranging from supermarkets to international beverage sales, to draw upon the best minds available in charting an aggressive, innovative retailing course. Toys "R" Us has plenty of executives with merchandising backgrounds within its ranks as well, but the goal was not to become pigeonholed into any one particular way of thinking about the business. It's an informal, shirtsleeves sort of a company, with no corporate airplane, just one company car with a full-time driver, no country club memberships, and rather austere offices. It doesn't want to lose sight of the fact that it is the toy purveyor to the middle class all over the world.

"Technology has been a big part of our success, and we had one of the first automated businesses at point-of-sale using a mainframe computer," said Goldstein, who is somewhat surprised that other retailers hadn't attempted to do the same earlier in order to make their businesses more efficient. "Now we've gone to satellite and have computer-to-computer communication with our major suppliers."

The satellite technology instantaneously links North America with the headquarters computer databases as well as customer transaction authorization networks in order to cut costs. It also enables television communication for all North American stores. Technology drives down costs in many ways. For example, when Goldstein started at the company, it had $1 billion in sales and 125 people in its payroll and personnel department. It now has $8 billion in sales, yet has fewer than 100 people in that same department.

"A major trend we hope to capitalize upon is that people don't want to shop as much anymore, but rather simply want to know where they can go to find the depth of merchandise to get what they need," Goldstein said.

Its rapidly growing holiday catalog is one attempt to get the company recognized. The first Toys "R" Us catalog, which came out in 1991, had 48 pages and $200 in sale coupons. Available only in the stores, it was circulated to three million customers. In 1992, the coupon value went to $313 and circulation was raised to six million. The company pulled a real surprise in 1993 by coming up with a 72-page catalog and $491 in coupons. Besides the three million in store circulation, it made the dramatic move of putting 52 million catalogs in Sunday newspapers around the country. It ran a clever television commercial with a newsboy tossing the paper at a house and breaking the pavement because it was so heavy. "The catalog was a marketing coup, with even radio disc jockeys Howard Stern and Don Imus talking about it on the air, so we have more surprises planned for the future," said Goldstein. "Years ago, the Sears Roebuck catalog was the toy catalog, but we tried a true toy catalog and the results are outstanding."

The efficiency of the Toys "R" Us operation makes it lethal competition in the United States, as the failed Child's World and Lionel chains found out. Its chief competition in the United States now includes Wal-Mart Stores, Target Stores, K mart, Caldor, and Fred Meyer, as well as the Kay-Bee Toy & Hobby Shop Inc. Wal-Mart and Target combined have a toy market share in the 21 to 23 percent range, thereby approaching the Toys "R" Us 25 percent level, and they're using expanded toy sections and competitive prices to compete effectively. K mart adds perhaps another eight or nine market share points. Toys "R" Us is generally expected to gain against competitors such as K mart, regional discount stores, catalog showrooms, national chains, department stores, and variety stores, though at a slower rate than in past years. Analysts' estimates put the projected Toys "R" Us share at about 29 percent of the market in 1996.

Improved merchandising and promotion will be big factors in extracting more money from the maturing U.S. toy market. Toys "R" Us stores average $300 of sales per square foot of selling space, while the most productive 200 stores average more than $400. New and remodeled Toys "R" Us stores featuring wider aisles, better signs, more attractive displays, and some carpeted areas are part of the plan to enhance sales. There's no question that they look a lot better and are more attractive places to shop, a necessity if Toys "R" Us is to compete with the clean, spacious, and well-lit environments of Wal-Mart and Target stores. The company had been remodeling about 15 older stores each year, but has stepped up the process to more than 25 annually. It's also taking more rapid markdowns on items, which translates to fewer unattractive clearance areas with tattered, older merchandise. The space saved by this move can be devoted to profitable boutiques. For example, Books "R" Us, which costs about $25,000 per store conversion, is expected to add $40 million in annual sales to the company, and considerably more as the concept is expanded. The company initiated its Geoffrey Helper program, which places additional sales assistants on the floor, in 1992. Yet another service available in a number of locations permits a customer to scan an item in order to validate its price and ascertain whether it's being offered at a special sale price that day.

The next important consideration is the ongoing international expansion. To be of any size in the coming century, the company believes, it will be necessary to be a truly global player. The U.S. retail market is "overstored" and will experience bloodletting, while the best of the retailers will confidently expand worldwide. "We have a head start in global expansion because we started 12 years ago and we're already in 16 countries," said Goldstein. "We'll be like McDonald's, all over the world."

While that's an admirable goal for a company with such a unique and recognized franchise, there are also some hard knocks in international investing, because it's difficult to predict how foreign economies will perform. For example, 1993 results for Toys "R" Us overseas were disappointing, due largely to weak economies, especially those of Germany, Japan, and Spain. A stronger dollar during the holiday sales season also made Toys "R" Us items more expensive in foreign countries, further hurting sales and profits. In addition, there were significant start-up costs in Australia, Belgium, the Netherlands, and Switzerland. Foot dragging by overseas governments and tough competitive efforts from the retailers already in those markets were other problems. The situation won't improve until the major European economies turn around, but 1994 earnings momentum should pick up, Goldstein predicted.

The potential is there. In Europe, the population and gross national product are higher than in the United States, so opening hundreds of stores makes good sense, he said. Japan has a population half the size of the United States but a gross national product that's larger, so there's huge potential for growth. Canada and Britain make up about 65 percent of international earnings, followed by Germany and Austria with 30 percent, and the rest distributed among the other countries. The company also recently signed franchising agreements in the United Arab Emirates and Saudi Arabia, where it will have control over the appearance and merchandise of the stores. Such arrangements are for parts of the world where the company can't legally have full responsibility for its operations. Meanwhile, Scandinavia in

1994, followed by Hungary, Greece, China, and Mexico in subsequent years, are the next expansion countries.

There's overseas competition, too. In France, there are large "hypermarkets" that sell a wide range of goods from food to clothing to toys. Their growth and its negative effect on small shops has made the French government slow to approve new retailing properties there. In other countries such as Britain, Spain, and Japan, the primary competitors are small shops and department stores, the type of traditional competition that Toys "R" Us likes best. It took Toys "R" Us executives three years to negotiate through a long list of Japanese rules and regulations, including those designed to protect shopkeepers from big retailers, to enter the Japanese market. Talks between Japanese and U.S. trade officials took so long that the company joined forces with - McDonald's Corp. to protest the difficult review process. Despite the $100 million spent before the first Toys "R" Us store was even opened, the investment is considered well worth the effort when viewed in the long term. Most companies wouldn't have had the patience, vision, or finances to tough it out. There are battles elsewhere. Established retailers in Germany and France have angrily opposed proposals to legalize the late-evening and seven-day-a-week retailing so common among American discount businesses. In Britain and France, small retailers have tried to persuade the government to limit how low the prices of the new discounters can go. In Australia, the Coles Meyer chain, which is 22 percent owned by K mart, has started up a toy store chain to go up against the new Toys "R" Us entry.

Toys "R" Us will take on all companies or countries. It is a powerful franchise earning 12 percent pretax margins in established markets and garnering success in each country it enters.

"We're a big cash flow generator, and while we've looked long and hard for acquisitions, nothing we find ever seems to be as good as our own Toys "R" Us business," said Goldstein, noting that the company plans to spend as much as $1 billion buying back its shares over several years. "We'll keep looking, but in the meantime we'll use our cash flow to grow, buy our own real estate, and buy back stock."

While the company's target is 20 percent earnings growth, in light of its enormous share of the toy market here, a robust 18 percent is more likely, Goldstein believes. There are inherent vagaries in the business, such as a year that may not offer up a lot of interesting new toys, the possible decline of a product area such as the once-booming video game business, or difficulties experienced by some overseas economies.

"We have a great work ethic here, and we really worry about where our money goes," said Goldstein. "If you want to grow like we want to grow as we enter the 21st century, you just can't become fat, dumb, and happy."

Goldstein, who practiced as an accountant for many years, wasn't always a lock to come to Toys "R" Us. When, earlier in his career, he decided to leave the Lerner Stores because he was unhappy with the direction the company was taking, he was torn between a position offered at The Limited women's apparel stores and the Toys "R" Us job.

"Both of my daughters were beyond the toy age and urged me very strongly to take the job with The Limited," he recalls with a laugh. "But I remember that when I told my seven-year-old nephew in a telephone call that I might be going into management at Toys "R" Us, there was a gasp of excitement, and the phone suddenly slammed to the floor."

The company is betting that the grandchildren and great-grandchildren of tomorrow will one day share that same excited affection for its business in countries around the globe.

Investment Close-Up: Toys "R" Us Inc.

461 From Road, Paramus, New Jersey 07652
(201) 262-7800

Toys "R" Us, the world's largest toy retailer, also operates a children's retail clothing business.

Chairman: Charles Lazarus
CEO and investor contact: Michael Goldstein
Total employees: 110,000

Stock: Traded on the New York Stock Exchange under the symbol "TOY." Price of $26 a share (5/16/95). No dividend. Price-to-earnings ratio of 14.

Sales and Earnings: Sales of $8.7 billion in 1994, with earnings of $532 million. Five-year annual sales growth of 13 percent, with earnings growth of 13 percent.

Earnings per Share Growth: Five-year earnings per share annual growth rate of 13 percent. Projected (Institutional Brokers Estimate System) five-year earnings per share annual growth rate of 16 percent.

Data from Bridge Information Systems Inc.

Toys "R" Us Inc.

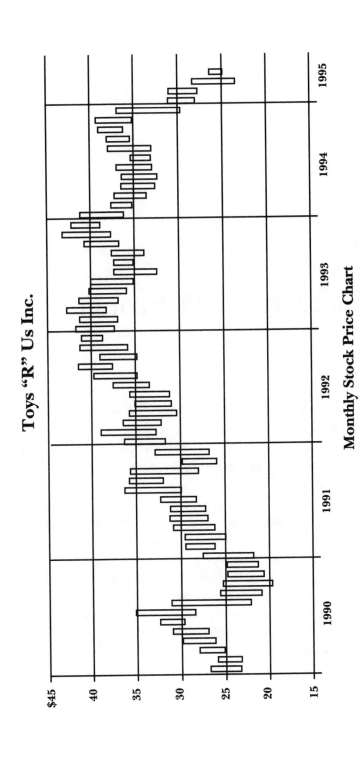

Monthly Stock Price Chart

12

Biotech Breakthroughs

There's an airlock and bench located between the laboratory and the final containment area where researchers must change into what they call a "full bunny suit" at Chiron Corp.'s research and manufacturing campus in Emeryville, California.

Such head-to-toe cover, resembling that of a space traveler, is sometimes necessary because potential contamination is a constant worry for those handling "live blood," either human or animal.

With serious diseases such as multiple sclerosis, hepatitis C, cancer, and AIDS on its agenda, leading biotechnology firm Chiron is recognized for having a productive scientific team, a broad product line, and a knack for forming profitable joint ventures.

The futuristic field of biotechnology will come into its own in the 21st century as breakthroughs to cure diseases and improve the food supply provide profits to investors willing to deal with inherent volatility. These stocks are definitely not for the faint of heart.

Companies such as Chiron, whose research is capable of producing breakthrough drugs, should prosper in a health care climate in which cost savings and disease prevention are of prime importance. Also offering promise in return for some investment risk are the stocks of firms genetically engineering new products such as the "Flavr Savr" tomato of agricultural biotech firm Calgene Corp., which received approval from the Food and Drug Administration in May 1994 after exhaustive review. Several other disease-fighting biotech firms discussed here also have potential. To spread the inherent risk in biotech, it's best to buy several different stocks.

There is ongoing controversy. Many biotech companies have taken investors on an erratic ride before their stocks financially crash and burn. It is also a field criticized by those unhappy with the concept of tampering with nature or concerned about the potential for scientific irresponsibility. Biotechnology basically involves making changes in living organisms by altering their genetic makeup. Recent advances have allowed scientists to enter and change the deoxyribonucleic acid (DNA) molecule. By spelling out the instructions for making proteins, DNA controls the characteristics of an individual organism. Primary goals of biotechnology research include curing human disease and creating superior food through hybrid plants or livestock.

In another wing of the Chiron manufacturing facility, five young people wearing hair nets were busily filling box after box with five vials of Betaseron, an MS drug that must be self-injected by patients every other day. The company won't be able to meet the phenomenal demand for the drug until 1995. Betaseron, the first new treatment for MS in a generation, received FDA approval in mid-1993. A computer lottery system was used in the fall of 1993 to select the first

20,000 people to receive the drug. The company obtained rights to Betaseron, expected to open a $1 billion market, in its 1991 acquisition of Cetus Corp. While not a cure, Betaseron may improve the natural course of MS as seen in brain scans after two-year treatment, reduce the number and severity of attacks, and shorten the length of hospitalization.

Founded in 1981, the now-global Chiron has sales of $454 million. It gained notoriety in 1987 for isolating and identifying the long-sought hepatitis C virus, a major cause of transfusion hepatitis. Millions of dollars were spent each year in that research, causing controversy with investors and the company's board. But determination paid off. Revenues from the sale of diagnostic tests for the virus have provided the financial strength for growth and diversification, including the acquisition of Cetus, which brought the company both Betaseron for MS and Interleukin-2, for the treatment of kidney cancer.

In 1995, Ciba Geigy Ltd. of Switzerland bought a 49.9 percent interest in Chiron for $2.1 billion. "We don't have the baggage of history here, and, in fact, when we started the company we were told we shouldn't even dream of becoming a pharmaceutical firm," recalled Edward Penhoet, president, chief executive, and one of the three Ph.D. founders of Chiron. "Why, it was as if everyone had already somehow decided that in the 21st century there would be only the same dozen pharmaceutical companies."

Chiron could become the first to market vaccines for genital herpes, which affects 25 percent of adults in this country, and for the hepatitis C virus, which infects about 150,000 Americans a year from blood transfusions. It is a leading supplier of blood-screening tests and surgical instruments to treat cataracts. It sells anticancer drugs, genetically engineered insulin, and a vaccine for hepatitis B. Its diagnostic test business is growing. Chiron's AIDS, malaria, and herpes vaccines are all in clinical trials. Also in the pipeline are new processes to deliver drugs and wound-healing agents to the eye. While other biotech firms typically have only one or two flagship drugs that make or break their future, Chiron is becoming a biotech conglomerate. It's also well connected with academic institutions, which helps with potential breakthroughs.

"The world is getting too efficient, and too many companies make the mistake of believing they can be the best at all aspects of a product," asserted Penhoet, who also continues to teach a class at nearby University of California at Berkeley. "Increasingly, companies must work together in collaborative efforts, which offer something to each of them and provide cross-fertilization of ideas."

While Chiron's reliance on industry partners had been criticized in the past, it now appears this system permitted it to turn its resources toward developing new drugs. It is well positioned as we head toward the 21st century of large managed health care systems in which such money-saving alliances are expected to be commonplace. Companies with fewer employees and more relationships will be the norm. It's a good idea not to bet the ranch on one or two ideas.

Recent examples are Chiron's joint business with Johnson & Johnson to market diagnostics for blood screening, and a similar venture in which Germany's Schering AG will market Betaseron. In the firm's earliest period, Chiron sold Merck & Co. the technology needed to produce a hepatitis B vaccine. It now sells all vaccine technology to the Biocine Co., a joint venture between Chiron and Ciba Geigy Ltd. In the cancer area, Chiron sells Interleukin-2, a genetically engineered protein developed by Cetus, and generic chemotherapy drugs to hospital pharmacies. When operating in a 50-50 joint venture, each company is much more likely to state the truth because what's decided affects them both equally, Chiron management believes. It also produces an important cross-fertilization of ideas and peer review.

On Penhoet's office wall is a framed picture of physician and clergyman Albert Schweitzer, a reference to earlier times in medicine before the application of biological and engineering research to solve health problems emerged as a modern growth industry. The Chiron goal is to fully understand how the body's immune system works in order to solve the problems that result in diseases.

The upbeat, smiling Penhoet loudly slapped the table in front of him as he emphasized that, in the modern era of health care reform, there will be a premium on innovative products because "you can't just sell every product like it's toothpaste anymore." Going forward, there will be a strong bias toward the prevention of diseases, since people around the globe are still vulnerable to infectious diseases. AIDS is an example of a disease for which the medical and scientific community was caught defenseless, he said.

The 300-seat auditorium on Chiron's Emeryville campus is more than an occasional meeting place. It's the regular location for a session each Tuesday morning at which scientists present their works in progress for peer review. Chiron includes more than 300 Ph.D.s among its workforce. It has an academic and cottage industry feel, emphasizing a flat organizational chart without a lot of layers.

"My advice to investors is not to buy biotech stocks unless they're willing to do their homework, to follow the opinions of the quality biotechnology analysts, and to size up the credibility of a company's management," said Penhoet. "Don't just jump on a train because it seems to be popular."

There's a great big red tomato that Calgene hopes will be popular in the 21st century.

An agricultural biotech firm featuring both products and promise, Calgene Inc. is a leader in genetically engineered foods and agricultural products. Academic research into plant biology isn't as advanced as it is in medicine, so companies must do more basic science on their way to innovations such as this new breed of tomato. It's grown from genetically engineered seed in which a patented gene is used to turn off production of polygalacturonase enzymes that help the tomato soften and spoil. It is then shipped without refrigeration.

A walk through the new 50,000-square-foot Calgene Fresh Service Center on Chicago's southeast side, specially designed as the shipment center for MacGregor "Flavr Savr" genetically altered tomatoes, feels like taking a step into the future. Prior to FDA approval of the new tomato, the facility handled and shipped regular tomatoes as a dry run.

The success of the gene-spliced tomato would mean year-round availability of full-flavored, vine-ripe tomatoes with extended shelf life. They'll stay fresh for two weeks after harvesting, which is nearly twice as long as regular breeds. The company believes consumers are willing to pay for such quality. Currently, 90 percent of all fresh market tomatoes in the $3.5 billion (wholesale) tomato industry are picked green, gassed with ethylene to artificially induce ripening, and refrigerated for shipping, which alters their taste and toughens their skin. Fifteen to 30 percent of tomatoes spoil before reaching the market. While 85 percent of American households eat tomatoes, consumption declines in the off season by 30 percent because of lack of quality.

Each step in this state-of-the-art Calgene facility's process is designed to preserve quality in the new supertomato. There's special harvesting for the tomatoes grown in Mexico, California, and Florida, a different trailer, and satellite communication on the trucks to control interior temperature. Tomatoes go through numerous stages at the plant and are first checked at the loading dock, then put into the ripening room if necessary, and set on a conveyor belt. A camera takes photographs of the tomatoes as they go to the sorting machine and a computer reads the information on size and color to decide which bin a tomato will be put into and whether it will bear the McGregor name.

"We can see the rating of the true color of every tomato, for the computer counts pixels (picture elements)," Thomas Churchwell, head of the Calgene Fresh subsidiary until 1995, said as he peered at the computer screen.

The second-tier tomatoes go into the market without the McGregor name, while the third-tier examples go to salsa makers. As they're boxed for grocery stores, a tag with the name of the employee is pressed on. There are 64 initial workers at this plant handling 40,000 pounds of tomatoes a shift, with more shifts and workers to be added when the new tomato gains steam in the marketplace.

"The 21st century will see new standards for fresh produce which is insect-resistant and disease-resistant," said Roger Salquist, chairman and chief executive of Davis, California–based Calgene, who has spent long periods of time in the nation's capital seeking approval for various examples of ag biotech products. "Greater concern about diet and health care means this unique technology will be growing in importance."

Once the "Flavr Savr" is up and running successfully, Calgene intends to use the same technology in other produce. Five years were spent testing the tomato, and the FDA examined it for more than three years. Dr. David Kessler, commissioner of the FDA, declared the tomato "as safe as any on the market." It thus became the first genetically engineered food cleared by federal regulators.

Calgene should be viewed by patient investors as a long-term choice, understanding that it will take a while to meet all the company's goals, since government approval and public acceptance will play a big part in the process. Company losses remain significant, but earnings per share for the full year are expected to be positive in 1996 and rise rapidly thereafter as new products are introduced.

The company has identified opportunities in markets with a combined value of nearly $6 billion. Edible and industrial oils and cotton are other big emphasis areas for Calgene. It has a strong technological and marketing lead in canola oil and seed, the most healthful and fastest-growing edible oil in this country. It owns 40 percent of the U.S. canola seed market. The firm's scientists have shown the ability to genetically modify the canola plant to produce new oils to specification, meaning applications in food ingredients, industrial lubricants, and cosmetic and detergent ingredients. Some of the new oils on the market in 1995 can be produced for 35 to 40 cents a pound, which will sell for 55 cents to $1.50 a pound for industrial lubricants and food ingredients and up to $10 a pound for cosmetic ingredients.

In a third area of Calgene expertise, cotton, the current problem is that growers lose 20 percent of their crop to pest and chemical damage, despite spending $500 million annually on field chemicals. The company is the second largest provider of cottonseed in this country. Its seed technology has been found to make cotton more resistant to herbicides and pests. The product, called BXN cotton, was introduced in 1994.

"The next wave will be genetically engineered cotton in the fiber business, for textile industry machines are operating at only 75 percent of capacity due to problems with the current fiber," said Salquist, who previously was chief financial officer of Zoecon Corp., the original developer of biorational pesticides.

Calgene has ongoing research relationships with Procter & Gamble, Nippon Steel, Rhone-Poulenc, Kirin Brewery, Pfizer Food Science, and Mobil Oil. More than $37 million has been invested in the company's research and licensing fees. It also owns 67 U.S. and foreign patents, with applications pending for another 182. The firm in 1991 was granted a U.S. patent covering "antisense" regulation of gene expression in plant cells, and, in 1993, it signed nine separate agreements with Monsanto covering patent conflict issues. The fact that an international company such as Monsanto wanted to cross-license technology with Calgene added validity to Calgene's sciences.

"As far as the shareholders are concerned, I think they should realize how important our patents are and understand that we're producing products where the value is higher," said Salquist, pointing out that investors should be long-term in their goals and accept some volatility. "Oh, I worry sometimes about fickleness in Washington or at the state levels, but that would just slow us a bit, because we're too far along for anything negative of major significance to occur."

The government has been positive about biotech. The FDA in 1992 announced that genetically engineered foods would be permitted on the market without special tests and without labels that identify the foods as products of gene splicing. Special labels will be required only when known allergens or toxins are combined with ordinary foods.

Not everyone is gung ho, however. Groups such as the Environmental Defense Fund, the Foundation on Economic Trends, and an organization of chefs and food purveyors called the Pure Foods Coalition have questioned the need for the new products. They're unhappy about the lack of labeling and concerned about whether some of the foods may contain new allergy-causing proteins. Another fear is that future genetically engineered products won't undergo the same scrutiny that the "Flavr Savr" did. Still, Calgene has sold all available Calgene Fresh tomatoes and still doesn't have the supply to meet the demand.

There are also smaller biotech firms worth considering

as investments. The smart way to do so is to buy a package of several promising companies, for there is undeniable risk involved. One big success, however, can make up for poor performance in the rest of the group.

For example, Agouron Pharmaceutical Inc. offers an opportunity to participate in rational drug design, which is the computer-aided design of drugs, with the focus on cancer, AIDS, and other serious diseases. The discovery of how the shapes of molecules influence the way they react includes developing software for modeling molecules. This approach is likely to grow significantly as we enter the next century, but for now it works better in a small entrepreneurial company because it requires integrating numerous scientific disciplines. Only four small companies are involved in computer-aided drug design, and there aren't many synthetic organic chemists with experience in the complex modeling process.

"We're working on 13 identifiable projects, from some in the early biology stage to two in clinical trials for treatment of solid malignant tumors," explained Peter Johnson, president and chief executive of La Jolla, California–based Agouron. "We estimate profitability won't come until 1996 or 1997, so our caveat to anyone investing is that it's a high-risk venture."

The company is focusing on inhibiting intracellular enzymes, with the first products to enter the clinic directed at thymidylate synthase (TS), an enzyme critical to the proliferation of cancer cells. It has also formed a strategic alliance with Japan Tobacco Inc. for the discovery, development, and sale of novel therapeutic drugs that act on key proteins related to the human immune system. Agouron stock jumped in price in March 1994 when the company's researchers discovered the atomic structure of an enzyme that plays a vital role in viruses involved in the common cold. Changes in the health care system should help a pioneering company like Agouron, Johnson believes, because it puts a high premium on breakthrough products, not just the "me too" products of the past that were sold by large sales forces.

ICOS Corp. is a development-stage pharmaceutical company founded by three of the leaders in commercializing biotechnology: George Rathmann, a founder and former chairman of Amgen; Robert Nowinski, a founder and former chairman of Genetic Systems; and Christopher Henney, a founder and former scientific director of Immunex. One of the investors in the private placement was Bill Gates, Microsoft chairman, who is on the ICOS board of directors and owns 8 percent of the company.

With that lineup, it's not difficult to see why this Bothell, Washington–based firm founded in 1989 has been able to attract a talented and ambitious group of scientists. The company has already completed a series of financings that make it one of the 35 largest biotech firms in terms of market capitalization. It enters into 50-50 collaborations with pharmaceutical companies, with Glaxo its first corporate partner in a project to discover phosphodiesterase inhibitors, enzymes that play a central role in cell activation.

"Our money is with our scientists, and we'll be around long-term because we have a strong board and management and are well financed," declared Rathmann, the ICOS chairman and chief executive. "We must figure how to exploit health care change with innovative products, for in the future brand names and company names won't be nearly as important anymore."

Early research efforts have emphasized developing effective therapies for treatment of chronic inflammatory diseases, specifically asthma, multiple sclerosis, and rheumatoid arthritis. Its humanized monoclonal antibody for treatment of MS is in clinical trial.

"Our focus is inflammation, biopharmaceuticals, and serious inflammatory diseases, not diagnostics or chemicals," explained Rathmann, pointing out that faster government approval is usually received when serious diseases are involved. "I'd tell the investor that the reality is that we have some powerful scientists and a long way to go."

Isis Pharmaceuticals is a development-stage company that is the scientific leader in antisense technology, which has the potential to treat an unlimited range of diseases. Antisense drugs are designed to bind to the messenger RNA, which stops the disease-causing protein from being produced. The company is a leader in the discovery and development of a new class of therapeutic compounds, its earliest disease targets being viruses, cancer, and inflammatory disease. For example, a compound to treat genital warts is in human clinical trials, while another in preclinical development is aimed at herpes simplex virus. Isis has a number of pharmaceutical company partners.

"We have two compounds in clinical trial, with three to be added by the end of 1995, and our earliest new drug application is the end of 1995," said Stanley T. Crooke, the founder, chairman, and chief executive of Carlsbad, California–based Isis. "As with any technology, there's a feasibility question and a range of opinions, but those who spend time with us come away believing."

If it works, Crooke notes, it will change the way that drugs are made in the future. The large buying groups in health care want innovative solutions, and this admittedly high-risk investment, which could face delays or problems in clinical trials, has "an incalculable upside," he added.

Another means of investing in biotechnology with greater diversity is by choosing a mutual fund that specializes in biotech. Boston-based Fidelity Select Biotechnology, managed by Karen Firestone, was the nation's best performing fund of any type for the five-year period 1988–1993, with a strong 273 percent gain. However, it was a real roller-coaster ride, with, for example, a gain of 99.5 percent in

1991 followed by a 10 percent loss in 1992. It fell 18 percent in 1994.

"The biotechnology industry is here to stay and will be important in the 21st century because it's becoming more sophisticated in finding novel ways to get the benefits of molecular compounds," said Firestone, whose top 20 stock holdings all have at least one product in the advanced phases of clinical tests. "But it's a new industry of trial and error, with two steps backward for every step forward, so I'd be sure to make a note of the difference between companies with products and those developing products."

Investment Close-Up: Chiron Corporation
4650 Horton St., Emeryville, California 94608
(510) 655-8730

Chiron is a leading biotechnology company that applies genetic engineering and other technologies to develop products that diagnose, prevent, and treat disease.

Chairman: William Rutter
President and CEO: Edward Penhoet
Investor contact: Larry Kurtz
Total employees: 6,300

Stock: Traded on NASDAQ under the symbol "CHIR." Price of $49⅝ a share (5/16/95). No dividend.

Sales and Earnings: Sales of $372 million in 1994, with earnings of $18 million. Five-year annual sales growth of 52 percent, with earnings growth of 5 percent.

Earnings per Share Annual Growth Rate: Five-year earnings per share growth rate of 34 percent. Projected (Institutional Brokers Estimate System) five-year earnings per share annual growth rate of 30 percent.

Data from Bridge Information Systems Inc.

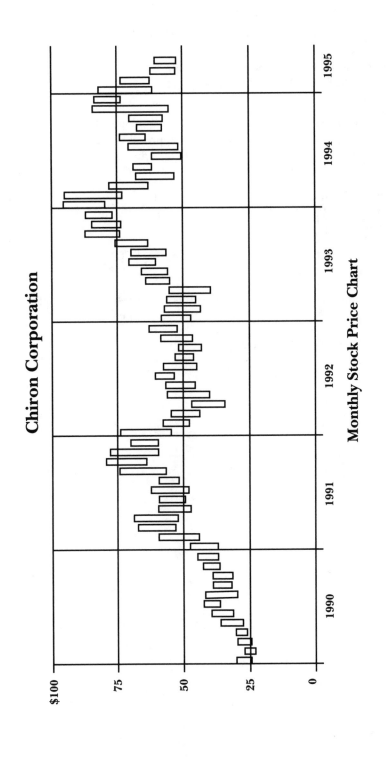

Chiron Corporation

Monthly Stock Price Chart

Investment Close-Up: Calgene Inc.

1920 Fifth Street, Davis, California 95616
(916) 753-6313

Calgene, a leader in the application of recombinant DNA technology to plants, received the first approval of a genetically engineered food from the Food and Drug Administration with its "Flavr Savr" tomato.

Chairman and CEO: Roger Salquist
Investor contact: Carolyn Hayworth
Total employees: 292

Stock: Traded on NASDAQ under the symbol "CGNE." Price of $6⅞ a share (5/16/95). No dividend.

Sales and Earnings: Sales of $37.7 million in 1994, with a loss of $43 million. Five-year annual sales growth of 9 percent.

Data from Bridge Information Systems Inc.

Calgene Inc.

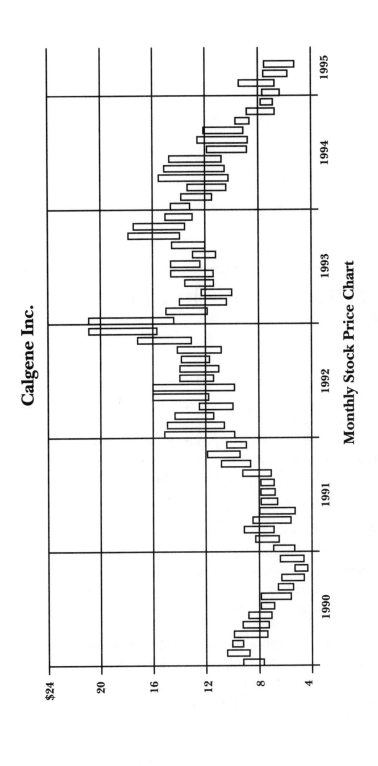

Monthly Stock Price Chart

13

Artificial Intelligence

There just may be a computer that has a better investment mind than your own.

Artificial intelligence promises to be a major investment force in the 21st century, and there are already mutual funds that have a profitable jump on this advanced technology.

Many investment analysts still avoid computers like the plague, preferring to rely on intuition when it comes to selecting stocks. Others claim they're quantitative analysts who go by the numbers, but they usually seem to call the shots themselves and make sure the computers know their place.

But Fidelity Investments portfolio manager Bradford Lewis considers the computer a close personal friend and a brilliant advisor. He's proud to call himself a computer "geek" as he happily outperforms stock market indexes with three stock mutual funds employing artificial intelligence. All three merit consideration based on method and results.

Complex "neural network" software that attempts to mimic the architecture and function of the human brain is the key to this process. The human brain is made up of as many as 100 billion cells called neurons, which act in groups known as neural networks. An artificial neural network is a model that patterns itself after this biological neural network. Artificial intelligence basically learns cause-and-effect patterns by looking at data over and over again. By detecting subtle pricing relationships that mere mortals might overlook, the network picks stocks likely to outperform the market.

We're not yet close to actually replicating the human thinking process of the biological neural system. After all, science still isn't 100 percent sure exactly how the human brain works to begin with. Nonetheless, decades of research into artificial intelligence has, particularly since the late 1980s, produced breakthroughs in the sophistication of this information technology and in our basic understanding of the relationships involved.

"I used to be a plain vanilla stock picker, spending my days doing things like visiting companies, but everything changed dramatically when I began using artificial learning in a big way," explained 40-year-old Lewis, portfolio manager of the innovative Fidelity Disciplined Equity, Fidelity Stock Selector, and Fidelity Small Cap Stock funds. "People err when they stick with one methodology, while my process is adaptive, retraining neural networks with new data every month."

This exciting technology marks not only a transformation in the computerization of investment, but a transformation in the way portfolios are constructed. Its progress will become faster and faster, thanks to the increasing speed of the new computers it will use.

Conventional computer investing programs are driven by fixed rules that require ongoing review and refinement as economic conditions change. Time-consuming, costly re-programming of the system is usually necessary. Neural networks, on the other hand, are able to relearn relationships automatically from new examples as conditions change. This shortens the screening process. The rapidly declining cost of computer technology has been of further advantage in this recent rise to popularity.

The concept of artificial intelligence may seem mysterious or other worldly to most people. There's also considerable misunderstanding about how it actually works. When I anonymously phoned the toll-free Fidelity information number out of curiosity to see how different representatives explain the process behind Lewis's three funds to potential customers, I received the following cautious responses:

Representative 1: "They're pretty much hush-hush about the whole thing. They don't give us much detail on it. They have proprietary models that meet the objectives of those funds, and maybe an econometric model too, but that's about all we know."

Representative 2: "For competitive reasons, they don't explain the process. They use quantitative and computer models for stock-picking, but it is proprietary and they don't really let out how it's done."

While no one's going to offer up all of the details of its neural network, the basic steps in the process are well worth understanding.

Quantitative analyst Lewis is formal in his approach to stock-picking, starting with hundreds of factors that could influence returns and then putting together hypothetical combinations. There could be hundreds of changes, or merely 5 to 10. Data such as projected per-share earnings, cash flow, book value, dividend payout ratios, and debt levels are typically fed to the neural network as historical data. It learns the relationships and the returns of the stocks. He is, in effect, training the network.

Current information is then fed into the network, and

it presents a forecast. He isn't actually telling the computer what type of stock to find, but rather asking it to figure out how the market is pricing stocks. This is based on an underlying belief that what worked in the stock market before will work again. The network tends to pick stocks that are inexpensive when compared to such benchmarks as book value and earnings. It also prefers higher earnings growth rates than the market.

"I don't play God by putting in my personal notions, but let the machine learn what's been useful," he said.

Lewis's computer in Boston calls a computer in New York at 3:30 A.M. each trading day and downloads 120,000 data items, spends a half-hour processing the information, and then prints out a 40-page report. It sorts the report by industries, then subsorts the stocks by the degree of under- or overvaluation based upon Lewis's model. This report will steer him toward stocks that are cheap within their industry group. When going through the reports, Lewis is looking not only for new buys, but also for potential sell ideas.

He has even fed historical information on weather trends to the computer in order to spot trends that could affect sales of soft drink manufacturers. But while it's important to properly train the network with sufficient information, he has to guard against overtraining it with too much. If he does, it goes "brain dead," as he puts it.

"Our performance will continue to improve with faster computers, since the faster the boxes, the more permutations we can factor into likely returns," added Lewis, whose computers recently favored the stocks of firms in finance the most. "Faster chips will definitely make a difference."

His exacting process results in a high 250 percent portfolio turnover annually, with a stock typically held four months. Volatility is about average. Because it's designed to catch trends, the system usually doesn't do as well in periods when the overall environment changes little. Lewis cautions investors to expect underperformance in very narrow markets when big stocks take the lead, since his models prefer mid-capitalization stocks, which are earnings driven.

The multibillion-dollar empire of Fidelity Investments is an excellent proving ground for investing by artificial intelligence. Its diversity of funds means it can more easily make room among them for more adventuresome concepts such as this one. "I'm lucky in that Fidelity Investments is technology-driven and has huge resources, for there's a lot of institutional inertia against this concept in the investing world," added Lewis.

A former Navy pilot who still flies a 1967 Piper Cherokee for sport, Lewis says he makes considerably more use of the operations analysis, modeling, game theory, and mathematics he learned at the U.S. Naval Academy than he does the theories he studied for his M.B.A. from the University of Pennsylvania's Wharton School. His computations five years ago employed conventional algorithmic models, but his methodology now changes on an almost daily basis as he learns more and more about neural networks.

Beyond theory, his funds are worthy of attention because they're by far the most successful quantitative funds around.

The Fidelity Disciplined Equity Fund, initiated in December 1988, seeks to beat the performance of the Standard & Poor's 500 each year and has done so for five straight years. The least risky of the funds Lewis manages, it keeps industry percentages as represented in the S&P 500, but diversifies away industry risks. For example, if banks are 2.5 percent of the S&P 500, it will allot 2.5 percent of the fund to banks, but perhaps will select smaller banks rather than the largest money-center banks. In that way, while it mimics the weightings of the S&P 500, it also adds value through its own stock-picking programs.

The more aggressive Fidelity Stock Selector Fund, begun in September 1990, omits some industries, prefers smaller capitalization stocks, and sets a longer-term performance goal of three years. It has beaten the market over the past three years.

Big names in technology, regional Bell holding companies, banking, pharmaceuticals, automobiles, and consumer products recently represented large positions in these portfolios.

Meanwhile, the Fidelity Small Cap Stock Fund chooses from the most attractive smaller stocks found in the Russell 2000. While Disciplined Equity and Stock Selector are no-load (no initial sales charge) funds, Small Cap has a 3 percent load. All three funds require a $2,500 minimum initial investment.

Initiated in mid-1993 at a high point in the popularity of small companies, Fidelity Small Cap Stock Fund drew an incredible response from new investors and shot beyond $500 million in assets in months. It tends to have more of a value emphasis than the other two funds and is likely to be traded less aggressively because of the high trading costs associated with small capitalization stocks. Lewis expects the annual portfolio turnover will consistently be less than 150 percent.

Some recent holdings in that fund have been stocks of entertainment, semiconductor, insurance, and technology companies. In discussing the fund's small-stock emphasis, Lewis explains that each day his computer spits out a list of 350 to 400 stocks to buy. He puts the list on a floppy disk, which he brings each morning to the Fidelity trading desk. Traders obviously aren't too crazy about filling that kind of demanding order, but the neural network could care less.

Most of the ideas for investment in the funds come straight from the computer models, but there can sometimes be problems that haven't yet shown up in the numbers. That's why the last column in Lewis's primary report is the analyst's rating. If there is some fundamental factor that looks really bad and a Fidelity analyst has a sell on the stock, Lewis won't own it. If he already owns it, he'll usually sell it and give the analyst the benefit of the doubt. He also screens for economic trends that affect specific industries.

From time to time, Lewis overrides the computer's advice altogether, with both good and bad results. For example, he bought stocks of defense electronics firms when Operation Desert Storm began, even though the computer gave no encouragement. But based on his military experience, he was sure that such weapons would be successful, and his hunch was proven right. In another instance, he bought stock of IBM against the computer's advice, and he lost money on the stock. You just can't let it take over completely, he reasons. Apparently, these inventive funds do not spell the end of conventional investment research as we know it.

"There will always be room for fundamental research and qualitative analysts," concluded Lewis, making an argument that computers and traditional analysis can coexist. "Why, Peter Lynch [the former Magellan fund manager noted for his spurning of most technical data] often talks to me about the trends I find in regard to certain stocks."

Artificial intelligence isn't really a new concept. It has seen its popularity wax and wane. After falling out of favor in the 1970s, the field has had a resurgence that began in the late 1980s, said Dr. Robert Trippi, visiting professor at California State University, San Diego, who has applied advanced computer technologies to the securities and real estate industries. The U.S. Department of Defense in 1989 began a five-year, multimillion-dollar program for neural network research to consider a wide variety of applications ranging from surveillance to weaponry. Financial organizations since then have been the second largest sponsors of research in neural network application.

"Within five years, all the money managers will be using some artificial intelligence, but right now a lot of people use the term for marketing hype, and a lot of the off-the-shelf software proporting to use AI is simplistic," said Trippi, coeditor of the book *Neural Networks in Finance and Investing* (Probus Publishing, Chicago: 1993). "But you'll definitely be seeing some breakthroughs in performance in the near future, which no doubt others will rush to emulate."

Artificial intelligence can enhance performance. Yet any investors being wooed by an advisor claiming to use neural networks in investment decisions should be careful that they're "hooking up with proven experts" before assuming any risks, he warned. Because of the proprietary nature of the individual neural network systems, specific explanations about how each one works often aren't made available. Furthermore, the complexity of the concept makes it difficult for the average investor to sort it out unless he or she is dealing with a manager and firm with solid track records. Be sure to request the educational background, professional history, and performance record of any manager you may be considering. Also find out the degree of risk likely to be associated with the investment. Don't put down serious money on a concept that may be no more than a buzzword.

The cutting edge of neural network research currently involves "stochastic (random variable) volatility modeling," an area in which Trippi is concentrating all of his efforts. Use of these models will make it possible to more accurately track many derivative instruments, such as stock index futures, and provide information necessary for more accurate forecasts.

A trading system for S&P 500 futures developed by Trippi uses several neural networks to come up with a composite recommendation for a given day's trading position. The technical variables for a two-week period prior to the trading day are fed into the computer. Some of the inputs include open, high, low, and close price information, and also statistics on price and volatility. The only actual information used from the current trading day is the opening price and the price 15 minutes after the market opened.

Each of the neural networks comes up with a long or short recommendation. This system is designed to be run overnight in the computer for use the following trading day.

By combining several neural networks, the system has outperformed the individual networks and the S&P 500 index itself. In eight weeks of trading, a gain of more than $14,200 was achieved. With an expected return of $317 per day, the potential annual return is $60,000 per contract. Trippi has plans to create a small investment fund that employs this strategy.

Within the general financial community, neural networks have already been developed for credit authorization screening, mortgage risk assessment, project management and bidding strategy, economic predictions, risk ratings of fixed-income investments, detection of regularities in security price movements, and portfolio selection and diversification, according to an article in the *Journal of Portfolio Management* by Trippi and Duane Desieno, president of Logical Designs Consulting Inc., La Jolla, California.

Neural networks can also help portfolio managers do the following:

• Generate improved risk ratings of bonds.

• Search for regularities in the price movements of an individual stock.

• Classify multiple stocks as to upside potential using fundamental and general economic data.

• Recognize a specific price pattern.

• Determine optimal buy and sell timing for an equity index.

• Drive a trading strategy for a nonfinancial commodity index.

Complex as it is, artificial intelligence will be used increasingly in investing as we enter the 21st century. It speeds up the decision-making process by making it possible to go through countless variables to come up with recommendations quickly. Such swift action in dealing with volatile global markets becomes more of a necessity each year. While a number of researchers and investment firms have also used neural networks on a more limited basis, Brad Lewis and his three large Fidelity funds provide an opportunity for neural networks to show off their impressive abilities to a wide audience. This high-tech investment concept is truly here to stay.

Investment Close-Up: Fidelity Disciplined Equity Fund
82 Devonshire Street, Boston, Massachusetts 02109
(800) 544-8888

Fidelity Disciplined Equity Fund seeks capital growth, normally investing at least 65 percent of its assets in domestic common stocks of companies with market capitalizations exceeding $100 million. Using computer models, it maintains representation in as many sectors as possible.

Portfolio manager: Bradford Lewis
Fund inception: 12/28/88
Total assets: $1.3 billion
Distributor: Fidelity Distributors

Shares: Traded under the symbol "FDEQX." Net asset value of $18.99 a share (3/31/95). No initial sales charge. Management fee of 0.30 percent of average net assets plus 0.52 percent group fee. Minimum initial purchase of $2,500.

Performance: One-year total return of 10.74 percent (through 3/95), three-year average annual return of 10.87 percent, and five-year average annual return of 13.88 percent. In 1994, fund value was down 1.54 percent in the first quarter, down 0.56 percent in the second, up 4.61 percent in the third, and up 0.56 percent in the fourth. First quarter 1995 was up 5.85 percent.

Portfolio: Composition was recently 83.6 percent stocks and 16.4 percent cash. Heaviest stock weightings were industrial cyclicals, consumer staples, and financials.

Data from Morningstar Inc.

Fidelity Disciplined Equity Fund

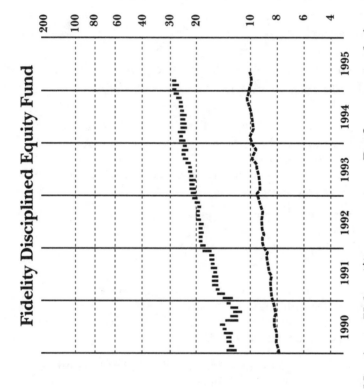

200
100
80
60
40
30
20
10
8
6
4

1990   1991   1992   1993   1994   1995

||||||||| Net Asset Value ($)   ------- Performance relative to S&P 500

Investment Close-Up: Fidelity Stock Selector Fund

This fund has the same address, telephone number, portfolio manager, and distributor as Fidelity Disciplined Equity Fund.

Fidelity Stock Selector Fund seeks capital growth, normally investing at least 65 percent of its assets in common stocks. It is actively managed and covers a broad range of foreign and domestic companies. Computer models consider both fundamental and technical factors.

Fund inception: 9/28/90
Total assets: $731 million

Shares: Traded under the symbol "FDSSX." Net asset value of $19.09 a share (3/31/95). No initial sales charge. Management fee of 0.30 percent of average net assets plus 0.52 percent group fee. Minimum initial purchase of $2,500.

Performance: One-year total return of 7.76 percent (through 3/95), and three-year average annual return of 10.45 percent. In 1994, fund value was down 0.33 percent in the first quarter, down 1.16 percent in the second quarter, up 3.30 percent in the third quarter, and down 0.96 percent in the fourth quarter. First quarter 1995 was up 6.58 percent.

Portfolio: Composition was recently 89.7 percent stocks and 10.3 percent cash. Heaviest stock weightings were industrial cyclicals, financials, and technology.

Data from Morningstar Inc.

Fidelity Stock Selector Fund

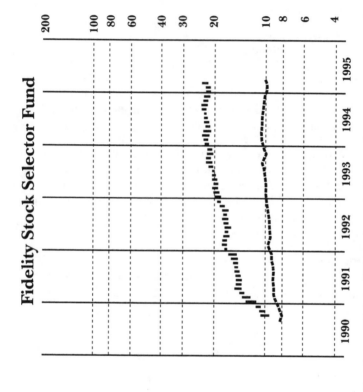

200
100
80
60
40
30
20
10
8
6
4

1990   1991   1992   1993   1994   1995

IIIIIIIIII Net Asset Value ($)   ------- Performance relative to S&P 500

Investment Close-Up: Fidelity Small Cap Stock Fund

This fund has the same address, telephone number, portfolio manager, and distributor as Fidelity Disciplined Equity Fund.

Fidelity Small Cap Stock Fund seeks capital appreciation, normally investing at least 65 percent of its assets in common and preferred stock issued by companies with less than $750 million in market capitalization. The fund also invests a portion in larger, more established companies. Computer-aided analysis of quantitative and fundamental factors is used.

Fund inception: 6/28/93
Total assets: $647 million

Shares: Traded under the symbol "FDSCX." Net asset value of $10.69 a share (3/31/95). Initial sales charge of 3 percent. Management fee of 0.35 percent of average net assets plus 0.52 percent group fee.

Performance: One-year total return of 2.50 percent (through 3/95). In 1994, fund value was down 3.51 percent in the first quarter, down 5.94 percent in the second quarter, up 7.32 percent in the third quarter, and down 0.76 percent in the fourth quarter. First quarter 1995 was up 2.30 percent.

Portfolio: Composition was recently 80.6 percent stocks and 19.4 percent cash. Heaviest stock weightings were technology, industrial cyclicals, and financials.

Data from Morningstar Inc.

Fidelity Small Cap Stock Fund

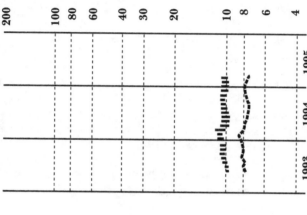

IIIIIIIII Net Asset Value ($)   -------- Performance relative to S&P 500

14

Crime Prevention

A visit through the Borg-Warner Security Corp. regional facility, which is surrounded by high barbed-wire fences, required a careful security check-in procedure for reasons that quickly became apparent.

The company's Wells Fargo armored trucks, insured to haul loads of currency ranging from $5 million to $20 million depending on size of the truck and number of guards on board, were being unloaded. Armed guards and security cameras were everywhere. I briefly handled a bag of $113,000 in cash from a local grocery chain that was being carried from a truck. Meanwhile, in the sorting room, stacks of legal tender were being counted, with some individual workers there counting more than $1 million in cash daily.

You can't be too careful these days.

Crime, unfortunately, has become a growth industry in this country. At the rate it's growing, it will be considerably worse in the 21st century. The evening news has become a police blotter. More than 14 million serious crimes were reported to the police in 1993, and it's conservatively estimated that such activity costs Americans more than $400 billion annually. Of the total, the price tag for business-related crime is $125 billion and projected to exceed $200 billion in the year 2000.

Fire is another concern. Incendiary and suspicious fires caused more than $2 billion in damage to buildings last year. Arson and suspected arson account for one of every three dollars lost in nonresidential building fires, according to the National Fire Protection Association.

Little wonder, in light of all these statistics and a general attitude of fear, that the $65 billion private security industry continues to grow at an 8 to 10 percent annual clip. The relentless quest for improved protection offers some solid stock opportunities.

Borg-Warner Security, with $1.8 billion in annual revenues, is one such investment. The world's largest security firm, it provides a wide range of services such as guards, electronic security systems, armored trucks, automated teller servicing, and cash management.

Another stock with potential is Central Sprinkler Corp., a maker of automatic fire sprinkler head nozzles and valves used in industrial, hotel, and residential applications to fight fire caused by arson or natural sources. It holds about 25 percent of the U.S. market. The company also distributes other components for sprinkler systems and markets a computer-aided design system for the design and installation of sprinkler systems.

"Crime is getting no better, and the acceleration of drugs and weapons on the street at a time when municipal budgets are already strained means people demand security more than ever," explained Donald Trauscht, who at the end of 1995 retires as chairman and chief executive of Chicago-based Borg-Warner Security. "Everyone these days wants to see someone in a uniform around and electronic security as well."

Worrisome FBI findings indicate that the number of juveniles arrested for homicide each year has soared 142 percent in the past decade, while violent crime has increased from 562 per 100,000 a decade ago to 758 per 100,000. FBI Director Louis Freeh, welcoming some recent percentage declines in burglary and robbery, still characterizes the national crisis as "staggering."

The World Trade Center bombing in New York City was yet another example of why security must be stepped up, Trauscht added.

Borg-Warner Security serves 160,000 clients from 600 offices throughout the United States, Canada, Britain, and Colombia. Average revenue growth over the past 15 years has been more than 15 percent, aided by the acquisition of more than 70 other security companies. Revenue growth of 13 percent and earnings growth of 15 percent are quite likely in the future, about half of that growth coming from acquisitions in the rapidly consolidating security industry.

"Our employees provided the first real security at Hurricane Andrew and at the L.A. riots for our corporate clients, and we patrol in unmarked cars for the city of Oceanside, California, keeping in close contact with the police," said Trauscht, who was wearing a lapel pin for the 1996 Olympics in Atlanta, where his firm will provide security. "We're a growth company, and, while I wouldn't expect a dividend from our stock, I believe we can produce 15 to 20 percent annual growth."

The company is a national leader in all security industry segments in which it competes, with the biggest revenue gains recently coming in armored trucks and alarms. It's one of the only security companies that can handle truly national accounts, as big corporations outsource their security needs.

Its corporate history includes the romantic adventure of Pony Express riders dodging arrows and bullets to deliver the mail and rifle-toting Wells Fargo agents protecting gold shipments. Tradition and adventure are a part of the firm's ongoing mystique.

Henry Wells and William Fargo formed Wells Fargo in 1852 to transport freight, currency, and gold between the East Coast and the California frontier. Next, in 1860, William Hepburn Russell established an overland mail route traveled by daring Pony Express riders between St. Joseph, Missouri, and Sacramento, California. Finally, in 1910, William Burns, the foremost American investigator of his day and first director of the government agency that became the Federal Bureau of Investigation, founded the Burns Detective Agency. During their long histories, Wells Fargo, Pony Express, and Burns set the industry standards for security.

Today Borg-Warner Security's guard services division includes Burns International Security Services and Wells Fargo Guard Services, which together provide 70,000 uniformed security officers. The company's largest division accounts for two-thirds of revenues and is likely to grow at a double-digit annual rate. It's a fragmented industry, the five largest guard service companies making up only about 20 percent of the market. Borg-Warner has captured about 9 percent of that market by developing a diverse client mix. Its guards protect commercial, industrial, and government facilities, monitor electronic systems, and control public and employee access to various facilities involving more than 13,000 clients. To its credit, the employee turnover rate is considerably lower than the industrywide average. An example of a unique specialized service is Burns International's nuclear business unit, which handles security at half the nation's nuclear power plants that use private security. Largest clients include Commonwealth Edison, Northeast Utilities, Carolina Light & Power, and Illinois Power Companies. Sporting events also include many Burns guards.

"The worst problem we face is that people want General Douglas MacArthur security but don't want to pay for it," said Trauscht.

Another specialty is Wells Fargo's investigative service, which does background checks and drug screening for employers nationwide. Able to handle large jobs as well as small temporary jobs, Borg-Warner Security is able to do on-site screening for four types of drugs in less than 10 minutes.

The company's second division, Wells Fargo Alarm Services, handles design, installation, and servicing of sophisticated electronic security systems and offers central monitoring for financial institutions, government and defense installations, and commercial and industrial clients. Borg-Warner is the second largest player in this $5 billion industry, its 4 percent share ranking only behind ADT Ltd. It has more than 120,000 alarm service customers. Individual systems may include intrusion and fire detection and building access control. Systems are either monitored at the customer's facilities or linked through telephone lines or long-range radio to monitoring stations.

The national monitoring center in Omaha, Nebraska, is dedicated to national retail chains and fast-food outlets. About two-thirds of Alarm Services revenues come from monitoring and service charges, another one-third from equipment sales and installation. It's the most profitable segment of Borg-Warner Security's business. A big plus is the company's software development group in Los Angeles. By shifting to highly secured digital transmission, it is streamlining costs and improving efficiency.

With about 13 million property crimes occurring annually in this country, with losses of more than $6 billion, studies have found that businesses with security systems are half as likely to be burglarized as those without them.

Meanwhile, a persistent problem in the security business has been the lack of quality guards or lack of proper background checks of those guards.

Years ago, a college classmate of mine got a night watchman job at a large factory basically so he could study and get paid for it. As I related to Trauscht, on my friend's first night on the job he was issued a uniform—and a gun. He was even permitted to take the gun home with him after work. There were no guidelines or training, and the company most certainly had no idea what this fellow's personal history might have been. We laughingly referred to him as "Kenny the cop" and drew humorous comparisons to Barney Fife on "The Andy Griffith Show." Viewed in hindsight, perhaps it wasn't such a laughing matter. Companies that simply hand out guns to anyone are asking for trouble.

"Half the states in the United States have no requirements for security people, and there are lots of mom and pop security businesses that handle the business in the same way that it was handled with your friend," said Trauscht. "We do things in a military sense here and have supported legislation to raise the performance of private security firms."

Borg-Warner Security has been the leader in pushing for stringent guidelines for screening prospective guards. It has already speeded up the process for checking out applicants through federal information on credit reports, driver's licenses, criminal records, and drug use. It set up its own national screening center in Nashville, Tennessee. It has been so successful that it's now a $10 million business serving outside clients as well.

The Bel-Air Patrol is another unique service of the alarm services division, providing residential alarm systems and guard patrol services to 26 Southern California communities such as Bel-Air, Beverly Hills, and Pacific Palisades. A central station in Oxnard, California, monitors systems of more than 7,000 residential customers. As more communities around the country cut back police staffing, private patrols are expected to grow significantly.

The company's third division is armored, automated teller machine, and cash processing services, which has far-flung responsibilities through 125 branch offices in the United States and Puerto Rico. Wells Fargo Armored Service Corp. transports more than $4 billion in currency, coin, and other valuables for financial institutions and commercial customers each business day. It has 2,200 armored vehicles operated by armed personnel. While it provides 65 percent of the revenues in its division, it has low profit margins and faces strong competition. Contracts are usually for multiyear terms with automatic one-year renewals. In 1993, the company landed a contract with NationsBank, which doubled the number of locations served. Large customers include Bank of America, K mart, Wal-Mart, Bay Banks, and First Union Corp. One problem has been the consolidation of U.S. banking institutions and the subsequent loss of clients.

As a safety precaution, all of the company's transport employees must wear bulletproof vests. Even most urban police don't require that.

Cash processing services are expanding. They include automated currency storage and preparation, micro-encoding of checks, deposit verification and consolidation, coin wrapping and storage, and food stamp processing. The company is the nation's largest servicer of ATMs, handling about 25,000 machines. An automated national dispatching center in Columbia, Maryland, coordinates customer requests, confirms data, and directs field technicians to malfunctioning ATMs. More than 100,000 ATM entries are handled each month. In 1993, the company formed a strategic alliance with NCR Corp. (now called AT&T Global Information Solutions) to offer financial institutions a complete range of ATM management and maintenance services. When customers phone a toll-free number with complaints, Borg-Warner Security guarantees a response time of 90 minutes or less.

Courier services is the company's fourth division. Pony Express Courier Corp., the nation's largest ground courier

company, transports time-sensitive, non-negotiable financial documents such as cancelled checks and small packages
such as urgent mail in 32 states. About 22 million shipments
are carried each year for Federal Reserve Banks, financial
institutions, and commercial customers. Among its largest
customers are Wachovia Bank, John Deere Co., First Interstate Bank, Fox Meyer Drug, and First Union National Bank.
Its fleet of 21,000 vehicles travel 225 million miles annually.
There's same-day and next-day delivery of shipments within
a 500-mile radius.

The present company's predecessor, Borg-Warner
Corp., was acquired in a $4.4 billion leveraged buyout in
1987. In January 1993, the company completed a recapital-
ization that included an initial public offering of shares of
Borg-Warner Security Corp. as a privately held firm and the
refinancing of some outstanding indebtedness.

One persistent concern about Borg-Warner Security is
its lack of net worth, due to costs associated with going public, the spinoff, and the additional writedown. There are also
possible liabilities facing Centaur, an old Borg-Warner insurance subsidiary that ceased writing insurance in 1984
and has been operating under rehabilitation since 1987.
Several lawsuits have been filed by insurance firms seeking
damages from the failure of Centaur to satisfy reinsurance
obligations. Although Borg-Warner Security doesn't believe
there would be a negative effect on its financial position if
decisions go against it, the situation is worth keeping in
mind. The company obviously requires a stable and growing cash flow to support its balance sheet. So far, it has it.

Fire is another concern of modern Americans. Automatic sprinklers are highly effective tools to save lives and
property in the event of fire, according to the National Fire
Protection Association.

When sprinklers are present, the chances of dying in a
fire are cut by one-third to two-thirds and property loss per
fire is cut by one-half to two-thirds. According to the In-

ternational Association of Fire Chiefs, there has never been a documented case of multiple death by fire in a working sprinklered structure.

That's a plus for Central Sprinkler, which sells its products to more than 3,000 contractors. It has taken its financial lumps during the long slump in the construction industry, though the situation began to improve in 1994. Most of its sales increase in the prior fiscal year were due to the acquisition of a distributor of fire sprinkler equipment and also a manufacturer of pipe couplings and fittings.

It will benefit from the fact that industrial and hotel sprinkler codes are becoming more stringent at the same time insurers and companies are attempting to lessen their risks. Residential sprinklers, now representing about 15 percent of its business, should increasingly become a profit center as more states adopt model fire codes. Sprinkler systems are vital in nursing homes and other facilities where residents are often unable to escape under their own power.

"In the 21st century, new construction simply won't go forward without a sprinkler system, and the competitor with the best marketing force and lowest cost will clearly benefit," predicted George Meyer, chief executive officer of Central Sprinkler, based in Lansdale, Pennsylvania. "Greater use of sprinkler systems in homes makes economic sense because it cuts insurance premiums and means fewer fire stations will be required by municipalities."

Purchased by current management in 1984 and taken public the following year, Central Sprinkler has a history of more than 60 years. Though a dominant company in its field, it faces competition from eight other manufacturers.

It has a strong balance sheet, making it capable of handling difficult times while gaining market share from weaker competitors that can't keep up. The strength of the retrofit sprinkler business in existing structures due to new ordinances helped the company's bottom line in the dry period for new construction. It has expanded its sales and marketing programs and is spending more money on new product development and promotion. A lot depends on the success of new products, where it has a reputation as an innovator. While Central Sprinkler's turnaround is likely to lag behind the overall construction market, shareholders will profit when a turnaround occurs. This is a stock whose profits over the long haul should be capable of growing at a 15 percent or better annual rate. A 10 percent rise in market demand tied to new construction has helped the company post strong increases in sales and earnings.

Domestically, quality-conscious Central Sprinkler is known for many device patents. Sprinklers capable of spraying a 130-foot area a year ago have been replaced with new models that cover 400 square feet. It has most recently been marketing smaller, more efficient ceiling sprinklers for large discount warehouse stores. The latest catalog includes "concealed" model sprinklers, which it was the first to introduce. Cover plates blend in with the decor, offering the designer the option of plated or custom-painted finish. The catalog also includes its Omega quick-response sprinkler, which operates five to six times faster than a standard sprinkler. It was initially introduced five years before similar products from other manufacturers.

The overseas market for sprinkler systems currently isn't as strong as the domestic market, because requirements vary considerably from country to country, with many, inexplicably, favoring sprinklers in factories rather than office buildings.

"The market for our product, as part of the general construction cycle, has been down 20 percent, but we've grown nonetheless," said Meyer, who notes that the company's stock shouldn't be viewed as a source of quick profit. "When the market comes back, our profit margins will improve significantly and so will our stock price."

Central Sprinkler is a stock for patient investors who can wait out cycles of the construction industry. However, just like Borg-Warner Security, it is a leading-edge company that will encounter strong demand as we enter the 21st century. After all, no advances to date seem capable of putting a permanent end to either crime or fire.

Investment Close-Up: Borg-Warner Security Corporation

200 South Michigan Avenue, Chicago, Illinois 60604
(312) 322-8500

Borg-Warner Security is the largest U.S. supplier of protective services, providing a broad line of guard, alarm, armored transport, and courier services.

Chairman, CEO, and president through 1995: Donald Trauscht (Chairman and CEO upon Trauscht's retirement: J. Joe Adjoran)
Investor contact: Joseph Allen
Total employees: 92,000

Stock: Traded on the New York Stock Exchange under the symbol "BOR." Price of $7½ a share (5/16/95). No dividend. Price-to-earnings ratio of 20.

Sales and Earnings: Sales of $1.8 billion in 1994, with earnings of $13.1 million. Five-year annual decline in sales of 4 percent, with earnings decline of 63 percent.

Earnings per Share Data: Projected (Institutional Brokers Estimate System) five-year earnings per share annual growth rate of 11.5 percent.

Data from Bridge Information Systems Inc.

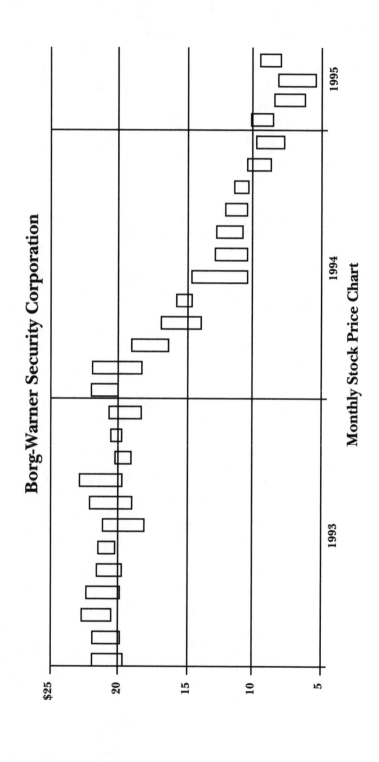

Borg-Warner Security Corporation

Monthly Stock Price Chart

Investment Close-Up: Central Sprinkler Corporation
451 North Cannon Avenue, Lansdale, Pennsylvania 19446
(215) 362-0700

Central Sprinkler is a leading manufacturer of automatic fire sprinkler heads, valves, and other components as well as a distributor of component parts of complete automatic fire sprinkler systems. A strong construction industry is the key to future results.

CEO: George Meyer
President: William Meyer
Vice president of finance and investor contact: Albert Sabol
Total employees: 778

Stock: Traded on NASDAQ under the symbol "CNSP." Price of $19¾ a share (5/16/95). No dividend. Price-to-earnings ratio of 19.

Sales and Earnings: Sales of $116 million in 1994, with earnings of $4 million. Five-year annual sales growth of 13 percent, with earnings decline of 10 percent.

Earnings per Share Growth: Five-year earnings per share annual decline of 21 percent.

Data from Bridge Information Systems Inc.

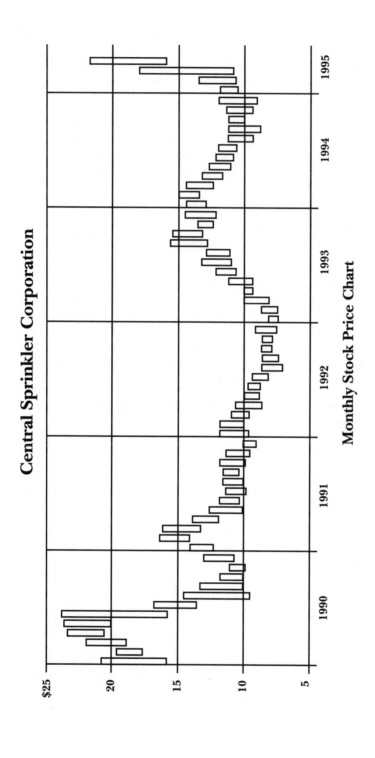

Central Sprinkler Corporation

Monthly Stock Price Chart

15

Hewlett-Packard

Just when you thought you'd seen it all, Hewlett-Packard Company comes up with a device to help you make printouts from your television screen.

Cable television subscribers using an interactive service will be able to print out all kinds of coupons, retail and restaurant promotions, maps, video images, invoices, and other information.

This innovative printer will also help deliver more magazine information to home subscribers, since a viewer can print out a copy of a magazine article available on the interactive system. The service will be a less expensive spinoff of the Hewlett-Packard Vidjet Pro, a video recorder–sized device for professional broadcast engineers. It allows video images from any source to be printed quickly on plain paper or transparencies.

"The communications revolution is a convergence of many areas, and the ability to compress and decompress television images through a color printer is just one of them," said Lewis Platt, who was named Hewlett-Packard chief executive in 1992 and received the additional title of chairman in 1993. "The 21st century will be a world where 'anywhere, anytime' communication will free you to have information wherever and whenever you need it."

Hewlett-Packard's interest in the technological future has been surprising. Written off by most experts as a conventional computer, printer, and workstation manufacturer that would have difficulty squeezing more profits out of those businesses, it is instead offering a surprising opportunity for investors who are willing to believe in its newfound vision. The new chairman has been trying a little bit of everything.

Platt's desire to lasso the future makes the stock an attractive long-term choice.

Within days of stepping up to the top management position of the Palo Alto, California–based company, Platt was making plans to use its unique blend of core technologies to join the communications revolution of the 21st century. Its impressive arsenal includes its respected family of computers, its test and measurement instruments, and its computer networking capabilities. These will be used to come up with brand-new products, a necessary step if Hewlett-Packard isn't to be left behind other high-tech companies that have been busily making deals for the new digital era.

"Five or six years ago, people didn't think Hewlett-Packard would be around now, but that belief changed with our recent successes," said Platt, noting that the company's worldwide PC sales are growing the fastest of the top computer companies, and its workstation and printer sales are also advancing at a healthy clip. "Founders Dave Packard and Bill Hewlett built the world's greatest measuring instrument firm, John Young (the previous CEO) built a great computer company, and now I think of this company as being in the third period."

One-third of Hewlett-Packard's research budget is now devoted to new products such as the video printer. Computers are vital to the new worldwide information structure, and his company will supply them, Platt contends. Computer peripherals, such as wireless handheld PCs and printers, are also important. The HP 100LX handheld PC, which is about the size of a calculator, can send and receive electronic mail when equipped with a modem, and is made through a cooperation effort with the company's wireless partners. For 1994, the company doubled the memory of the HP 100LX and lowered the price of its one-megabyte version to $549. The company has also added to the HP 100LX a wireless voice-mail subscriber service called HP-StarLink, which transmits voice and data messages, as well as news, sports, and financial updates. In addition, Hewlett-Packard and Novell Inc. have bought minority stakes in Geoworks of Berkeley, California, a developer of operating systems for small handheld devices, in order to offer specialized information appliances for business users such as real estate agents, doctors, and nurses.

Platt's goal is to have one handheld computing device to combine functions of handheld computers, personal digital assistants, and cellular phones, with the capability to print out documents on the printer in your office. The company is willing to develop partnerships with other companies in order to get into new market quickly.

The cable TV printer was developed for Time Warner's interactive television network project and is initially being made available free of charge to 4,000 households in Orlando, Florida, in the test program begun in the fourth quarter of 1994. There are other innovations as well.

For example, Hewlett-Packard is supplying its largest computers to Pacific Telesis Group for an interactive television system in which movies, shopping catalogs, and other programs can be ordered. It is also selling cable television boxes to Tele-Communications Inc. for its interactive television service in 1995. Comcast, another large cable company, has also placed a significant order for the boxes. A prototype physician's workstation is being used by the U.S. Department of Veterans Affairs Medical Center in Palo Alto. It collects patient and medical information from computers throughout the V.A. and exhibits it on one computer screen to address a patient's needs.

"An example of how the new communication can be of benefit is the fact that, if I travel to New York today, become ill, and am rushed to a hospital there, I'm an unknown human being and they'd have no knowledge of me," said Platt, an engineer with 28 years of experience at the firm. "That's not a good world, because the hospital should be able to tap into my medical base for the vital medical information about me. In the future, it will."

The company's unique diagnostic system, designed for Ford Motor Co. dealers, combines instruments that monitor a car's internal operations with a personal computer. The system includes a "flight recorder" that plugs into the data link found in most Fords and stores the vital information for analysis at the garage. In addition, the company is studying a device that would allow researchers to collect soil samples near a toxic waste spill, analyze them immediately, transmit the results to a laboratory, and return a recommendation within minutes.

Hewlett-Packard and Finland's Nokia Telecommunications joined in an agreement in 1994 to develop intelligent network systems that will make advanced telecommunications services such as telephone calling-card validations available to business and residential users. It's estimated that intelligent network equipment in Europe alone will reach $5 billion by the year 2000, with such services accounting for 15 percent of all call-charge revenues. Also in 1994, Hewlett-Packard and Northern Telecom announced an alliance to outfit corporate buildings with powerful structured wiring systems capable of handling "information super-highway" traffic. Meanwhile, a new joint venture with Swedish telecommunications giant Ericsson is addressing the growing demand for network management systems among telecommunications operators and service providers around the world.

Platt's vision for future profits has been explained in "coffee talks" with employees around the world. While not everyone in the company's scientific community is necessarily excited about it all or exactly sure what the vision entails, it does offer an opportunity to create new products rather than simply upgrade existing ones.

"I put it all under the heading of HP-MC^2, or Hewlett-Packard equals measurement, computing, and communications," said Platt, who has created an MC^2 Council of his top technical and marketing staffers to help delineate markets for future growth. "My hope is to be able to capitalize on our strong capabilities and our successes as a company."

The beginnings of Hewlett-Packard marked the very beginnings of what was to become known as Silicon Valley. It was founded in 1939 by William Hewlett and David Packard, two Stanford University electrical engineering graduates who built their first product in a rented Palo Alto garage. It was an electronic test instrument called an audio oscillator that gave higher performance than competing instruments in measuring the frequency of sound, and, most important, it cost less as well.

The partnership's first big break came when Walt Disney Studios purchased eight of the first model and used them in the production of the stereophonic sound presentation of the classic animated film *Fantasia*.

The company then, as now, was product driven. Government orders for other measurement products during World War II resulted in an increase in staffing to nearly 100 people working two shifts a day, with annual sales of nearly $1 million. After the war, it introduced the first of its line of microwave measurement products and by the end of the decade was annually bringing 20 new instruments onto the market. The first public offering of Hewlett-Packard stock was in late 1957, and it was listed on the New York Stock Exchange in 1961. In the 1960s, the first HP mini-computer and first high-tech desktop calculator were introduced, and it also gained worldwide recognition when two of its "atomic clocks" coordinated the national time standards of various countries to within a millionth of a second. The company's electronics technology was also extended to the fields of medicine and analytical chemistry.

When Apollo II landed on the moon in 1969 and U.S. astronauts Neil Armstrong and Buzz Aldrin leaped about on the moon's surface, Hewlett-Packard diodes and switches helped guide and control the journey. International orders for its products grew to 30 percent of the total. The HP-35, the world's first scientific pocket calculator, was introduced in 1972 and made the engineer's slide rule obsolete. The company subsequently branched into business computing with the HP 3000 mid-range computer. It also introduced powerful desktop workstations and networking products to connect computers. Hewlett-Packard pioneered inkjet printing technology with the introduction of the HP Thinkjet printer in 1984 and introduced the HP LaserJet printer— the most successful single product in the company's history—a year later. The company surpassed $10 billion in total orders for its products for the first time in 1988.

"It was a period of strong growth and good financial performance that gave us the resources to do things for the future," noted Platt, whose firm currently enjoys a strong financial position at a time when troubled competitors are going through difficult reorganizations.

Hewlett-Packard is dominant in laser printers. Whenever you shop for a laser printer, it seems that sales personnel virtually across the board recommend the HP first and urge you to take a look at the quality of its copies. As a matter of fact, the manuscript for this book was printed on a Hewlett-Packard LaserJet. The company keeps improving this popular product to stay ahead of the competition. For example, the newest HP LaserJet 5P is a 600 dpi printer, meaning that it lays down 600 dots per inch both horizontally and vertically. Prior generations of laser printers in the $800 to $1,000 range have typically been 300 dpi machines. Anyone who wanted the greater print quality of 600 dpi had to pay significantly more. In addition, new fuser (the device that uses heat to bond laser toner particles to paper) and paper-path technologies allow it to print single envelopes more easily, as well as items as small as mailing labels and 3 × 5 cards.

The world's leading maker of color printers sold two million color DeskJet printers worldwide in 1993, a 122 percent increase over the prior year. Color printer sales are growing faster than sales for all other types of printers, and HP is responsible for most of those sales. The firm's black-and-white DeskJet 500 remains the bestselling printer in the world.

While Hewlett-Packard is the nation's second largest computer maker in terms of revenue, its personal computer business wasn't a strong force until the middle of 1992. Its PC line in the early 1980s didn't gain a large following, primarily because it wasn't compatible with the IBM PC, and even after it switched to IBM compatibility in the mid-1980s the sales remained weak. Because it offered overpriced and narrowly marketed machines, the company lost market share to lower-priced competitors such as Compaq Computer Corp., even though its quality and reliability were high.

With PC sales growing faster than any other part of the hardware industry, Hewlett-Packard finally decided that enough was enough and began to cut prices and market aggressively. Coincidentally, a general PC price war among other computer makers began in the summer of 1992, forcing the price of high-end computers down from more than $5,000 to less than $2,000. Consumers increasingly decided to go with brand names because the price advantage of "clones" made by smaller firms wasn't that much anymore. Hewlett-Packard benefited from this brand-name rush. In addition, it began making more PCs and expanding its sales outlets to include large national dealers. Intensifying its efforts, the company shortened its new-product cycle from 18 months to 6 months. It also added features on some machines, such as its "coffee break" button which lets a user blank the screen for a period of time without turning off the whole machine so no one else can look at what's on it. That has proven particularly helpful in offices that deal with confidential financial information.

The dramatic result of all these positives was more than a doubling of Hewlett-Packard's worldwide PC sales, to about 640,000 in 1993 from 305,000 the prior year. No other company of its size has grown so quickly in PC sales. It remains to be seen whether it can meet its goal of becoming one of the top five PC makers in sales, thereby moving up from its current position as number seven. After market share gains from the smaller competitors, head-to-head combat between the largest computer makers will likely make share gains more difficult.

In early 1994, the company launched new low-cost desktop workstations with prices beginning below $4,000 and business servers costing less than $6,000. These computers are powered by a new high-performance HP microprocessor that is one-third the cost and one-half the size of chips made by archrival Intel Corp.

Not only PCs, but printers and workstations carry lower gross profit margins than other products Hewlett-Packard makes. The minicomputer business and the company's new cable set-top box operations could similarly be hit with stiff pricing competition.

Hewlett-Packard's computers based on its present PA-RISC architecture are designed to be easily upgraded for more power, which has kept its computers at the front of the performance curve. However, to move into the next generation of hardware technology, Hewlett-Packard has begun research on what's called Very Long Instruction Word computing, designed to speed up computers by taking tasks from the microprocessor and moving them to the software. Platt predicts HP Wide Word computers will be available within two years. HP and IBM, acting in tandem, also plan to introduce products next year to increase the speed and capacity of computer local area networks sixfold to tenfold. Those networks link several machines, allowing them to share files and printers. Hewlett-Packard and Intel Corp. will cooperate on microprocessor-based advanced technologies. Hewlett-Packard has also acquired 15 percent of Taligent, a joint-venture company of IBM and Apple Computer that is working on operating software.

"In terms of our company's profit centers, my goal is to make sure that we have a reasonable balance of profitability without much to distinguish one area from another, although computers and computer peripherals are growing the fastest," explained Platt.

To get a handle on the future, Hewlett-Packard has also joined a consortium on how the information superhighway may be assembled and used. The consortium consists of universities, government laboratories, telephone carriers, and computer companies. It will create a prototype capable of transmitting a large volume of data and attempt to prove the number of ways that the network is useful. Firms such as HP will provide computers, while AT&T and Sprint Corp. provide communications lines.

"When we talk about a national information infrastructure, I get concerned when the hype raises a lot of expectations that will not be met at first, meaning that we have to go through some consumer disappointment," Platt added. "For example, genetic engineering was a victim of such hype in its early days, but look at all of its accomplishments now that a little time has gone by."

Net revenues increased 23 percent in 1994, with earnings per share rising 32 percent. Demand for the company's printers and network products remains strong, and cost-control efforts offset the downward pressure on margins. Order growth has also been good. Revenues are expected to grow at a pace of somewhat less than 20 percent, with earnings per share rising a solid 15 percent. That makes its stock well worth considering.

"Hewlett-Packard stock is that of a mature $20 billion growth company that's deep in financial resources and also has depth of management," Platt explained. "To provide shareholder value, we are emphasizing return on sales, putting a new emphasis on return on assets, and also looking for solid growth."

A positive attitude toward employees, despite the inevitable workforce cuts of the computer industry, is another important factor at Hewlett-Packard. *Personnel Journal* named the company the winner of its top award for general excellence in human resources management, the 1993 Optimas Award, and cited it for its efforts to improve workforce balance and diversity. The HP corporate objectives initially published in 1957 and updated from time to time emphasize trust and respect for individuals, a high level of achievement and contribution, uncompromising integrity, teamwork, flexibility, and innovation.

In a 1982 speech at the University of Notre Dame, cofounder William Hewlett made the following comments—which are still included in an HP brochure to employees—

about the firm's ongoing attitude toward its workforce and financial dealings:

> It is important to remember that both Dave [Packard] and I were products of the Great Depression. We had observed its effects on all sides, and it could not help but influence our decisions on how a company should be run. Two thoughts were clear from the start. First, we did not want to run a hire-and-fire operation, but rather a company built on a loyal and dedicated workforce. Further, we felt that this workforce should be able to share to some extent in the progress of the company. Second, we wished to operate, as much as possible, on a pay-as-you-go basis, that our growth be financed by our earnings and not by debt.

That basic philosophy has provided a strong financial underpinning for the ambitious 21st-century goals that new boss Lewis Platt now has for the company. It already does many things well and has a strong base of technology and products. That puts it on a firm financial footing when it tries new concepts, not all of which will be big successes.

Oh, by the way, Bill and Dave's initial garage workshop in Palo Alto has been designated California registered historical landmark No. 976 as the birthplace of "Silicon Valley."

Investment Close-Up: Hewlett-Packard Company

3000 Hanover St., Palo Alto, California 94304
(415) 857-1501

Hewlett-Packard manufactures a broad range of electronic instruments and computer systems.

Chairman, president, and CEO: Lewis Platt
Investor contact: Steve Beitler
Total employees: 98,400

Stock: Traded on the New York Stock Exchange under the symbol "HWP." Price of $71 a share (5/16/95). Dividend of 80 cents a share, which has grown at a 29 percent annual rate over the past five years. Price-to-earnings ratio of 20.

Sales and Earnings: Sales of $25 billion in 1994, with earnings of $1.6 billion. Five-year annual sales growth of 17 percent, with earnings growth of 21 percent.

Earnings per Share Growth: Five-year earnings per share annual growth rate of 16 percent. Projected (Institutional Brokers Estimate System) five-year earnings per share annual growth rate of 14 percent.

Data from Bridge Information Systems Inc.

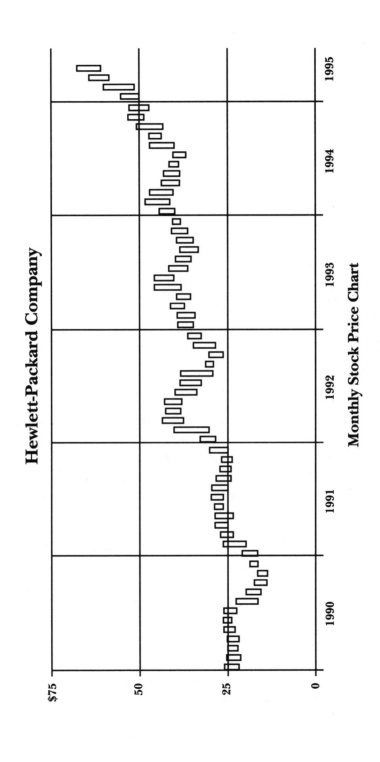

Hewlett-Packard Company

Monthly Stock Price Chart

16

Real Estate Investment Trusts

As his lengthy "road show" drew to a close, C. Ronald Blankenship was taking a deep breath and relaxing over breakfast in a downtown Chicago hotel. He'd made presentations in Los Angeles, New York, Boston, Philadelphia, Newark, Minneapolis, Appleton, Wisconsin, Milwaukee, and Chicago.

Depending on how large each group was, he'd used slides or a flip chart book to present important graphics as he explained investment strategy and the real estate markets. He'd open the floor for questions. His audiences consisted of insurance companies and pension funds with plenty of money to invest. Soon he'd be on a conference call to some cities he hadn't visited personally.

Blankenship, as the chairman of El Paso, Texas–based Security Capital Pacific Trust, was preaching the gospel of the real estate investment trust, or REIT, a company that holds a real estate portfolio and is traded publicly as a stock.

REITs, investing in real estate, mortgages, or both, have become attractive to average investors because they pay out most of their income as dividends, currently averaging about 6 percent. Over the past 15 years, the average annual total return (yield plus price appreciation) of equity REITs has been a strong 15 percent. Investing in an REIT is much like investing in a mutual fund, in that you're pooling your money with other investors. There's liquidity, since about one-third of REITs are listed on the major stock exchanges, the rest over the counter. It's a chance for the average investor to become a commercial real estate mogul on a small scale, dabbling in ownership of apartment buildings, shopping centers, office buildings, and warehouses without having to worry about fix-ups and daily management.

The past several years, equity REITs have been a hot investment, their market capitalization growing by $9 billion to $39 billion in 1994. There's been a flood of new initial public offerings, totaling more than 42 in 1994. That's recognition that the securitization of real estate through REITs is an important trend that will accelerate as we enter the 21st century.

Security Capital Pacific Trust (the result of the 1995 merger of Property Trust of America and the private REIT Security Capital Pacific Inc.), Weingarten Realty Investors, and United Dominion Realty Trust represent three good investment choices in proven REITs whose future prospects are impressive.

"The REIT market was overheated for a while, and a lot of people were really scared about it, but it's now gaining some discipline again and starting to differentiate between the degree of quality of the various products available," said Blankenship, whose REIT's dividend yield is nearly 7 percent. "There has also been a significant growth in the analyst community that follows REITs, from just several analysts three years ago to the current situation with virtually all Wall Street firms having REIT analysts."

Most REITs have their own specialty and geographic region.

Security Capital Pacific Trust invests primarily in apartment complexes in 11 western states, a region with good job growth. It also owns some shopping centers, motels, and office buildings. The company emphasizes "affordable," but not subsidized, buildings and bases this specialty on the fact that 75 percent of renters earn less than $30,000 annually, with most of them actually in the $21,000 to $26,000 range. The desire of many companies to buy high-end rental properties really isn't in line with actual income levels of renters, Blankenship emphasized.

"Ours aren't beautiful properties on magazine covers, but we don't really want the 'trophy' properties," Blankenship said in his quiet, articulate Texas drawl. "We want Sam Walton's customers in our apartments."

Speaking of discount stores, Weingarten Realty Investors of Houston specializes in "value-oriented" shopping center properties in Texas, Louisiana, Arkansas, Oklahoma, New Mexico, Tennessee, and Arizona, along with a few apartment complexes and other properties. The REIT is now the lifeblood for such commercial projects.

"We're one of the largest equity REITs, and it lets us raise capital at more advantageous prices," said Stanford Alexander, chairman and chief executive of Weingarten, whose REIT has a yield of around 7 percent. "For the investor, an REIT is a vehicle with good current yield and growth potential, and our properties are so diversified and spread out that no one thing is capable of really hurting this company."

Stores such as Walgreen's, Kroger, Randall's Food Market, Albertson's, K mart, Wal-Mart, and Marshall's serve as anchors for its 100,000- to 400,000-square-foot centers. Bright photos of The Gap and other stores fill the company's annual reports, including some impressive "before and after" shots. The corporate goal is to add value to each center. If, for example, one has several vacancies when Weingarten buys it, the company will probably remodel it and will also improve the mall's overall merchandise mix.

"It's a great niche because we're catering to consumers who are value-oriented, a trend that won't ever go away and a retailing format that won't change," explained Alexander, who has held the position of chief executive since 1962. "The general economy is important to our business, but we've had 92 percent occupancy in our Texas locations despite some of the difficult economic problems that have occurred here."

United Dominion Realty Trust, based in Richmond, Virginia, specializes in apartments and also has some shopping centers. They're located in the southeastern part of the country in a geographic area that stretches from Delaware to Miami. It has tended to buy older properties in less than peak shape and renovate them, an ability that not all real estate companies possess.

"The traditional sources of real estate financing have disappeared, with syndications gone, insurance companies withdrawing, and foreign investors leaving as well," explained John McCann, president and chief executive of United Dominion, which has a dividend yield of more than 6 percent. "The REIT provides liquidity as a freely traded stock, and the trend is clearly toward the public markets financing real estate."

McCann notes that the partners of many older real estate partnerships are getting old, and the properties are selling. The buyers of these properties are REITs. Future growth will be driven by a need for affordable housing. The new nationwide emphasis on adding jobs in the lower-paying service industries means most growth will occur in the "lower portions" of the economy, he said.

"In the next century, immigration to this country will also be greater and will increase the demand for apartments," he added. "No matter how low interest rates get, it is still always cheaper to rent."

The apartment business is looking better, and rents have begun to rise. That's because the supply of new apartments in this country has seriously lagged behind population growth ever since the 1986 Tax Act, which signaled the end of tax advantages associated with income-producing real estate. Nationwide apartment starts of nearly 700,000 in 1985 gradually fell to less than 200,000 annually. Apartment construction isn't popular in many municipalities at a time when antigrowth initiatives and restrictive zoning are important factors. New apartments are criticized because they increase demands on local infrastructure, especially school systems. In addition, lower-income families and minorities comprise a disproportionately large share of apartment renters, so local residents may often use antiapartment zoning ordinances to preserve the "existing nature" of their communities.

The lack of new apartment construction puts existing buildings at a premium, as does the trend away from traditional household patterns. Rising divorce rates, the greater frequency of single parents, and the higher number of unrelated individuals living together all reinforce apartment demand.

Be a careful investor when considering REITs, weighing the positives and negatives. REITs are a good portfolio diversification tool, and the depressed real estate markets appear to be gradually recovering. They offer the advantage of being a liquid form of investment in real estate, which historically has been an illiquid asset. Besides the 6 percent average dividend yield—which in riskier examples can be as high as 9 percent—there's also price appreciation to figure into the equation. Those REITs investing in apartments and discount shopping centers seem to be the strongest lately, while lower-level malls, office complexes, and industrial properties aren't held in as high regard by many investment analysts. However, attractiveness also takes into account who's running the REIT.

A real advantage to REITs is that they can be easily bought from stockbrokers for the usual brokerage commissions associated with stocks. Then, as an investor, you basically collect income that the trust earns from rent and other sources. Hefty dividends make REITs especially attractive to income investors, and there's a reason why these dividends are so generous. REITs are actually required by law to distribute at least 95 percent of their taxable income as dividends to shareholders. Since they pay out so much of earnings, they're not taxed before they're distributed, and investors get a bigger share of profits than they do with conventional stock. In addition, when you collect your dividends, you may also be able to defer paying taxes on a portion of them. As much as half of their cash distributions may be sheltered. When the trust sells properties, you receive the profits from the sale, collected either through special dividends or, if the proceeds are reinvested, higher earnings per share. That can boost the price of your REIT stock.

Here's a word of warning: If you're considering yanking money out of a bank certificate of deposit or selling your bonds to obtain a better yield from an REIT, realize that there is risk involved and the value of your investment could go down, as it can with any stock.

For example, REIT prices react negatively to increases in long-term interest rates. It's also worth noting that REITs have experienced a lengthy bull market, so corrections along the way are quite possible. When properties owned by an

REIT increase in value, the market also bids up the price of its shares. For example, REITs boomed in the early 1970s, but crashed when many construction and development loans failed. REITs were also hard hit in 1990 when federal regulators started dumping foreclosed commercial properties on the market at low prices. An uptick in interest rates in late 1993 similarly sent the market into a short correction. This cyclical nature has continued, though the real estate industry may now be somewhat less volatile because REITs now represent a growing portion of it.

These days, especially with all of the new REITs now available, you must be selective. Most experts advise that you never invest in an REIT that's being introduced as an initial public offering, because you may have no idea how the properties will perform or how well the REIT will be managed. Instead, wait at least four to six weeks until all the "hot money" in such deals has staked out its position. The price will probably be lower at that point as well. The individual investor isn't on an equal footing in IPO ("initial public offering") deals, which are heavily dominated by large institutions. You're generally better off buying older REITs because they sell at the deepest discount from the property's appraised values. That means you're buying properties for significantly less than their resale value. In addition, older REITs have properties that are producing income, and their management generally is more likely to have valuable experience. The first investors in REITs pay large set-up fees, but you'll avoid these start-up expenses if you buy shares later.

No matter what someone offering you the investment may imply, all REITs are not alike, and it's therefore important to choose an REIT from a strong company with a proven track record. Lately, a greater number of real estate developers have been behind new REITs, and many may not have the same expertise of companies that have extensive experience in buying and selling properties over many years. Examine the REIT's annual report to glean all the possible information about what the company buys and how it has performed. Examine the history of its stock value and its dividends. Look for dividend growth. Avoid REITs in which investors are being paid through the sale of properties or by dipping into reserves. Look closely at the REIT's board of directors to see whether they have solid investment backgrounds. Find out the company's strategy for growth, whether there's significant inside ownership, the net operating income adjusted for capital expenditures, and how much variable debt it handles. When assessing the long-term value of an REIT, decide whether the dividend is a real measure of true operating profits or whether it overstates or understates true operating cash flows. If the dividend exceeds operating cash flows, dividend growth could underperform the company's growth in earnings and profitability. Investment analysts generally focus on operating cash flows—rather than earnings—as a true measure of REIT profitability.

A research study by the Kidder, Peabody investment firm pointed out that investors should avoid the following negative traits of some REITs:

- Over-leverage. Strong operators with clean balance sheets will take advantage of weak operators with over-leveraged balance sheets that need to sell for debt-related reasons.

- Conflict of interest. Bad times can bring out the worst in self-interest.

- Passive holders. Unlike the boom times of the 1980s, a company must actively add value in order to excel and keep investor money in the process.

- Convoluted structure. Many older deals are complex, with multiple parties having different levels of equity, security, preferred or subordinated returns, and back-end returns. These complicated structures must be simplified.

While REITs will perform like a stock, they also have the characteristics of real estate. That means that, over the long haul, they will reflect the values of the real estate. A rise in long-term real estate values would therefore bode well for well-managed REITs.

"It makes sense to invest in companies with fully integrated management, and ours is able to 'do it all' from acquisitions to development, to asset management, accounting, and raising equity, without needing any consultants or hired guns to get the job done," said Blankenship. "Our focus is a good one, we're conservative in our business with low leverage, and we have no floating rates to contend with."

Security Capital Pacific Trust is an REIT designed for the investor seeking growth potential, he added. To ensure shareholder value, the company does the necessary research and has the expertise to buy strong assets that have stable cash flow and growth for the investor.

Some recent company acquisitions, expansion of existing properties, and new developments illustrate where the money is going. Security Capital acquired Corrales Point, a 208-unit middle income property in Albuquerque, New Mexico, located near large employers such as Honeywell, Digital Equipment, Motorola, JC Penney, Levi Strauss, and Intel. Haystack Apartments, another recent purchase, is a 272-unit middle income property in Tucson, Arizona, with good access to employment centers such as the University of Arizona, Hughes Aircraft, Tucson Medical Center, and U.S. West. Another purchase, Southern Slope, is a 142-unit upper middle income property in one of the most exclusive suburban residential areas in Tulsa, Oklahoma, a quarter-mile from St. Francis Hospital, one of the state's largest hospitals. Meanwhile, nine acres of land were purchased in Scottsdale, Arizona, to develop 208 units to be operated as part of the 264-unit San Marquis apartment community.

At the same time, the company began development of four new Homestead Village properties, three in Houston and one in San Antonio, each consisting of 134 units. Homestead Village is an affordable housing complex catering to budget-conscious residents seeking accommodations on a short-term basis.

"We have a strong market research team, we're in a great part of the country, and we have the ability to develop, acquire, renovate, and modernize properties," said Alexander of Weingarten Realty Investors, whose company is constantly diversifying its property mix. "Our company is a long-term investment in a vehicle with good current yield and growth potential, and isn't for the investor who only cares about quarter to quarter."

Weingarten's broad base of retail tenants offers considerable downside protection for its stock. An example of new development is the Village Arcade shopping center, built in conjunction with Rice University in an established, affluent area near the school and the Houston Medical Center. The Gap store there is the second highest producing Gap in the nation and has already been expanded twice. There's also a Baby Gap, a Foot Locker, and La Madeleine French Bakery in that center. Recent projects in affluent Houston suburbs include completion of the King's Crossing center that's anchored by Randall's, the Cypress Pointe anchored by Kroger and Venture, and the Northwest Crossing anchored by Target and Marshall's.

United Dominion Realty, whose shares have provided

investors with a 10-year average annual total return of 22 percent, also recommends that its investors buy and put its shares away. An individual retirement account, a Keogh account for the self-employed, or a company 401(k) plan would be good places for its REIT shares, McCann believes. "If you bought and owned our stock for any three-year period you did very well," said McCann, who expects the real estate market will be somewhat less cyclical in the future than it has been in the past. "A consolidation of apartment owners will occur, and the major players will be the half-dozen REITs that have been around the longest."

While buying a variety of apartment communities in locations such as Wilmington, North Carolina, United Dominion has also completed its renovation and rental of Plum Chase apartments in Columbia, South Carolina, and the expansion of a supermarket in Village Square Shopping Center in Myrtle Beach, South Carolina. In 1994, United Dominion bought 47 properties for $400 billion.

Besides equity REITs, there are also mortgage REITS, which don't have as good a long-term record. Rather than buy properties, these invest in mortgages or construction loans and generally have some sort of equity or income participation in the property. Their behavior is more like bonds than stocks. There are also hybrid REITs, which are a combination of equity and mortgage REITs.

The securitizing of America's commercial real estate is accelerating and provides opportunity for those willing to accept the vagaries of interest rates and housing cycles to obtain yield and price appreciation.

Investment Close-Up: Security Capital Pacific Trust (formerly Property Trust of America)

1790 Commerce Park Drive, El Paso, Texas 79912
(915) 877-3900

Security Capital Pacific Trust is a real estate investment trust that invests mainly in equity ownership of a variety of income-producing properties.

Chairman: C. Ronald Blankenship
President, CEO, and investor contact: James Polk III
Total employees: None. Run by employees of several other corporate entities.

Stock: Traded on the New York Stock Exchange under the symbol "PTR." Stock price $18 a share (5/16/95). Dividend of $1.15 a share, which has grown at an 11 percent annual rate over the past five years. Price-to-earnings ratio of 24.

Sales and Earnings: Sales of $186 million for 1994, with earnings of $56.8 million. Five-year annual sales growth of 95 percent, with earnings growth of 29 percent.

Earnings per Share Growth: Five-year earnings per share annual growth rate of 33 percent. Projected (Institutional Brokers Estimate System) five-year earnings per share annual growth rate of 18 percent.

Data from Bridge Information Systems Inc.

Security Capital Pacific Trust
(formerly Property Trust of America)

Monthly Stock Price Chart

Investment Close-Up: Weingarten Realty Investors

2600 Citadel Plaza Drive, Houston, Texas 77292
(713) 866-6000

President and CEO: Stanford Alexander
Vice president, secretary, and investor contact: M. Candace DuFour
Total employees 145

Stock: Traded on the New York Stock Exchange under the symbol "WRI." Price of $36⅞ a share (5/16/95). Dividend of $2.40 a share, with a five-year annual growth rate of 5 percent. Price-to-earnings ratio of 22.

Sales and Earnings: Sales of $121 million for 1994, with earnings of $44 million. Five-year annual sales growth of 12 percent, with earnings growth of 29 percent.

Earnings per Share Growth: Five-year earnings per share annual growth rate of 13 percent.

Data from Bridge Information Systems Inc.

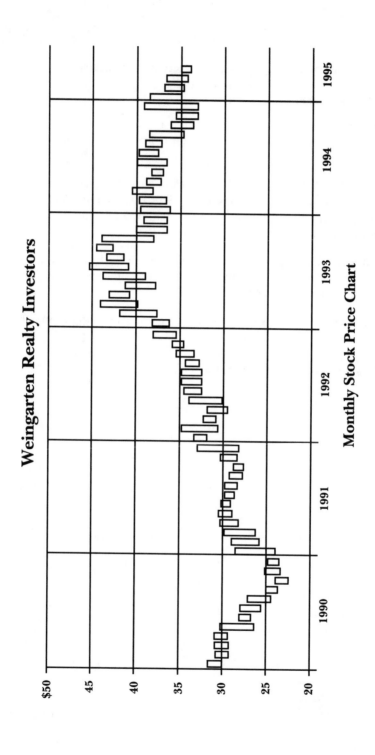

Weingarten Realty Investors

Monthly Stock Price Chart

Investment Close-Up: United Dominion Realty Trust Inc.

10 South Sixth Street, Richmond, Virginia 23219
(804) 780-2691

President and CEO: John McCann
Investor contact: Christine Johnson
Total employees: 900

Stock: Traded on the New York Stock Exchange under the symbol "UDR." Price of $14½ a share (5/16/95). Dividend of 90 cents a share, which has grown at a 6 percent annual rate over the past five years. Price-to-earnings ratio of 32.

Sales and Earnings: Sales of $140 million for 1994, with earnings of $19.1 million. Five-year annual sales growth of 27 percent, with earnings growth of 21 percent.

Earnings per Share Growth: Five-year earnings per share annual growth of 9 percent. Projected (Institutional Brokers Estimate System) five-year earnings per share annual growth rate of 15 percent.

Data from Bridge Information Systems Inc.

United Dominion Realty Trust Inc.

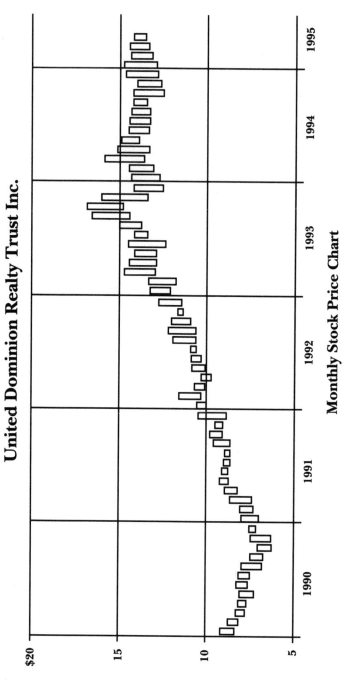

Monthly Stock Price Chart

17

Flexible Technology

It's all done with mirrors at Texas Instruments Inc.

The large video screen featured dramatic footage of tropical parrots with the vivid color, brightness, and overall clarity that's usually confined to glossy photos in a slick magazine.

Inside the projection machine responsible for this stunning image was a digital micromirror device, known as a DMD, that contained more than 300,000 tiny, movable aluminum mirrors and a wealth of electronic logic, memory, and control circuitry. Each mirror is told whether to tilt 10° or stay in the same position by a digital command. The longer the mirror reflects the light, the brighter the image. These mirrors move at about 20 millionths of a second, tricking the human eye into believing that the light bursts are moving pictures.

That's not the kind of innovation that would have been expected from semiconductor giant TI in the past, for it had seemingly lost sight of its market opportunities.

Thermo Electron Corp., meanwhile, features a futuristic management structure that almost appears to have been constructed through the use of mirrors.

The unusual strategy of this environmental instrument, recycling, and biomedical firm involves "spinning out" promising businesses. Creating an entirely new company with each spinout, it retains a majority of the equity in the new company and offers new stock to the public. Unlike the traditional corporate spinoff, the new unit also gets to keep the proceeds of the stock sale.

The result is a smaller, entrepreneurial company with the financial wherewithal of a large company. The Thermo Electron family of companies includes 11 public subsidiaries in which the parent retains majority ownership. Everything from magazine fragrance strips to artificial heart-assist devices are included in its product lines. In some cases, ambitious employees of Thermo Electron Corp. have cooked up brilliant ideas for which they've been rewarded with the opportunity to run their own public company through a spinout.

Flexibility will be an important factor in the 21st century, as many companies fall by the wayside because they lose sight of their markets and stick with the old ways of doing things. Technology lends itself to obsolescence.

Texas Instruments is a turnaround situation, a company that stumbled in the past, its inventories filled with products for which there was no demand. It could easily have become a relic. But by determining what it did wrong and righting its course, it has developed the ability to listen more closely to customers. It is enjoying record profits and is once again comfortable in the role of innovator.

Thermo Electron, well positioned in an industry that should benefit from a modern emphasis on pollution control, alternative energy, recycling, and public safety, is built around the concept of flexibility. It also harbors a deep-seated belief that change is inevitable and always unpredictable. So it seeks a piece of the action in a wide range of technological endeavors without allowing itself to become a lumbering corporation that takes itself too seriously and refuses to acknowledge the potential for making mistakes.

At Texas Instruments (TI), the high-quality images from its experimental digital micromirror device can be projected, printed, or displayed.

In contrast to the cathode-ray tubes used in high definition television receivers, DMD-based systems are flicker-free and brighter and display more lifelike colors. The reduction in visual "noise" makes it possible for viewers to perceive more detail in foreground and background scenes as well. The images also appear to have greater depth than CRT images. These DMD chips can be mass-produced in standard semiconductor production facilities, making them more cost-effective than exotic technologies. Besides high-definition TV, other equipment on the upcoming information superhighway that might use the chips include facsimile machines, copiers, computer printers, x-ray systems, and computer displays. As maker of these chips, developed by one of its engineers, TI believes there's a potential $1 billion industry for them. While this invention is still in its embryonic stage, the company says it could easily make large quantities to sell to manufacturers.

Meanwhile, TI and Sprint combined their technology strengths to bring to market in 1994 the first widely available voice recognition calling card, called Sprint Voice Foncard. The Sprint customer phones an 800 number and verbally gives the system his or her identification number. Using digital signal processors and voice technologies, the system recognizes the digits and verifies the caller's voice by comparing it to a previously recorded template of the phrase. If legitimate, the caller is authorized to place calls. There's also a spoken speed dial feature, which permits the caller to simply say, for example, "call doctor" and immediately have that prearranged number called.

This Dallas-based company is in an excellent financial position to expand its future, coming off a period of 30 percent gains in semiconductor revenues and an uplifting run of record profits. Its semiconductors are used in computers, telecommunications networking equipment, consumer electronics, industrial electronics, and the automotive markets. The company projects that the $60 billion semiconductor industry will grow to more than $200 billion by the turn of the century. In recent years, TI has improved its once-sagging fortunes and would fare much better in any cyclical semiconductor market slowdown than it did in the past.

Worldwide overcapacity in the chip industry and a subsequent cutback in defense business resulted in drastic restructuring measures at the company. However, its product line has now been improved, its management is much admired, and its finances are in fine shape.

The opportunities this global company's stock offers to investors is significant as well. To improve shareholder value, it has set a goal of a sustained after-tax return of 8 to 10 percent on total assets, while maintaining dividends in the historical range of about one-quarter of earnings.

"As we look at the 21st century, we see a higher content of semiconductors in computers and telecommunications, which means more business with the Bell companies, the cable folks, and developing countries that are building communications infrastructures," explained Jerry Junkins, the chairman, president, and chief executive of Texas Instruments. "We've become much better aligned with the markets for our products the past several years, and we've now got a much tighter engineer-to-engineer link with our customer base."

The excellence is already there. TI's Defense Systems & Electronics Group won the 1992 Malcolm Baldrige National Quality Award, and the company in its literature extols the importance of teamwork. It lists the "old way" of doing things as focusing on results, viewing training as an expense, emphasizing individual performance, and working with customers outside the firm. Its "new way" is to focus on the processes, view training as an investment, stress team performance, and work with customers before and after the product's development. As Junkins puts it: "We now expect each individual to do what's right for the customer without having to ask permission."

Texas Instruments has joined the assault on Intel's dominance in personal computer microprocessors with its new Potomac chip line, designed to provide laptops and smaller computers with greater computing performance, including the ability to run Windows software at high speed, while shrinking size, reducing weight, and extending battery life.

The firm is always looking ahead. Completing a decade of work, Texas Instruments said it has demonstrated in the laboratory a new type of semiconductor device that works three times as fast as conventional computer chips. The new chip, operating at room temperature, uses quantum-mechanical techniques that reduce by as much as 50 times the size of some of the semiconductor's parts. Smaller parts speed up the chip's performance, since electrons don't have to travel as far to do the same work. These could eventually replace today's semiconductors, but the devices are still too expensive to make and probably won't be available for four or five years. Other semiconductor manufacturers, including Japan's Fujitsu Ltd., have shown that quantum-mechanical devices can work in very cold temperatures, but TI is the first to demonstrate the chips at room temperature.

In response to increased semiconductor demand and a need to stay ahead of shortening product cycles, the company is building a development and manufacturing facility in Dallas that could wind up costing as much as $1 billion. It will be one of the first facilities in the electronics industry to have a product development center, an equipment evaluation center, and a state-of-the-art manufacturing plant all inside one building. With rising wages in Europe and a strong yen in Japan, Junkins believes the Dallas plant will be competitive. This symbolizes the comeback of the company and a new emphasis on higher-margin specialized chips rather than commodity memory chips. The plant will produce advanced and specialized computer chips as well as integrated chips that combine multiple functions on a single chip. These semiconductors, with dimensions of 0.25 microns and less, are two generations ahead of the current 0.50-micron state-of-the art chips. (The measure 0.25 microns is 400 times smaller than the diameter of a human hair.)

Semiconductors will remain the principal product for Texas Instruments, with 15 percent annual growth in that business likely. The company's semiconductor integrated circuits and electrical control devices account for 53 percent of sales; defense electronics a declining 27 percent; digital products such as computer hardware and software 18 percent; and metallurgical materials 2 percent. More than one-third of total sales are overseas.

By the turn of the century, electronic equipment and information services will be among the largest industries in the world, predicted Junkins. More of the semiconductor market is already outside the United States than inside, and this trend will accelerate. High-volume production is so expensive that only those firms with the strongest financial resources will succeed. The decline in defense electronics spending will continue, Junkins expects, although once that market stabilizes there should be a need for productivity-enhancing systems to offset the dramatic reduction in military personnel. Finally, long-term demographic trends such as the aging of the U.S. workforce will put special emphasis on retraining current workers for new jobs and new skills.

"When you look at Texas Instruments as an investment, look ahead and not behind, for there used to be rotten inventory by us and our customers, but there's now a lot less slack in the system," said Junkins. "The investor must keep

an eye on the marketplace and look at the technology and products, and at this point it sure looks like a lot of semi-conductors will be needed."

To understand Thermo Electron, the study of some basic "astronomy" is required.

That's because the company depicts itself as a solar system, with planets orbiting around the core company. Investors traveling in this solar system had better take their pocket calculators along for the trip, for over the past decade the number of Thermo Electron subsidiary companies in which it has majority ownership has grown to 11. It also has six wholly owned private units and a majority stake in four more private companies. All of these entities generate a dramatic rush of product ideas.

"Our structure created in the last 10 years is the appropriate one for the 21st century, for it combines small companies with the financial resources of a large company," said Dr. George Hatsopoulos, chairman, president, and chief executive of Thermo Electron Corporation in Waltham, Massachusetts. "The conclusion is that the only way to survive throughout the coming century is to create the ability to create new businesses."

That's because the cycle of a typical business from small size to larger size to ultimate decline used to take 70 to 80 years, but the cycle is now becoming shorter and shorter, he noted. The computer industry is in decline after only 30 years of existence, he believes. With more technology, there are more educated people involved in the process, and there is more competition. That means a company's time in the sun can be quite limited.

Financial results of this company, founded by Hatsopoulos in 1956, are impressive over the past decade. Among Fortune 500 companies, Thermo Electron ranked number one in terms of gain in earnings per share for the 10-year period from 1983 to 1993, boasting a compounded annual rate of 97.1 percent. The second-place firm, Compaq Computer, was far behind, with a 46.5 percent compounded annual rate for that period. Despite paying $174 million in cash for acquisitions in 1994, Thermo Electron ended the year with more than $1 billion in cash and marketable investments. The company announced plans to repurchase up to $50 million of its own securities and those of its subsidiaries in 1995 in order to boost share value. The annual appreciation of the stock of its spinout companies has also been strong.

Representatives of many major U.S. companies have visited Thermo Electron's headquarters for tours and informal lectures in order to decide whether its innovative approach can be transferred elsewhere. Yet despite strong financial results and considerable corporate acclaim, the company won't rest on its laurels.

"The classic error that companies such as IBM, Digital Equipment, and Xerox make is that they believe their markets will last forever, and they're wrong," warned Hatsopoulos, who was born in Greece in 1927, received a Ph.D. from Massachusetts Institute of Technology, and has enjoyed diverse careers as a professor, businessman, inventor, and chairman of the Boston Federal Reserve Bank. "I tell people to expect that their markets will disappear tomorrow, since every business is vulnerable and a company must be able to change 'on a dime.'"

When President John F. Kennedy announced that he wanted America to go to the moon, Thermo Electron developed thermionic and thermoelectric technologies to provide power in space. As the energy crisis unfolded after the 1973 Arab oil embargo, the firm's technology center studied energy conservation and the production of more efficient industrial equipment. In the early 1980s, when the environment became a greater issue, the company used its resources to address environmental questions through improved monitoring devices. In fact, when the Chernobyl nuclear accident occurred in the Soviet Union, it was detected with Thermo Electron radiation-monitoring instruments used by Swedish scientists. Later, a worldwide rise in terrorism symbolized by the bombing of Pan Am Flight 103 in 1988 prompted the company to develop technology to detect explosives. The increase in drug abuse in the 1990s has led to the firm's systems for detecting certain illegal drugs.

Of course, not every project has to be of earthshaking importance. Prospects for significant profits are enough. An example is the development of a perfume sample strip for magazines called Scent Seal that has no smell until the airtight label-thin seal is peeled away. It has proven quite profitable since its introduction in *Vogue* magazine in 1993, providing more than $7 million in profits. Leading perfume houses such as Chanel, Christian Dior, Yves St. Laurent, Nina Ricci, and Giorgio Beverly Hills quickly began using the product.

The firm received Food and Drug Administration approval of a skin preparation and special laser to be used in the removal of unwanted hair. It is made by the publicly traded firm ThermoLase Corp., a spinoff company. That same laser laboratory is researching ways to turn previous defense technologies, such as high-definition radar and microwave cameras, into future use in business or residential security. In addition, a new imaging system to use digital images to make breast cancer diagnosis quicker and more accurate was introduced in 1993. Elsewhere, low-emission natural gas engines are operating in 100 school buses in California, in U.S. Postal Service and United Parcel Service trucks in several cities, and in truck and bus fleets in this country and abroad.

"You never really know what tomorrow will bring, so you must be ready," philosophized Hatsopoulos.

With that flexible philosophy and the goal of entrepreneurship in mind, Thermo Electron's many spinouts began in 1983 with Thermedics Inc. (52 percent owned by Thermo Electron), which specializes in biomedical products and explosives detection. Thermedics won FDA approval of an artificial heart pump to keep cardiac patients alive while awaiting a transplant. The pump has since been used by more than 100 trial patients over the past decade.

"Our artificial left ventricular heart-assist device, which has received an approval recommendation from a panel of the Food and Drug Administration, may have market potential in the billions of dollars," predicted Hatsopoulos. "I expect that within two or three years the artificial heart business could grow at a very high rate."

When a company is open-minded and playing all the angles, one discovery leads to another. After discovering a means of testing blood for the angina drug nitroglycerin, Thermedics used this as a starting point in developing devices to detect traces of explosives made from that chemical. As a result, it now sells bomb detectors to police and airports. A developmental contract has been awarded by the Federal Aviation Administration for work on a walk-through explosives detector to be used at airports. After further research, its detection procedure is now also able to uncover cocaine, methamphetamines, and heroin.

Other 1980s spinouts included Thermo Instrument Systems Inc. (83 percent owned by Thermo Electron) in environmental monitoring, analytical instruments, and environmental services; Thermo Process Systems Inc. (80 percent owned) in soil-cleaning technology and furnaces; Thermo Power Corp. (60 percent owned) in natural gas engines, nonpolluting air conditioners, and refrigeration; and Thermo Cardiosystems Inc. (58 percent owned by both Thermo Electron and Thermedics) in heart-assist devices.

During the 1990s, additional spinouts have included Thermo Voltek Corp. (71 percent owned by Thermo Electron and Thermedics) in electronic test gear and power supplies; ThermoTrex Corp. (50 percent owned by Thermo Electron) in imaging, optics, direct-energy conversion, mammography, and biopsy; Thermo Fibertek Inc. (81 percent owned) in paper recycling equipment; Thermo Remediation Inc. (65 percent owned by Thermo Process Systems) in contaminated soil cleanup and waste fluids recycling; Thermo-Lase Corp. (spun out in mid-1994 and 69 percent owned by ThermoTrex) in long-term hair removal; and Thermo Ecotek Inc. (97 percent owned) in environmentally sound power plants and fuels.

Some spinouts have actually spawned their very own spinouts, and the company is also actively buying up companies to add to its existing businesses each year. In a recent six-month period it acquired seven smaller companies. Because of this aggressive nature, some experts prefer to label Thermo Electron as a publicly traded venture capital group or a conglomerate organization. "Acquisitions and outstanding, exciting innovations are our bread and butter for the future," Hatsopoulos said.

Not every one of the myriad of Thermo Electron acquisitions made over the years has been successful, and not all technologies have come through as hoped. The overall structure is complicated and requires greater administrative costs. But Hatsopoulos believes it's more than worth the extra effort and is instrumental in rapid growth. While the spinouts are left to emphasize technology advances, the parent company takes care of capital investment decisions, accounting, legal, and other corporate services. Each of its separate companies is able to gain financial clout in the markets and governmental approvals for its products more quickly than if it were part of a large corporation.

Growth has been dramatic. After just missing the Fortune 500 list in 1988 by placing 501st, Thermo Electron was ranked in 309th place for 1993 and had annual revenues of $1.2 billion. It is one of the world's largest manufacturers of analytical instruments, which provides the largest portion of its profits. Hatsopoulos does admit to some concern about the company's size and the ability to keep it a "close-knit" group of people as it has grown from 2,000 to 12,000 employees and plans to become much larger. But that concern doesn't last long as he considers the future.

"We're number one in 70 percent of our industries, and the only way to continue providing returns in the top 5 to 10 percent of firms around the world is to keep investing short term, mid term, and long term," Hatsopoulos concluded. "For the 21st century, we hope to continue stockholder return of 20 percent or better, as we have done the last 10 years."

Companies can live or die by technology. But neither Texas Instruments nor Thermo Electron is likely to go the way of the buggy whip. Their flexibility is the key to survival.

Investment Close-Up: Texas Instruments Inc.
13500 North Central Expressway, Dallas, Texas 75265
(214) 995-2551

Texas Instruments is one of the world's largest producers of semiconductors, which provide about half of revenues, with the balance derived from defense electronics, software, and calculators.

Chairman, president and CEO: Jerry Junkins
Investor contact: Max Post
Total employees: 56,500

Stock: Traded on the New York Stock Exchange under the symbol "TXN." Price is $118½ a share (5/16/95). Dividend of $1, which has grown at a 6 percent annual rate over the past five years. Price-to-earnings ratio of 14.

Sales and Earnings: Sales of $10.3 billion in 1994, with earnings of $691 million. Five-year annual sales growth of 11 percent, with earnings growth of 701 percent.

Earnings per Share Growth: Five-year earnings per share annual growth rate of 128 percent. Projected (Institutional Brokers Estimate System) five-year earnings per share annual growth rate of 14 percent.

Data from Bridge Information Systems Inc.

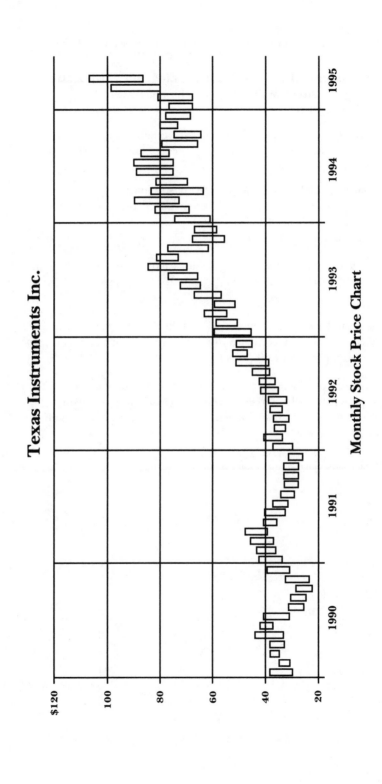

Texas Instruments Inc.

Monthly Stock Price Chart

Investment Close-Up: Thermo Electron Corporation
81 Wyman Street, Waltham, Massachusetts 02254
(617) 622-1000

Thermo Electron manufactures environmental and analytical instruments, biomedical equipment, cogeneration systems, and process equipment.

Chairman and president: George Hatsopoulos
Executive vice president, chief financial officer, and investor contact: John Hatsopoulos
Total employees: 12,000

Stock: Traded on the New York Stock Exchange under the symbol "TMO." Price of $57½ a share (5/16/95). No dividend. Price-to-earnings ratio of 26.

Sales and Earnings: Sales of $1.58 billion in 1994, with earnings of $103 million. Five-year annual sales growth of 22 percent, with earnings growth of 30 percent.

Earnings per Share Growth: Five-year earnings per share annual growth rate of 19 percent. Projected (Institutional Brokers Estimate System) five-year earnings per share annual growth rate of 19 percent.

Data from Bridge Information Systems Inc.

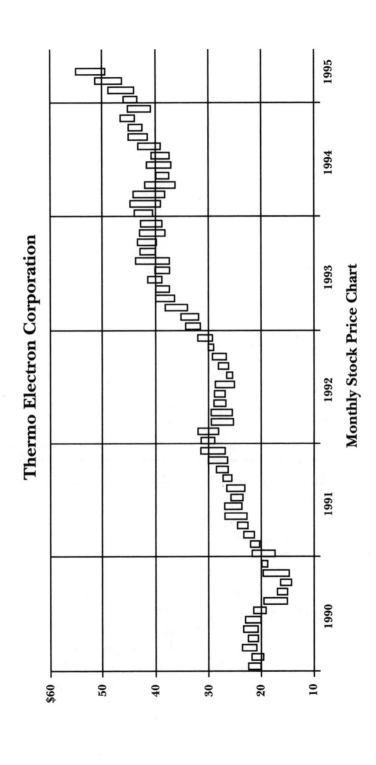

Thermo Electron Corporation

Monthly Stock Price Chart

18

Value Funds

Most value investors toss around pennies like they're manhole covers.

Their stingy philosophy is gaining momentum as we head toward the 21st century: Buy the "right" downtrodden stocks that are selling for considerably less than their net worth but have excellent potential for recovery.

More and more companies will be making mistakes and heading in wrong directions as they try to stay ahead of the coming changes in our global economy and industries. Their errors in many cases won't be fatal. Their misguided courses will be correctable, their franchises remaining intact. Such firms offer stock-buying opportunities for the value investor. Even some companies that fail and fall into bankruptcy could offer an eventual chance to make some profits.

Value, for all its old-fashioned virtues, surprisingly is now a hot modern investment strategy. While it has historically excelled in flat and declining markets and underperformed in strong bull markets, value investing is increasingly being looked upon as a worthy "all-weather" concept. It also gives you the warm satisfaction of not having overspent.

The evidence is lately mounting that value theories aren't just the bailiwick of investment fuddy-duddies anymore, as some mainstream critics have claimed in the past. A research study by Frank Russell & Co. put 1,000 large stocks into two groups, one emphasizing value and the other striving for growth. Over the past 15 years, the value portfolio was ahead in cumulative return. Meanwhile, a study by the National Bureau of Economic Research concluded that, over time, value stocks beat growth stocks by a comfortable margin. While growth stocks did indeed grow, they often didn't grow fast enough to justify the prices that some overexcited investors had paid for their shares. In the 1992 through 1994 period in particular, value-oriented stocks greatly outperformed growth stocks.

These aren't the kind of stocks whose names their owners bring up at cocktail parties. Their shareholders usually keep them to themselves because they're considered "dogs." But investors may later have opportunity to smile knowingly about the profits made because they were patient and unwilling to pay too much. Buying low and selling high has always been an obvious goal, but the basics of value investing are becoming a respected art. At the very least, value investing offers a hedge for any portfolio that already holds high visibility popular names. You definitely won't have the problem of duplication of investments held elsewhere.

Some stock mutual funds that emphasize value investing currently offer eye-popping returns that will become even more noteworthy in the future. Their assets will be rising in the future not only from the rewards of shrewd stockpicking, but from new money of those won over to this strategy. It requires breaking from an American investment attitude that emphasizes short-term results.

Some basics of buying shares of distressed companies:

- Buy stock of companies in industries that are temporarily out of favor. Realize that all groups have their ups and downs.

- Try to buy $1 worth of assets for 50 cents. If you don't pay much, you don't have much to lose.

- Seek out companies with good management and little debt whose stock is selling cheaply because of weak earnings or restructuring efforts. It helps if management itself owns a stake in the company.

- Don't be scared off by restructuring, spinoffs, or bankruptcy. Such events may afford you the chance to buy real value at bargain-basement prices.

- Sit tight and be patient. Very patient. Keep telling yourself that Rome wasn't built in a day.

Some value funds offering excellent opportunities to turn misfortune into fortune are Third Avenue Value Fund, averaging a 14 percent annual return over the past three years; New York Venture Fund, averaging 10 percent; Mutual Beacon Fund, averaging 17 percent; and Vanguard Windsor II, averaging 8 percent.

Their stubborn portfolio managers laugh at how much other managers that emphasize growth are willing to shell out for some stocks. This contrarian emphasis means rejection of the trendy and a willingness to play the role of vulture. They must have solid training and be willing to work outside of the mainstream. Since they do their own homework, they are very sure of themselves.

"My portfolio has absolutely no correlation with the S&P 500 index, for value investing to me means determining whether the stock price relates to the quality and quantity of a company's assets," explained Martin Whitman, portfolio manager of Third Avenue Value Fund.

"The investor should basically consider whether, if he

could own the company, he'd really want to own it," advised Selby Davis, portfolio manager of New York Venture Fund.

"It's this simple," said Michael Price, portfolio manager of the Mutual Beacon Fund. "Just ask: what's the company worth?"

"No investor has ever said he bought overvalued securities, but my approach is good returns with limited risk," said James Barrow, the portfolio manager of Vanguard Windsor II.

In the boom market of the past 20 years, most of corporate America, including real estate, automobiles, and steel, has undergone some low points, and that's the best time to buy. There will always be speculative excesses and initial public offering booms, so it's important not to be swayed by them, but to keep score on the closing prices of stocks and carefully concentrate on the fundamentals.

Adept at finding bargains with his bottom-up approach, Whitman will take a good, hard look at any company in any industry if the price and prospects are right. He says he does business analysis rather than stock analysis. His portfolio is compact, with less than 30 stock names. There's always a substantial cash position when no appropriate investments are available. But when he does come up with something he likes, he'll invest immediately—no matter how the overall stock market or the industry in question are performing at the moment. Wall Street's obsession with quarterly earnings and dividends is totally ridiculous, he believes, and his holdings tend to be illiquid with no dividend to provide any sort of cushion. Some stocks involve companies whose troubles obscure their true worth, while others aren't in financial distress but have merely been overlooked. He also likes buying shares of initial public offerings, but only after they've had their initial price run-up and subsequent drop and are settling into a steady growth pattern as well-financed public companies.

"I've got $3.7 million of my own money in this fund,

so I'm definitely looking for value," declared Whitman, who has taught a finance course at Yale University for 20 years and likes to wear white gym socks and black sneakers in his Manhattan office because comfort makes more sense to him than traditional Wall Street style. "My advice to investors is not to take advice from anyone who buys when a stock is popular and doesn't know a lot about the company."

For example, Whitman bought stock in downtrodden Apple Computer because of its new products and the fact it was adequately financed. He admired Digital Equipment Corp. due to its growth-oriented service business and strong financial position. His largest recent holding was First American Financial. Even if a few of the companies he buys don't make it, he reasons, they'd still be extremely attractive acquisition candidates. Debt-free real estate companies such as Forest City Enterprises are other holdings. SunAmerica, specializing in annuities, looked good to him because of the profit margins in its business. St. Joe Paper was attractive because its vast Florida land holdings are worth more than its stock price. Some high-yield bonds are included in his fund, but they must be inexpensive and their yield at least 10 percentage points higher than investment-grade bonds. These are credits in which the companies are still making their interest payments, and their protective covenants assure Third Avenue Value of senior claims on its assets if the company should go into default.

Sometimes his investment style has had its pitfalls. For example, as manager of Third Avenue's predecessor, Equity Strategies Fund, Whitman became so heavily invested in Nabors Industries, a restructuring oil services company, that the fund lost its subchapter-M status, causing it to close. It became the holding company controlling Nabors Industries and was liquidated, albeit at a significant profit. Whitman is making sure that scenario never happens again. His prospectus for Third Avenue restricts him to less than a 25 percent position in any one issue, and, while he participates in restructurings when managing private accounts, his role with companies in his fund is strictly passive.

Whitman's New York–based Third Avenue Value Fund requires a 4.50 percent load (initial sales charge).

The fact that they "aren't making buggy whips these days" is an underlying philosophy of New York Venture Fund's Davis. He focuses on industries or companies that are unlikely to become obsolete in the future. That does require some crystal ball work, but he's more than up to the task. He has a reputation of being a master of "all-weather" funds that are oblivious to market conditions. Considering himself a "value growth" investor, he's willing to accept a price/earnings ratio that's equal to the growth rate in earnings. However, the higher the growth rate, the less he's willing to pay for the stock because the less sustainable its growth will be. When he buys a 20 percent grower, he'll rarely buy it for 20 times earnings.

Striving to be a "perpetual" holder of stocks, Davis buys and watches value compound over time. A "generational" view of investing, rather than a quarterly view, is required. Any investor in his fund should have a 10-year time horizon, he believes. The portfolio is constructed as a garden, in which he "plants some new flowers from time to time while occasionally uprooting a few mature plants" as well. When selling a position, he'll do so gradually. His trick to obtaining a growth company cheaply is to buy when other investors haven't yet recognized that it is in a growth industry. He's convinced that the less-rapid-growth economy of the future will provide the best chance of growing to niche and smaller companies, as well as special situations and entrepreneurial businesses.

"Eighty percent of company managements are bluffers that can't back up their statements with a track record, and the goal is to separate winners from bluffers," said Davis, a low-key fellow who now runs several funds from Santa Fe, New Mexico, with two sons helping him with the task.

He loves companies whose management owns a stake so that it's shareholder-minded; that are leaders in their industry when that industry is out of favor; that are able to put excess cash to good use; and that can remain fast growing even though its stock has been battered by bad news. He particularly likes a firm to have attributes of a growth company even though it appears to be something else, such as a cyclical company. That way, most analysts won't recognize its potential, and you can get a good deal. A company with "fewer, rather than more" employees is also preferred.

Firms providing financial services are the foundation stone of capitalism, mobilizing capital and making a return on it. So, in global investment banking, Davis bought shares of J. P. Morgan, Morgan Stanley, and Salomon Brothers because they offered higher rates of return on their businesses than other U.S. firms. Insurer American International Group boasted international exposure, while Chubb Group featured a high-margin franchise. Equitable Co. and Primerica Corp. looked like potential superpowers in future years. Banking holdings have included First Bank System, State Street Boston, and Wells Fargo. Intel Corp. provides inexpensive growth, while Archer-Daniels-Midland has a terrific balance sheet and a feed grain supplier business that benefits from the fact that "the world has to eat."

"You can make a big mistake in projecting today's conditions out into the future and assuming the very same growth rate is attainable for decades," explained Davis. "But if I can find a stock that's 7 to 15 percent below its actual value, I'm better off and not just jumping on the bandwagon at the point when growth is actually beginning to slow down."

New York Venture Fund has a 4.75 percent load. Davis began managing the no-load Selected American Shares in

mid-1993 when the fund's board of directors became dissatisfied with Kemper Corp.'s management of it. It features many of the same stocks as New York Venture, but with a greater emphasis on income.

"I'm always in the same investment church and it's the one that says to buy at a discount to intrinsic value," said Price of Mutual Beacon Fund, who likes to deal in bankruptcies and arbitrage and spends much of his day seated at the trading desk talking with his staff about whether to buy or sell certain stocks. "The ability to value companies and their assets is a higher one than the ability to predict future earnings on a new drug."

This no-load fund went through a difficult period from 1989 through 1991. His quest for bargains left it out in the cold as recession-wary investors paid up for companies with strong, reliable earnings growth. While it lagged behind the average value portfolio during 1991's bull market, it has since made up for lost time and underscored the need to view value funds as long-term holdings.

Finding pockets of opportunity in which you can buy $1 worth of assets for 50 cents is Price's goal. Two-thirds of the assets in his fund are classically defined value stocks that meet that specific criterion. He pays little attention to a company's profit estimates for the next quarter or year, but does analyze the price/equity and price-to-cash-flow ratios. As a stock approaches his estimate for the firm's asset value, he will gradually sell his stake. The remaining third of the fund invests in companies involved in bankruptcy reorganization or deals such as takeovers, recapitalizations, spinoffs, or other restructuring.

Drug, health care, and real estate firms became attractive in Price's eyes when the groups were out of favor. He liked Catellus Development for its California real estate and Borden Inc. because it had been poorly managed but had strong assets. Other out-of-favor choices include

U.S. West, Litton Industries, Sears Roebuck, and Philip Morris. He expects a massive restructuring of Kodak that will likely result in selling off a number of its businesses, so it can stick with its profitable film and imaging divisions. He also held Sears as it spun off its Allstate and Dean Witter Discovery financial services businesses. The remaining Sears business gave him the opportunity to own a large stream of revenues very cheaply at a time when management is aggressively focused on getting more earnings out of those revenues. Price's biggest holding, Sunbeam-Oster (formerly Allegheny International), sought bankruptcy protection. Three of the Mutual Series funds joined another investor in buying the entire company in 1990. Sunbeam is again publicly traded, and the Mutual Series stake, which cost about $30 million, was recently valued at around $600 million.

Arbitrage deals include merger situations such as buying the stock of Dreyfus Corp., which was being acquired by Mellon Bank Corp., in order to wind up with Mellon Bank stock quite cheaply. He often keeps close to 20 percent of his fund in cash so he'll be ready if opportunities arise. He also bought American Express Corp. before it spun off Lehman Brothers so that he could, in effect, buy American Express for about $7 a share less than it was actually worth.

There are many ways to cast about for a value.

When I spoke with Vanguard Windsor II's Dallas-based portfolio manager Barrow, he was getting ready to leave on a flight that would take him to Cabo San Lucas for some marlin fishing. He and some friends take a three-day fishing trip there each year. I asked him if there are any similarities between marlin fishing and value investing.

"No, there's no value in marlin fishing whatsoever, because we turn all the marlins loose after we catch them, since they aren't that good to eat and they're marvelous creatures that deserve their freedom," said Barrow. "On the other hand, when we buy overvalued securities, we hold on tight for a long time."

Low price-to-earnings stocks selling for 30 to 40 percent below market price, with dividend yields 30 percent higher than the average market yield, are his focus. Barrow wants good returns with limited risk.

In the 1980s when the average stock portfolio gained 15 percent a year and bonds gained 11 percent, value stocks had difficulty keeping up. But in the current period of yields just over 10 percent for both stocks and bonds, it's possible to do much better, Barrow believes. Because of the characteristics that Windsor II emphasizes in selecting stocks, the profile of the fund is much different from the profile of the broad market indexes. Its prospectus warns that such portfolio biases will cause the fund to perform quite differently at times in relation to the broad market indices. Barrow bought stocks in the financial, drug, and oil companies because these firms have, in his opinion, been undermanaged. He makes a discipline of not holding more than 15 percent of the portfolio in any one industry. Choices such as Phillips Petroleum, Amoco, Texaco Inc., and Exxon Corp. were extremely undervalued, he believes, and opportunities in natural gas are a big part of that play. In drugs, American Home Products, Eli Lilly, and Bristol-Myers Squibb are "better than utilities" for yield, he believes. Financial stocks such as Aetna Life & Casualty, American Express, Bankers Trust, Chase Manhattan, and Chemical Banking Corp. are other favorites.

"You're born with an investment philosophy, and growth investing is very different from value investing," concluded Barrow. "You just do what feels right."

For a growing number of American investors, value investing feels right. Both historic results and future trends seem to be in its favor. The cup is half full, not half empty.

Investment Close-Up: Third Avenue Value Fund

787 Third Avenue, Fifth Floor, New York, New York 10017
(800) 443-1021

Third Avenue Value Fund seeks long-term capital appreciation by
investing in domestic and foreign securities, including common
and preferred stocks and high-risk, high-yield debt securities. A
substantial portion of assets may be invested in securities having
relatively inactive markets. Accepting a high degree of risk, the
fund may leverage its portfolio with up to 50 percent of its net
assets.

Portfolio manager: Martin Whitman
Fund inception: 11/01/90
Total assets: $193 million
Distributor: M. J. Whitman

Shares: Traded under the symbol "TAVFX." Net asset value of
$18.26 a share (3/31/95). No initial sales charge. Management fee
of 0.75 percent. Minimum initial purchase of $1,000.

Performance: One-year total return of 9.19 percent (through
3/95). Three-year average annual return of 13.98 percent. In 1994,
fund value was down 2.89 percent in the first quarter, down 1.06
percent in the second, up 5.97 percent in the third, and down 3.22
percent in the fourth. First quarter 1995 was up 7.61 percent.

Portfolio: Composition was recently 85.4 percent stocks, 2.8
percent cash, and 8.3 percent other securities. Heaviest stock
weightings were in financials and technology.

Data from Morningstar Inc.

Third Avenue Value Fund

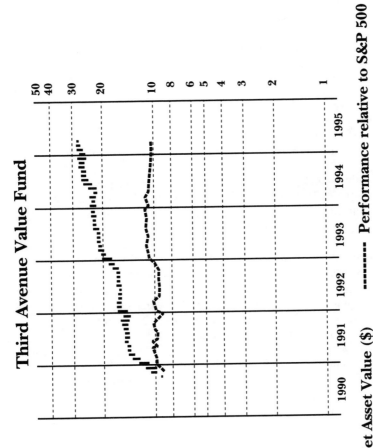

|||||||||| Net Asset Value ($)   ------ Performance relative to S&P 500

Investment Close-Up: Mutual Beacon Fund

51 John F. Kennedy Parkway, Short Hills, New Jersey 07078
(800) 553-3014

Mutual Beacon Fund seeks capital appreciation, with income a
secondary consideration. It invests in common and preferred stocks
and corporate debt securities of any credit quality that are trading
below their intrinsic value. The fund may invest up to 50 percent
of assets in securities of companies involved in mergers,
consolidations, liquidations, and reorganizations.

Portfolio manager: Michael Price
Fund inception: 8/01/61
Total assets: $2.4 billion
Distributor: Heine Securities

Shares: Traded under the symbol "BEGRX." Net asset value of
$32.97 a share (3/31/95). No initial sales charge. Management fee
of 0.6 percent of average net assets. Minimum initial purchase of
$5,000.

Performance: One-year total return of 11.29 percent (through
3/95), three-year average annual return of 17.13 percent, and five-
year average annual return of 13.30 percent. In 1994, fund value
was up 0.83 percent in the first quarter, up 1.99 percent in the
second, up 5.19 percent in the third, and down 2.36 percent in the
fourth. First quarter 1995 was up 6.25 percent.

Portfolio: Composition was recently 70 percent stocks, 20 percent
cash, and 10 percent bonds. Heaviest stock weightings were in
financials, services, and health.

Data from Morningstar Inc.

Mutual Beacon Fund

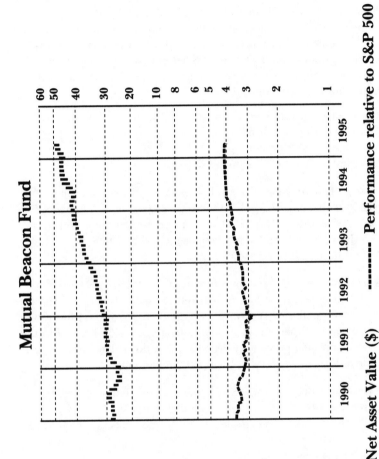

|||||||||| Net Asset Value ($)   ------- Performance relative to S&P 500

Investment Close-Up: New York Venture Fund

124 E. Marcy Street, Sante Fe, New Mexico 87501
(800) 279-0279

New York Venture Fund seeks growth of capital, with income not a
significant factor. It normally invests in common stocks or
convertible securities, predominantly those of companies with
market capitalizations of at least $250 million. It may put up to 10
percent of assets in restricted securities, and may lend securities
and write covered call options.

Portfolio manager: Shelby Davis
Fund inception: 2/17/69
Total assets: $1.23 billion
Distributor: Selected/Venture Advisers

Shares: Traded under the symbol "NYVTX." Net asset value of
$12.34 a share (3/31/95). Initial sales charge of 4.75 percent for
Class "A" shares. (Class "B" shares have deferred loads and Class
"C" shares have level loads.) Management fee of 0.75 percent.
Minimum initial purchase of $1,000.

Performance: One-year total return of 12.29 percent (through
3/95), three-year average annual return of 14.39 percent, and five-
year average annual return of 14.55 percent. In 1994, fund value
was down 3.42 percent in the first quarter, up 1.30 percent in the
second, up 1.89 percent in the third, and down 1.60 percent in the
fourth. First quarter 1995 was up 10.58 percent.

Portfolio: Composition was recently 92.7 percent stocks, 3.9
percent bonds, 3.0 percent convertible securities, and 0.4 percent
cash. Heaviest stock weightings were in financials and technology.

Data from Morningstar Inc.

New York Venture Fund

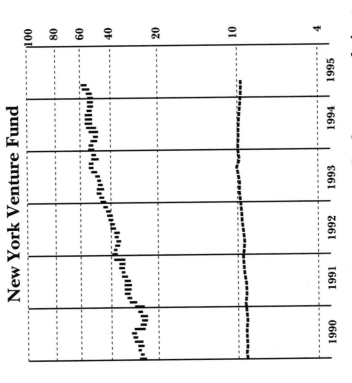

100 ─
80 ─
60 ─
40 ─

20 ─

10 ─

4 ─

1990   1991   1992   1993   1994   1995

▌▌▌▌▌▌ Net Asset Value ($)   ------- Performance relative to S&P 500

Investment Close-Up: Vanguard Windsor II Fund

Vanguard Financial Center, P.O. Box 2600, Valley Forge,
Pennsylvania 19482
(800) 662-7447

Vanguard Windsor II seeks long-term growth of capital and
income, with current income secondary. It invests primarily in
undervalued, income-producing stocks characterized by above-
average income yields and below-average price-to-earnings ratios.

Lead fund manager: James Barrow
Fund inception: 6/24/85
Total assets: $8.5 billion
Distributor: Vanguard Group

Shares: Traded under the symbol "VWNFX." Net asset value of
$17.38 a share (3/31/95). No initial sales charge. Management fee
of 0.63 percent. Minimum initial purchase of $3,000.

Performance: One-year total return of 13.65 percent (through
3/95), three-year average annual return of 11.32 percent, and five-
year average annual return of 10.86 percent. In 1994, fund value
was down 4.47 percent in the first quarter, up 2.61 percent in the
second, up 2.84 percent in the third, and down 1.98 percent in the
fourth. First quarter 1995 was up 9.87 percent.

Portfolio: Composition was recently 92 percent stocks and 8
percent cash. Heaviest stock weightings were in financials, energy,
and consumer staples.

Data from Morningstar Inc.

Vanguard Windsor II Fund

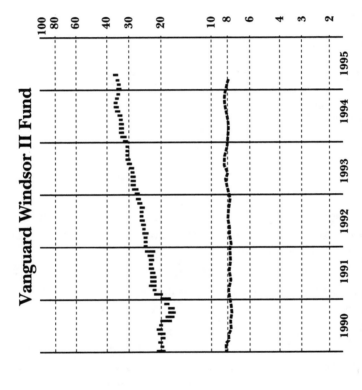

||||||||| Net Asset Value ($)   -------- Performance relative to S&P 500

19

Telecommunications Warriors

The telecommunications business has become a global battlefield as we approach the 21st century. Show no quarter. Take no prisoners.

MCI Communications Corp., the brash upstart whose legal maneuvering led to the breakup of mighty AT&T, isn't content with continuing to gain market share in the long-distance telephone business through savvy marketing.

It has initiated an aggressive $20 billion spending plan to upgrade its fiber-optic network and says it will "wage war" on the regional Bell companies in local phone service. It also intends to build a long-distance network with Mexico.

Sweden's L. M. Ericsson Telephone AB, lacking the large home market of its rivals, is taking on all comers around the globe. It has long controlled 40 percent of the world market for traditional analog cellular transmission equipment and lately has captured a 60 percent lead in the rising market for digital cellular gear.

The aggression of these telecommunications firms provides risk, but could also represent long-term profits for investors who are willing to deal with the potential volatility of their stock. Investors should spread the risk among several stocks as they make a bet on the future that will be intriguing to monitor.

Item: MCI's six-year spending plan to improve its fiber-optic network through a program called networkMCI will also try to break the regional Bell companies' monopoly over local phone service with its MCImetro plan. Access fees those companies charge for completing long-distance MCI calls constitute as much as 45 cents of every revenue dollar MCI takes in. Twice what the company previously expected to spend by the year 2000, the ambitious $20 billion plan signals a commitment to prepare for the multimedia age. It will gladly battle the Bells, which themselves are planning to invade the long-distance business.

Item: MCI is building a long-distance network called AVANTEL in Mexico with Grupo Financiero Banamex-Accival, Mexico's largest financial group. The joint venture is estimated to cost $1 billion, of which MCI will invest $650 million for a 45 percent stake. The investment could increase in the future. The $6 billion Mexican long-distance phone market is expected to explode as the government opens the market to competitors by 1996.

Item: MCI will invest up to $2 billion in the Rupert Murdoch–run News Corporation over the next four years, accumulating as much as a 13.5 percent stake in the media giant. This global joint venture, announced on May 10, 1995, will create and distribute News Corporation electronic information, education, and entertainment through the digital network operated by MCI. Initially businesses will be targeted for the services, to be followed later by individuals.

As the nation's second largest long-distance company, MCI is not awed by risk or strong competition. Its emphasis is on growth, not dividends, and it has a history of doing much better than anyone ever thinks it will.

"MCI Communications is in the catbird's seat for the 21st century because of our culture, our flexibility, and our entrepreneurial spirit that makes things happen," asserted Bert Roberts Jr., chairman and chief executive of MCI Communications. "The lines of local or long-distance service may be replaced by multimedia, but the industry will remain strong nonetheless."

Its canny ability to find financial partners is remarkable. In 1992, MCI and Stentor, an alliance of major Canadian telephone companies, announced a strategic initiative creating the first fully integrated international network linking the United States and Canada. Then, in 1993, British Telecommunications PLC agreed to pay $4.3 billion for a 20 percent stake in MCI as part of a global communications alliance. MCI and British Telecom have already launched their first jointly developed telephone products through a sophisticated worldwide communication services venture dubbed Concert, which competes against AT&T's multicompany alliance. They've also lined up Nippon Information & Communication Corp. as their distributor in Japan.

That doesn't mean MCI has given up on its main moneymaker, long-distance service. This Washington, D.C.–based company's long-distance business is growing at twice the industry average, due to enormous gains from its innovative Friends and Family consumer program launched in 1991 and new corporate business in the toll-free 800 and data-transmission markets. It has snared 19 percent of the $60 billion long-distance market and is gaining about 1 percent in market share annually. However, AT&T, which is able to spend about six times as much on ads as MCI does, has lately shown some renewed life with its aggressive True Rewards consumer program. MCI gained an early jump in such special programs because of the sophistication of its billing system, in which computers can keep track of millions of "calling circles" and issue highly customized bills. It is now enhancing its flagship Friends and Family plan with its Best Friends plan, which lets users save up to 40 percent on calls made to one specified number.

MCI already has the lowest cost structure of any carrier, a situation that would be enhanced if MCI can build its new local networks. It's estimated that even a 5 percent reduction in the $5 billion that MCI spends annually on access fees would let the new MCI local networks pay for themselves in only a few years. How that initiative will shake out is still not certain. Meanwhile, its upgraded fiber-optic network should enable it to carry more traffic at faster rates. It will use synchronous optical network (SONET) technology, already in about half of MCI's existing network, which should eventually permit it to make available broadcast-quality videophones, electronic data interchange, long-distance medical imaging, movies on demand, and personal communication services.

"The ability to merchandise and sell is our forte, and while the business market was once our most important, now the consumer side is the most profitable business," said Roberts, an electrical engineering graduate who worked in computer and software positions before joining MCI's sales and marketing department in 1971, where he coordinated litigation against AT&T. "In the future, a shift to wireless and multimedia will show the fruits of all our efforts."

MCI loves to capitalize on its image as the good guy in the white hat. Founded in 1963 as Microwave Communications Inc., MCI's primary goal was pursuing legal angles to unravel the Bell System's long-distance monopoly. When I asked Roberts who his competition is, he quickly replied "AT&T," without acknowledging any other competition, such as Sprint. The company has been responsible for a significant number of firsts. It was the first long-distance carrier to offer coast-to-coast service over its own facilities in competition with AT&T in 1985; the first to offer alternative nationwide toll-free 800 service in 1987; the first with nationwide caller-paid 900 interactive long-distance service in 1988; and the first to offer long-haul synchronous optical network (SONET) routes in the United States in 1990.

I recall a television interview I conducted several years ago with William McGowan, MCI's visionary, nonconformist former chairman, in which he told me with a broad smile that the company initially was "just a law firm with an antenna on top" before the break-up ruling. McGowan, who died in 1992, symbolized the pride and "David vs. Goliath" personality of the company, which still exists in the executives McGowan handpicked to run it. In a financial pinch, the company in its early days had to issue employee checks on a monthly basis so it could meet its payroll. There are still fewer layers of management than at other companies. Offices at MCI headquarters don't have doors, and employees are encouraged to call their bosses with ideas. What other CEO besides Roberts has willingly had a pie smashed in his face at a company event? He's helped to revive MCI after a period in which it had started to stagnate.

"Many companies such as GM and IBM got complacent, built bureaucracy, and lost vision, so our challenge internally is to think small and entrepreneurial even though we're a big $13 billion company now," said Roberts. "We have the network, sales, and marketing, and AT&T is our competition, so we know what to do."

The company did, however, find it necessary to reorganize its business in 1993 with three new operating groups to tie its structure more closely to its goals. MCI Communications Services Group will maintain the company's focus on profitable market share growth in the domestic long-distance business. MCI International Group assumes full responsibility for the expansion of the company's global reach and presence. The Strategy and Technology Group will seek to exploit emerging technology such as multimedia and wireless services, including PCS.

MCI intends to be a major player in whatever forms of communication are important to customers, whether wireline or wireless, global or domestic. It faces tougher competition from AT&T in the form of chairman Robert Allen than was the case in the past, but there may be more than enough business for both of these rivals in the 21st-century world of instant communications. How fast Roberts can meet his lofty goals remains to be seen. He clearly believes he's fighting a war that the company intends to win.

Telecommunications supplier L. M. Ericsson Telephone AB has put itself in a unique position.

So high are the expectations for its performance in the worldwide telecommunications field that when president Lars Ramqvist announced 1993 earnings would probably "somewhat more than double" the previous year, the stock suddenly nosedived. Investment analysts, you see, had expected that profits might triple or quadruple. Worried American investors unloaded their shares of the company, which are sold as American Depositary Receipts in this country.

While it may not be able to muster the political clout of the United States, France, or Japan, which is a handicap in winning big contracts around the world, Ericsson's need to expand beyond its small Swedish homeland has given it the tenacity and flexibility to do battle anywhere around the globe. What is wanted, it will provide. In the 1990s, it has cut its worldwide payroll by 11 percent over three years, yet added 2,000 engineers and other professionals and invested $220 million in new facilities in order to get a technological edge on the competition.

Ericsson is now one of the hottest players, ranking sixth in revenues among the world's equipment suppliers. Its cellular business now actually accounts for more of the firm's revenues than wire-based public telephone network equipment, its mainstay since the company's founding in 1876. The company is determined to turn this mobile competence into a broad range of wireless communications, ranging from cordless phones to the new PCS. Plans by network operators to combine mobile and fixed systems so callers can be reached anywhere also gets its creative juices flowing.

The company is in the middle of all the action. When the World Trade Center bombing occurred in New York, Ericsson immediately provided advance delivery of 90 portable radios that were scheduled to be delivered to the center's security a few weeks later. They were immediately programmed and used to support the evacuations.

"The key trend of the future is mobility, since people want freedom to communicate at home, in the jungle, or at their vacation home with pocket phones that are becoming smaller and smaller with features such as built-in planning calendars," said Carl Wilhelm Ros, executive vice president and CFO, speaking by phone from the Stockholm headquarters. "But, of course, you can always turn off the phone if you want to be alone undisturbed with your fiancé."

A slick company magazine, *Ericsson Connexion*, exemplifies the corporate vision. A recent cover story was "Freeways to the Future," illustrated by a view of a modern city with bright blue, green, purple, and red rays projecting toward it to symbolize high-speed communication signals. The signs above this freeway featured off-ramp arrows indicating "copper wire," "fiber optics," or "coaxial cable." The magazine's articles on riding the information highway posed the likelihood of schoolchildren being able to practice foreign languages or carry out joint classroom projects with students in other countries; people with troublesome ailments being examined and diagnosed "in person" by medical specialists thousands of miles away; and catalog shoppers touching a picture of a cashmere sweater and seeing a short high-definition video clip of someone wearing it.

The first nontechnical travelers on this highway are likely to be businesspeople, the magazine explained. With multimedia computers linked together, colleagues at remote locations could send "video faxes" to one another or hold spur-of-the-moment videoconferences at their desks. In mid-meeting, they could call up reports, spreadsheets, or other computerized data at the touch of a button and share them instantly with the group. In the home, movies on demand ordered digitally from the network could mean the end of videocassettes in plastic boxes. The network could let you play video games head-to-head with friends in other cities. You'll see each other not as animated characters but as yourselves in live, full-motion video.

This is a nimble company whose mind is on the present as well as the future. A $400 million order from Japan Telecom broke the lock on that country's cellular market, which had been shared by NEC, Fujitsu, and Motorola, making Ericsson the only supplier shipping complete digital systems to the world's top three markets. It surprised competitors in 1992 by offering a 12-ounce mobile-phone handset and confounded them further in 1993 with a 25 percent price cut. It nabbed the contract for the world's first PCS network with a London system begun in 1993. Its next goal is to move into new multimedia switches that handle a mixture of voice, video, and data, plus the high-speed transmission systems.

"The strength of Ericsson is that we have all of the technologies, so we can choose any standard and follow the market that operators want," explained Ros. "We're one or two years ahead of the competition in digital cellular systems, providing a good connection as you drive from one cell to another, and our general switching know-how is why we're so successful in radio communications and personal telephony."

This company has a sense of style. After positioning his company for success over a turbulent three-year period, president Ramqvist sold $2 million in his company's stock to buy a 1,500-acre private hunting reserve with a 16th-century chateau near the Baltic Sea. But he hasn't lost the drive that gave him the confidence to commit 16 percent of the firm's sales to research and development, thereby producing systems that conform to differing cellular standards around the world.

That world is Ericsson's oyster. While Sweden accounts for 10 percent of its sales, other European countries represent 31 percent, the United States and Canada 12 percent, Latin America 8 percent, Asia 23 percent, and the rest of the world 7 percent. It has more than 70 percent of Europe's digital cellular equipment orders, plus 59 percent of combined analog and digital systems. In the United States, 32 percent of cellular subscribers use Ericsson equipment. The company expects the number of worldwide cellular subscribers will quadruple by the 21st century to 350 million. Aware that its transmission, switching, network management systems, and broadband systems for multimedia delivery have lagged, it entered into partnerships with Hewlett-Packard, Texas Instruments, General Electric, Toshiba, and Raychem.

The acquisition of McCaw Cellular by AT&T will have an effect on Ericsson, since it has been a big supplier of equipment to McCaw. But while that business may eventually be taken over by AT&T's own equipment business, other companies in the field may decide to take their equipment purchases away from their enormous new competitor and give the business to Ericsson instead. The company offers a wide variety of cellular phones in this country, including a portable flip phone capable of operating on both analog and digital systems. Weighing 8.9 ounces, it comes with features such as caller identification and message waiting. While digital offers more sound clarity and lower monthly rates, the phones themselves are more costly than the analog phone. Ericsson recently won contracts for digital communications systems for public safety agencies in Los Angeles, Dade County, Florida, and Polk County, Iowa.

The company has also unveiled a prototype handheld satellite telephone in Paris for the proposed global digital satellite-based telephone service under development by the International Maritime Satellite Organization, also called Immarsat-P. If it actually becomes reality, that service would be a direct competitor to the Iridium satellite network developed and run by Motorola. In addition, computer chip maker Intel Corp. has joined with Ericsson and Germany's Siemens to explore development of integrated telephone/personal computer technology and service.

All is not perfect, however. Ericsson has experienced some problems obtaining large orders for central office switches because it doesn't have access to large export credits like its rivals. Obtaining trade financing for China and other markets has proven difficult. Furthermore, earnings comparisons no longer benefit from year-to-year earnings gains stemming from devaluation of the Swedish krona. But these are realities of the modern marketplace that must be accepted. Company management doesn't want investors to head for the hills each and every time something negative comes up.

"We love to have long-term investors, because we can promise a good long-term investment but can't do the same in terms of short-term speculation," said Ros. "If we take care of profits and spend them on the right markets and products, we'll do what's expected for shareholder value."

The prospects of telecommunications giants MCI Communications and Ericsson are bright, although investors in their stocks will have to be as adventuresome and determined as the companies themselves.

Investment Close-Up: MCI Communications Corporation
1801 Pennsylvania Avenue, Washington, D.C. 20006
(202) 887-2028

MCI is the second largest U.S. long-distance telephone carrier, providing domestic and international services and featuring strategic alliances around the globe.

Chairman and CEO: Bert Roberts Jr.
Investor contact: Connie Weaver
Total employees: 41,000

Stock: Traded on NASDAQ under the symbol "MCIC." Price of 21\frac{11}{16}$ a share (5/16/95). Dividend of five cents a share. Price-to-earnings ratio of 16.

Sales and Earnings: Sales of $13.3 billion in 1994, with earnings of $795 million. Five-year annual sales growth of 14 percent, with earnings growth of 21 percent.

Earnings per Share Growth: Five-year earnings per share annual growth rate of 3 percent. Projected (Institutional Brokers Estimate System) five-year earnings per share annual growth rate of 14 percent.

Data from Bridge Information Systems Inc.

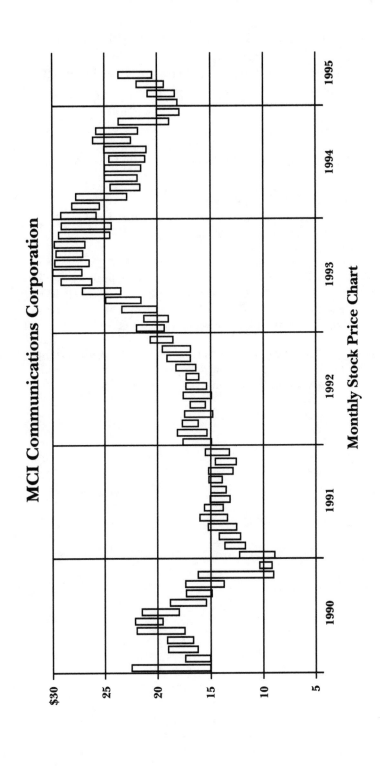

MCI Communications Corporation

Monthly Stock Price Chart

Investment Close-Up: L. M. Ericsson Telephone AB

Telefonplan, S-126 25 Stockholm, Sweden
U.S. address: 100 Park Avenue, New York, New York 10017
(212) 685-4030

Ericsson is a leading international supplier of systems and services for the handling and transmission of voice and data in public and private communications networks.

President and CEO: Lars Ramqvist
Executive vice president and CFO: Carl Wilhelm Ros
U.S. investor contact: Lars Jonsteg
Total employees: 76,000

Stock: Traded on NASDAQ as an American Depositary Receipt under the symbol "ERICY." Price of $69¾ a share (5/16/95). Dividend of 64 cents a share, which has grown at an annual rate of 1.7 percent over the past five years. Price-to-earnings ratio of 29.

Sales and Earnings: Sales of $11 billion in 1994, with earnings of $751 million. Five-year annual sales growth of 6 percent, with earnings growth of 54 percent.

Data from Bridge Information Systems Inc.

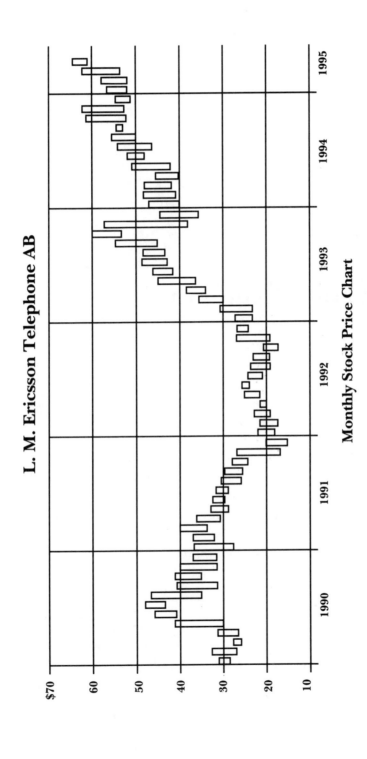

L. M. Ericsson Telephone AB

Monthly Stock Price Chart

20

Closed-End Funds

Dare to be different: The closed-end fund is a hybrid investment that's drawing increased attention as the 21st century draws near.

The returns, the total assets, and the number of funds have been on an upward spiral that makes them worthy of careful consideration by modern investors looking for something unique. Though they may seem tricky at first, they offer an opportunity to snap up some real bargains.

There's a closed-end fund for virtually every investment goal, though those investing in a single country or region have been gaining the most attention lately with their eye-popping returns. Unlike a conventional open-end mutual fund that issues unlimited amounts of shares and redeems them on demand, a closed-end fund issues only a fixed number of shares at an initial public offering. These shares are then traded on the New York, American, or NASDAQ exchanges just like any public company. Shares are bought through a stockbroker, and regular brokerage commission charges must be paid.

Shares, however, can't be bought directly from the closed-end fund itself. After the initial offering the fund is closed; it doesn't issue new shares unless it has a secondary offering later. It doesn't redeem shares, either. The number of closed-end funds has skyrocketed from 54 with assets of $7 billion in 1985 to more than 526 with assets of more than $128 billion today. The average total return for closed-end funds was nearly 21 percent in 1993, but a negative 14 percent in 1994.

A distinct advantage of a closed-end fund is that it often permits investors to buy assets for less than their true value. Here's why: The fund's share price on the exchange will fluctuate and differ from the net asset value (N.A.V.) of all the securities in its portfolio. So a fund selling for a stock price that's higher than its N.A.V. is trading at a premium, while a fund selling for a price lower than its N.A.V. is trading at a discount.

A fund trading at a 10 percent discount, for example, lets investors buy $1 worth of assets for only 90 cents. On the other hand, a fund trading at a 10 percent premium requires that you pay $1.10 for every $1 in assets. Closed-end funds typically sell at a discount, but if a fund is particularly attractive or in demand it will sell at a premium. Premiums usually don't last long, because they basically indicate the fund is selling for more than its portfolio is actually worth. A smart investor who buys the "right" closed-end fund at a discount could profit one day by selling it at either the level of its N.A.V. or, better yet, at a premium. When you combine a possible gain in both N.A.V. and stock price, you could experience a double pop of profit on your sales transaction. Of course, there's the potential for downward movement, too.

Another advantage of a closed-end fund's fixed number of shares is that it gives its portfolio manager a stable pool of assets to invest without having to worry about raising cash or investing new amounts without warning. The stability of assets also makes them the preferred vehicle for single-country funds, because a developing country's stock market has the assurance that this large amount of foreign capital won't be removed suddenly on shareholder request.

"A plus of a closed-end fund is that it makes a long-term strategy possible, because investors aren't constantly taking their money away," agreed William Gedale, president of General American Investors, which was established in 1927 and ranks as the nation's oldest closed-end fund.

If you're willing to do your own homework, you can make a wise investment in a closed-end fund. Study the goals, management, and portfolio of the fund you're considering, then consider its price history in terms of its N.A.V. and discount. These investments are often preferred by folks who like to trade and by investors interested in a specific foreign country.

General American Investors, H&Q Healthcare Investors, H&Q Life Sciences, Jundt Growth Fund, Latin American Discovery, Emerging Mexico, and The Brazil Fund are among closed-end fund selections worth considering. While some are attractive because of their recent discounts, the investor must always do an up-to-the-minute check of how each strategy, portfolio, and discount looks at the time money is being committed.

"Our philosophy is to emphasize long-term trends by carefully viewing each company and its talent," explained Gedale. "With any trend, the key is being there, and, for example, we never buy stock in any overseas company that we haven't seen personally."

This New York–based fund is looking for 50 percent appreciation over three years in each of its holdings. It turns over stocks about every four or five years, with some held for 15 years or longer. General American sees the long-term biology revolution in terms of profits and holds stock in companies such as Chiron Corp., Glaxo Holdings PLC, Pfizer Inc., and Merck & Co. It has also had success in finding retail companies that bring value to the consumer, among them Home Depot, Wal-Mart Stores, and Toys "R" Us. It has also invested in foreign companies for some time, most recently in southern Europe. "We found the Italian maker of eyeglasses Luxottica Group, which makes Armani and Valentino frames, when it was going public, and learned how it sold its product and the high service levels it provided," said Gedale, an upbeat, gregarious man who obviously loves his work. "We invested in Banco Popular Espano because we found it had gradually become the third largest bank in Spain by emphasizing consumer loans."

Long-term media and information prospects led General American to invest in Walt Disney Co. because of its media distribution system and its goal of "ramping up" for 40 to 60 films a year, Gedale explained. Disney's 50 years in the animation business gives it an edge in financially successful full-length animation films "in which the actors don't demand anything," he said. Elsewhere, Sara Lee Corp. and Rubbermaid Inc. feature creative people and offer economic opportunity in basic consumer businesses.

These have been frustrating times for the health care and biotechnology industries, but the price of their closed-end funds may now be right.

"The number of Americans over age 80 is growing, and they use more health care, while technology is increasing life spans and developing therapies for many diseases," said Alan Carr, portfolio manager of the H&Q Healthcare Investors and H&Q Life Sciences closed-end funds in Boston. "This means a potential for new markets and new technologies as health care becomes a $1.5 trillion business by the year 2000."

H&Q Healthcare Investors, the older of the two funds he manages, is broader based and includes health management and medical services stocks. The more adventuresome fund, H&Q Life Sciences, owns a number of agricultural and environmental stocks. Both funds share stakes in public biotech holdings such as Affymax, Genzyme Corp., Chiron Corp., Calgene Inc., and Plant Genetic Systems. His core biotech positions are often in the form of convertible debentures and preferred stock, which initially carry lower risk and the potential for further gain if converted into common stock. Life Sciences and Healthcare Investors have the ability to put up to 40 percent of their portfolio in restricted venture capital–type securities.

"This is a volatile universe that's less so with some diversification, but in the early stages events such as acquisitions and mergers can drive these stocks," said Carr, who believes biotechnology will change the way that many things are done in the near future. "Despite the risk element, this is an enormously exciting area, with, for example, more than 40 companies working on the best ways of stopping inflammation."

Restricted securities must be held for a few years before they can be sold into the public market, and Carr has reaped significant profits from startup investment such as Shaman Pharmaceuticals in tropical cures and Biotage, a maker of pharmaceutical test equipment. Carr has spent better than three decades in high-tech investing. This closed-end fund is for the patient who are willing to bet that health care firms will successfully withstand any government changes to their industry.

Forward thinking may pay off.

"We try to invest in the geniuses of the world by owning the 30 to 50 fastest growing companies in America," said James Jundt, chairman of the Minneapolis-based Jundt Growth Fund. "We bought Wal-Mart Stores when it was much smaller, and we bought Microsoft 10 years ago when it was smaller."

In the last four years, companies such as IBM, Merck, and Philip Morris have seen their growth end as it became clear that they're not where the future is, Jundt said. He also doesn't like oil and gas or real estate. Instead, he has put 25 percent of his portfolio into communications companies, primarily firms in the wireless field, such as Motorola and Intel. "There will be a day when everyone has a phone in their pocket, for the era of the Dick Tracy two-way wrist radio is here," Jundt said. "In addition, the era of the department store is dead because interactive TV firms will take their place."

The companies in his portfolio tend to be higher-multiple stocks. They're growing at five to six times the growth rate of corporate America, and they're held until they stumble. Historically, the fund has been down slightly in periods when growth wasn't good, but up significantly in years when it was good. Recent additional holdings include Vodaphone Group PLC, L. M. Ericsson Telephone AB, Motorola Inc., Oracle Systems Corp., and United Healthcare Corp. An interesting aspect of this closed-end fund is that it holds annual tender offers to buy back its stock at net asset value, thus allowing shareholders to realize the value of any existing discount. "If you believe that marginal tax rates will go up, go with growth stocks," Jundt said. "I don't think that you'll get double-digit returns from the overall stock market, but growth stocks should do well."

International investing, as noted earlier in this book, offers both rewards and volatility. Closed-end funds offer another good way to take advantage of the new overseas opportunities.

"The stage is set for solid economic growth in Latin America into the 21st century as countries break from the state's role in the economy and push toward competition," said Jay Pelosky, Morgan Stanley's director of strategy and research for Latin America. "The biggest beneficiary of the

Berlin Wall falling is Latin America, because of the real-ization that only the free market works."

Morgan Stanley's Latin American Discovery Fund is a contrarian closed-end fund, avoiding well-known, well-loved markets and searching out the less admired examples. The economic leaders in Latin America are Chile, Mexico, and Argentina, while the laggards are Brazil and Venezuela, Pelosky believes. The fund is usually fully invested. There are many Latin American positives in terms of growth po-tential, including the fact that 50 percent of the population is under the age of 25 and there's a growing literacy rate. He considers Brazil the biggest prize in Latin America be-cause, whenever that country begins to work properly and "stops thinking it must do everything its own way," it will outshine even Mexico. Significant portfolio holdings have included Telebras, Austral de Inversiones, Petrobras P.N., Electrobras P.N., and Brasmotor P.N.

"We're long-term believers in Brazil, which has a so-phisticated private sector that has done well despite the fact that the public sector there is crummy, and we're convinced that it will explode economically at some point," explained Pelosky, whose New York–based fund has also had excellent results by putting a portion of its portfolio in Peru. "We're leery of the traditional big, solid companies because they got that way due to their government ties in the past, and they'll probably have a hard time adjusting to the new competition."

The lands south of the border offer many new prospects these days, despite trauma in Mexico in 1994 and 1995.

"Mexico has done its homework and will start growing at a 4.5 to 6 percent annual rate over the next decade," predicted Pablo Mancera, portfolio manager of Emerging Mexico Fund, in a telephone interview from his Mexico City office.

The country had been operating many plants that had

100-year-old machinery, but now that has been replaced by state-of-the-art equipment. Many companies and industries will grow much faster than the Mexican gross domestic product, he predicts. That could mean 20 percent growth at some firms, so the investor is buying a long-term bargain in exchange for some short-term volatility.

"The North American Free Trade Agreement is like building a new bridge in the acceleration of progress, and hopefully a more democratic Mexico can integrate into North America without losing its traditions and way of life," Mancera said. "Infrastructure, communications, and consumer products are all greatly needed areas that provide investment opportunity."

Top-quality companies that will attract international partners are the best choices for his New York City–based fund, he believes. In retailing, Grupo Industrial Bimbo has an alliance with Sara Lee, while Grupo Carso has interests in tobacco, retailing, and communications. Cifra has a joint venture with Wal-Mart Stores, and Sears Roebuck de Mexico (75 percent owned by Sears Roebuck) is growing fast. Grupo Dina, an assembler of buses and trucks, is taking away Mercedes Benz's market in Mexico. "In the past, it was difficult to go to second-tier companies in Mexico because there was no liquidity, but that has changed," said Mancera. "The general interest in Mexico is really helping because there's research now from all the big U.S. companies."

It may be time to trust some countries that haven't been trustworthy in the past.

"The argument is persuasive that there will be significant progress in personal income and living standards in Brazil as we approach the 21st century," said Ed Games, portfolio manager of The Brazil Fund Inc., which experienced a sharp rise in value after the Brazilian government launched an anti-inflation program July 1, 1994. "If Brazil could put its house in order, its stock market would rise from

$90 billion to $225 billion, but that would require a strong executive to overcome the uniquely tribal politics of that country."

The volatile New York City–based Brazil Fund has had a chaotic history: up 40 percent in net asset value in 1993 due to the strength of the Brazilian bolsa, up 7 percent in 1992, up 131 percent in 1991, and down 80 percent in 1990. Telecommunications is the largest sector, followed by food and beverages, petroleum, and banking. Its portfolio isn't actively traded. Holdings include Telebras, petroleum firm Petroleo Brasileiro SA, Banco Itau SA, and Companhia Souza Cruz Industria e Comercio, a tobacco company controlled by B.A.T. Industries.

"Brazil isn't well respected, but I think we'll see a period of virtually no inflation, rising optimism, and a more open economy," said Games. "After all, it has become the second largest economy in the Western Hemisphere despite the fact that the country has been acting like a drunken sailor."

Some other closed-end funds worthy of consideration include:

- Salomon Brothers Fund. Invests in common stocks with above-average earnings and dividend growth potential, with long-term capital appreciation and reasonable income its main objectives. Turnover in this large, diversified New York–based fund has lately been high, with large purchases made in industrial cyclicals, retail trade, and technology stocks. In 1992, after the fund's longtime manager John Weed retired, assets were divided evenly between managers Allan White and Ross Margolies to foster a competitive spirit.

- Tri-Continental Corp. Largest domestic closed-end and diversified investment management company, with long-term appreciation and income growth its major aims. It emphasizes larger capitalization issues, which have recently lagged behind mid-capitalization and small-capitalization stocks. It also made a few wrong stock picks that didn't pay off. The fund is best for conservative portfolios when its price is right. To add a foreign flavor, portfolio manager James Crawford has added some American Depositary Receipts to the portfolio of this New York–based fund.

- MFS Charter Income. Seeks to maximize current income, allocating one-third of assets each to U.S. government, foreign government, and high-yield corporate fixed-income securities. No one sector can take up more than 50 percent of assets of this Boston-based fund, which was begun in 1989. It may also use options or futures. To ease volatility, portfolio manager James Swanson has shortened the duration of the fund's longest Treasuries. It is also maintaining a conservative stance in the foreign and high-yield markets as well. The fund uses covered-call writing, a practice that can backfire when interest rates fall.

- Putnam Master Income Trust. Seeks high current income consistent with preservation of capital. The fund diversifies its assets among U.S. government securities, high-yield corporate securities, and foreign-government securities. Returns are in the upper half of the bond group, yield is above average, and it has delivered this performance with less risk than most competitors. The biggest boost has come from the strength of the junk bond market, where it keeps 40 percent of its portfolio. This Boston-based fund started in 1987 has lately shifted its foreign focus to short-to-intermediate bonds. This should improve total returns, but may cut into its income.

- Gabelli Equity Fund. Seeks long-term growth of capital with income as a secondary objective. Invests in equity securities that famous portfolio manager Mario Gabelli believes are priced lower than their underlying assets. Favorable price-to-earnings ratios and debt-to-equity ratios, as well as the quality of management, are additional criteria. The fund, started in 1986 and based in Rye, New York, can invest one-fourth of assets in foreign securities. About 40 percent of the fund's assets are committed to the theme of interactive media. Gabelli's value style involves buying stocks priced below their private market value and waiting for some external catalyst to lift prices to higher valuations. Ongoing merger activity in the field has helped boost the fund's performance.

- New Germany Fund. Invests in equity and equity-linked securities of companies domiciled in Germany with capital appreciation as its goal. Emphasizes companies positively affected by economic and other reforms in the former East Germany and other parts of Eastern Europe, with about 83 percent of its assets invested in German securities. This New York–based fund, run by John Abbink, may also invest in put and call options on German stocks and in index and bond futures and options.

- Templeton China World Fund. Launched in September 1993, this fund, which invests at least 65 percent of assets in the stocks of Chinese companies, has quickly become popular. That definition includes companies organized under the laws of the People's Republic of China or having a principal office in China, Hong Kong, or Taiwan, having their principal trading market in China, Hong Kong, or Taiwan, or deriving at least 60 percent of revenues or having at least half of their assets in China. China's double-digit growth rate and

growing consumer base have appeal, and the Hong
Kong market offers investors liquid stocks to benefit
from China's potential. Emerging market guru J. Mark
Mobius (see earlier chapter on international investing)
of the St. Petersburg, Florida, Templeton Funds is the
portfolio manager.

- Asia Pacific Fund. Can invest at least 80 percent of
  assets in companies in Hong Kong, Korea, Malaysia,
  the Philippines, Singapore, Taiwan, and Thailand.
  There's no limit on the percentage of assets that may
  be invested in any one country at any one time. This
  New York–based fund was started in 1987 and long-
  term capital appreciation is its emphasis. In 1993, it
  ranked in the top 1 percent of all closed-end funds.
  Enthusiasm for China sent the Hong Kong market
  skyrocketing, and Malaysia, the fund's number two
  market, also prospered. With portfolio manager
  David Brennan keeping so much of the fund's assets
  in Hong Kong, it is vulnerable to a correction in that
  market.

- First Philippine Fund. Can invest at least 80 percent of
  assets in stocks of Philippine incorporated companies
  that generate at least half of revenues from operations
  within the Philippines. This New York–based fund with
  long-term capital appreciation as its goal was initiated
  in 1989 and can invest up to 15 percent of assets in
  non-publicly traded securities. Despite its strong
  increase in net asset value and track record as one of
  the best performing closed-end funds in its region, it is
  trading at a discount due to concerns about factors
  such as the country's persistent power blackouts. The
  government and private industry are building
  generators to try to help this power crisis. Portfolio
  manager Roberto Ticson underweights some of the
  blue-chip companies of the Philippines.

- Scudder New Asia. With long-term capital appreciation as its goal, at least 65 percent of the fund's assets will be invested in stocks of Asian companies, which include Japan, Hong Kong, Singapore, Malaysia, the Republic of Korea, Taiwan, India, the Philippines, Thailand, Indonesia, and Sri Lanka. Started in 1987, this New York–based fund, managed by Andrew Economos, didn't do quite as well as some other Asian funds because of its stake in sluggish Japanese small capitalization stocks. It is expected to emphasize the Pacific's smaller markets with the themes of economic integration, infrastructure improvements, and increased domestic demand.

Don't buy newly issued closed-end funds, because the offering price includes the cost of the offering and commissions. If you wait awhile, you'll probably be able to buy the fund at a lower price. In addition, some closed-end funds guarantee a set percentage payout each year to keep the discount from becoming too deep, but that could actually erode your investment if the fund doesn't make enough and it must dig into your principal.

Remember to keep all of these variables in mind as you invest in closed-end funds. They're going to become bigger and bigger, so you should know their intricacies. Sometimes different *can* mean better.

Investment Close-Up: Closed-End Funds

General American Investors
450 Lexington Avenue, Suite 3300, New York, New York 10017
(800) 436-8401

General American Investors seeks long-term capital appreciation, investing primarily in common stocks considered to have better-than-average growth potential. It is permitted to use leverage and to underwrite securities. Heaviest portfolio weightings were recently in health care and services.

Fund inception: 1/30/87
Portfolio manager: William Gedale
Total assets: $526 million

Traded on the New York Stock Exchange under the symbol "GAM." Market price of $19 a share (3/31/95) and net asset value of $22.61, resulting in a discount of 16 percent. Three-year annualized decline of 4.27 percent in market price and gain of 2.88 percent in N.A.V. Five-year annualized return of 11.12 percent in market price and 11.50 percent in N.A.V.

H&Q Healthcare Investors
50 Rowes Wharf, 4th floor, Boston, Massachusetts 02110
(800) 327-6679

H&Q Healthcare Investors seeks long-term capital appreciation and will normally invest at least 80 percent of assets in health services and medical technology companies with above-average growth potential. It may invest up to 40 percent of assets in venture capital or other restricted securities.

Fund inception: 4/22/87
Portfolio manager: Alan Carr
Total assets: $94 million

Traded on the New York Stock Exchange under the symbol "HQH." Market price of $13.88 a share (3/31/95) and net asset value of $17.10, resulting in a discount of 18.9 percent. Three-year annualized decline of 12.63 percent in market price and decline of 1.35 percent in N.A.V. Five-year annualized return of 13.05 percent in market price and 14.72 percent in N.A.V.

H&Q Life Sciences Investors

This fund has the same address, telephone, and portfolio manager as H&Q Healthcare Investors.

H&Q Life Sciences Investors seeks long-term capital appreciation, with at least 65 percent of assets in U.S. and foreign health care companies, as well as agricultural and environmental management firms. It may also invest in preferreds, convertibles, and junk bonds of health care issuers.

Fund inception: 5/01/92
Total assets: $75 million

Traded on the New York Stock Exchange under the symbol "HQL." Market price of $9.63 a share (3/31/95) and net asset value of $11.29, resulting in a discount of 14.8 percent. One-year decline of 7.23 percent in market price and decline of 0.96 percent in N.A.V.

Jundt Growth Fund

1550 Utica Avenue South, Suite 500, Minneapolis, Minnesota 55416
(800) 543-6217

Jundt Growth Fund seeks long-term capital appreciation by investing at least 65 percent of assets in equity securities with significant growth potential. It will generally contain 30 to 50 medium to large companies with projected revenue growth of 15 percent or greater. The fund may invest up to 20 percent of assets in foreign securities with similar characteristics. Heaviest portfolio weightings were recently in technology and retailing.

Fund inception: 11/27/91
Lead Manager: James Jundt
Total assets: $224 million

Traded on the New York Stock Exchange under the symbol "JF." Market price of $14.38 a share (3/31/95) and net asset value of $15.33, resulting in a discount of 6.2 percent. Three-year annualized return of 3.55 percent in market price and 4.58 percent in N.A.V.

Latin American Discovery Fund
1221 Avenue of the Americas, New York, New York 10020
(212) 296-7100

Latin American Discovery Fund seeks long-term capital appreciation, normally investing at least 80 percent of assets in Latin American equity securities, including American Depositary Receipts and sovereign debts. The fund invests at least 55 percent of assets in Argentine, Brazilian, Chilean, and Mexican equities.

Fund inception: 6/16/92
Portfolio manager: Robert Meyer
Total assets: $88 million

Traded on the New York Stock Exchange under the symbol "LDF." Market price of $11.63 a share (3/31/95) and net asset value of $10.44, resulting in a premium of 11.4 percent. One-year decline of 28.43 percent in market price and decline of 44.23 percent in N.A.V.

Emerging Mexico Fund
1285 Avenue of the Americas, New York, New York 10019
(212) 713-2000

Emerging Mexico Fund seeks long-term capital appreciation, primarily from investment in Mexican equities. The fund will usually invest at least 65 percent of assets in Mexican equities, the balance in peso- or U.S.-dollar–denominated fixed-income securities. The fund may invest up to 25 percent of assets in unlisted securities, private placements, joint ventures, and partnerships.

Fund inception: 10/11/90
Portfolio manager: Pablo Mancera
Total assets: $52 million

Traded on the New York Stock Exchange under the symbol "MEF." Market price of $7.63 a share (3/31/95) and net asset value of $5.62, resulting in a premium of 38 percent. Three-year annualized decline of 13.03 percent in market price and decline of 22.20 percent in N.A.V.

The Brazil Fund
345 Park Avenue, New York, New York 10154
(800) 349-4281

Brazil Fund seeks long-term capital appreciation, normally investing at least 70 percent of assets in common and preferred stocks of companies registered with the Brazilian Securities Commission. The balance is held in debt securities of the Brazilian government, Brazilian corporations, and U.S.-dollar–denominated money-market accounts. The fund may engage in futures and options transactions for hedging purposes.

Fund inception: 4/08/88
Lead manager: Ed Games
Total assets: $272 million

Traded on the New York Stock Exchange under the symbol "BZF." Market price of $24.88 a share (3/31/95) and net asset value of $23.06, resulting in a premium of 10.6 percent. Three-year annualized return of 17.55 percent in market price and 10.49 percent in N.A.V. Five-year annualized return of 21.76 percent in market price and 7.91 percent in N.A.V.

Data from Morningstar Inc.

Afterword

Relax, time travelers: Just getting to the 21st century will be half the fun. Most of the time, anyway.

It won't always be easy. The recent volatility and vagaries of world economies, financial markets, technological change, and health care modernization will remain with us and perhaps even accelerate. Don't let a one-day event or market gyration throw you off course, and don't become one of those investors who's always complaining, "If only years ago I had just . . ."

It's a bit like the *Back to the Future* thrill ride at Universal Studios in Florida, which subjects you to traumatic drops and heart-stopping soaring sensations as your "flying" DeLorean automobile barely averts what appear to be giant asteroid showers and nearly crashes in make-believe ravines. Once you catch your breath, you bravely tell yourself that you were never really frightened at all. You're perfectly safe and enjoyed the trip. Energized, you get back in line to do it all over again.

The need for global and personal communications, entertainment, innovative products, infrastructure rebuilding, property development, breakthrough medical treatments, computerized advances, care for the elderly, and retirement security won't go away. Reap rewards from these and from other growing endeavors rather than sticking with outmoded companies and industries that are likely one day to do a disappearing act.

Even well-positioned investment choices have experienced shifts in fortune in the past, and no one can promise a future without risk. Pick and choose among the 20 hottest investments according to your own comfort level, keeping in mind that at least a portion of your portfolio should be geared toward growth and the future. Some are adventuresome picks, others fairly conservative. Don't invest in anything you don't basically understand or agree with. Don't unload money-market funds, certificates of deposit, or blue-chip stocks if that's where you're most comfortable. But do leave room for some adventure.

When selecting investments likely to prosper in the coming century, study the story behind each company or mutual fund. Pay close attention to what its chief executive or portfolio manager is saying and decide whether you share management's dream for the future. This book features interviews with the best and the brightest, executives whose thinking is focused and whose companies are definitely not fly-by-night operations. Next, ask the nine basic investment questions listed in the beginning of this book. Examine financial track records to see whether a choice is one you can live with. Diversify among several selections to cut your risks, since not each and every hot company or fund will ultimately be a winner.

The investment emphasis should never be this quarter's earnings or next week's stock price, but steady, long-term gain from a selection that's in the right place at the right time and capable of charting its course successfully. Adjust your portfolio when necessary, but don't jump out of an investment once the going gets tough. That's usually the worst time to sell.

From early visions of steam-belching contraptions and shiny robotic machines to murky science fiction films, the millennium has been long awaited. Now the investment trip through the 21st century is shaping up as a truly exciting and rewarding one.

Index

Abbey Healthcare, 93
Abbey Pharmaceutical Services,
   93
Acorn International Fund, 29, 33
ADRs. *See* American Depositary
   Receipts
Aetna Life Insurance and Annuity
   Co., 122
Affymax, 294
Agouron Pharmaceutical Inc.,
   177
Alexander, Stanford, 228, 229,
   235
Allen & Co., 61
Allen, Robert, 7, 57–60, 62–63,
   66, 281
Allianz Life Insurance Co., 123
Alzheimer's disease, 91
American Depositary Receipts
   (ADRs), 37–39
American Pharmaceutical
   Services, 93
Annuities, 119
Apple Computer, 262

Argentina, 34
Arson, 200
Artificial intelligence, 184–97
Asia Pacific Fund, 301
Asia-Pacific region, 34, 50
ATMs, 205
AT&T, 7, 15, 56–68, 108, 276–81,
   285
Australia, 35, 50

Baby boom, 9
Bane, Keith, 113
Bank of Singapore, 39
Barrow, James, 261, 266–67
Barton, Bill, 143, 145–46
Bel-Air Patrol, 204
Bell Atlantic, 6–7, 58
Bell Sports Corp., 8, 44–54
Best of America IV/Nationwide
   variable annuities, 122–23
Betaseron, 169–70
Bicycling, 47
Biotechnology, 168–82
Blackburn Designs, 48

Blankenship, C. Ronald, 226–28, 234
Books "R" Us, 157, 162
Borg-Warner Security Corp., 199–206, 209
Brazil, 34–35, 296
Brazil Fund Inc., The, 298, 306
British Steel, 39
British Telecommunications PLC, 278
BSI brand, 47
Burns International Security Services, 202
Burroughs Wellcome, 139–40

Cable & Wireless, 39
CableComm, 108
Calgene Corp., 169, 172–76
Campanias de Telefonos de Chile, 39
Canada, 35
Cardura, 134
Carr, Alan, 293, 294
Cellular phones, 5, 104–5, 277, 284–85
Central Sprinkler Corp., 200, 207–9, 211
Cetus Corp., 170
Challenge computer systems, 21
Charles Schwab & Co., 8, 70–75, 81
Chile, 34
China, 31, 34, 38, 62
Chiron Corp., 168–72
Churchwell, Thomas, 173–74
Ciba Geigy Ltd., 171
Clark, James, 19
Clinton, Bill, 14, 106–7
Closed-end funds, 9, 290–306
Collins, George, 78–80
Comcast, 216
Compaq Computer, 249–50
Computers, 219–21
Concert, 278–79
Conservera Campofrio, 32
Corporate alliances, 6–7
Crime prevention, 10, 199–211
Crooke, Stanley T., 179
Cukurova Elektrik AS, 31
Currency fluctuations, 33

Davis, Selby, 261, 263–65
Diflucan, 132–33
Digital Equipment Corp., 262
Digital micromirror device, 243, 245
Dino-Light helmet, 46–47
DNA, 169

Ek Chor Motorcycle, 39
Electronic Data Systems Corp., 15
Emerging Mexico Fund, 297, 305
Envoy personal digital assistant, 108
Europe, 35, 50

Feller, Jack, 143, 149, 150
Fidelity Disciplined Equity Fund, 188, 193
Fidelity Retirement Reserves variable annuities, 120–21
Fidelity Select Biotechnology, 179
Fidelity Small Cap Stock Fund, 189, 197
Fidelity Stock Selector Fund, 188–89, 195
Filmes Lusomundo, 32
Financial services, 70–85
Finland, 35
Fiondella, Robert, 120
Firestone, Karen, 179–80
First Philippine Fund, 301–2
First Team Sports, 48
Fletcher Challenge, 39
Flexible technology, 243–54
Ford Motor Co., 216
401(k) plans, 121
France, 35, 164
Freeh, Louis, 201
Fujitsu Ltd., 247

Gabelli Equity Fund, 300
Galvin, Paul V., 111
Galvin, Robert, 111
Games, Ed, 298
Gates, Bill, 178
Gedale, William, 292, 293
General American Investors, 292–93, 303
General Electric, 284, 285

Genesis Health Ventures, Inc.,
    92–93, 99
Geoworks, 215
Germany, 35
Glaxo, 178
Goldstein, Michael, 157–61,
    163–65
Gore, Al, 5, 14
Granite Construction Inc., 143,
    146, 149, 150, 154
Grupo Financiero Banamex-
    Accival, 277–78

Handheld computers, 215
Hatsopoulos, George, 249–54
Health care, 10
    long-term, 87–101
Health Care & Retirement Corp.,
    88–89, 91–92, 97
Health maintenance organizations
    (HMOs), 130–31
Henney, Christopher, 178
Hewlett, William, 217, 222–23
Hewlett-Packard Co., 7, 23,
    213–24, 284
Hong Kong, 34
H&Q Healthcare Investors,
    293–94, 303
H&Q Life Sciences, 293–94,
    304

IBM, 61, 108, 221
ICOS Corp., 177–78
I.D.O., 107
In the Line of Fire, 16
Indy desktop system, 16, 22
Information superhighway, 5,
    283
Infrastructure, rebuilding of, 10,
    142–54
Initial public offerings, 232
Intermodal Surface
    Transportation Efficiency Act
    of 1991, 145
International investing, 26–39
Iridium global satellite
    communications system,
    105–6, 285
Isis Pharmaceuticals, 179
Italy, 35

Jackson, Bo, 129
Jameison, Richard, 121
Japan, 34, 50, 106–7, 148
Japan Telecom, 283
Johnson & Johnson, 171
Johnson, Peter, 177
Jundt, James, 294–95
Jundt Growth Fund, 294–95, 304
Junkins, Jerry, 246–49

K Mart, 161–62
Kaplan, Dave, 45
Kasler Holding Co., 143, 146–47,
    149, 150, 152
Kessler, David, 174
Kids "R" Us, 158, 160
Kuntz, Edward, 90–91, 93

Laser printers, 218–19
Latin America, 34, 295–96
Latin American Discovery Fund,
    296, 305
Lazarus, Charles, 159–60
Lee, Terry, 45–46, 50, 52
Lewis, Bradford, 184–90, 193
Liberty Media Corp., 61
Living Centers of America Inc.,
    90–91, 93, 101
L. M. Ericsson Telephone AB, 7,
    217, 276, 281–86, 288
Loevner, Kirk, 22
Long-term health care, 87–101
Loral, 61, 108
Los Angeles earthquake, 142
Lotus Development Corp., 61

MacGregor "Flavr Savr" tomatoes,
    172–74
Malaysia, 34
Malcolm Baldrige National
    Quality Award, 67, 104, 246
Managed care, 10
Mancera, Pablo, 297
McCann, John, 229–30, 236
McCaw Cellular, 284
McCracken, Edward, 16–20, 23
McGowan, William, 280
MCI Communications Corp., 7,
    63, 107, 276–81, 286
McKinnell, Henry, 130–32, 138

Medco Containment, 139
Medicaid, 95–96
Medicare, 95–96
Merck & Co., 139, 171
Merrill Lynch & Co., 8, 75–78, 83
Merrill Lynch Pacific Fund, 36–37, 77
Mexico, 28, 34, 147, 277–78, 296–97
Meyer, George, 207–8
MFS Charter Income, 299
Mobius, J. Mark, 28–30, 32, 33
Monsanto, 174–75
Motorola Inc., 7, 61, 103–15, 277, 285
Mutual Beacon Fund, 260, 265, 270
Mutual funds, 9, 78
    for international investing, 27

Nabors Industries, 262
Nationwide Life Insurance Co., 123
NCR Corp., 59
Netherlands, 35
Neural networks, 185–88, 191–92
New Germany Fund, 300
New Perspective Fund, 37
New York Venture Fund, 263–65, 272
Next Computer Corp., 221
Nextel Communications Inc., 107, 277
Nintendo, 16
Nippon Information & Communication Corp., 279
Nippon Telegraphic & Telephone Corp., 15
Nokia Telecommunications, 216
North American Free Trade Agreement, 34, 297
Northern Telecom, 216–17
Norvasc, 133–34
Novell Inc., 61, 215
Nowinski, Robert, 178

Ormond, Paul, 89
Oscar Mayer SA, 32
Owens-Illinois Corp., 92

Pacific Telesis Group, 58, 215
Packard, David, 217
Pelosky, Jay, 295–96
Penhoet, Edward, 170–72
Personal digital assistants (PDAs), 108
Peru, 296
Pfizer, 129–40
Phoenix Home Mutual Insurance Co., 120
Platt, Lewis, 214–18, 221–23
Pony Express Courier Corp., 205–6
PowerPC, 107
Price, Michael, 261, 265
Price, Thomas Rowe, 78, 79
Procardia XL, 132, 136
PT Barito Pacific, 30–31
Putnam Master Income Trust, 299–300

Ramqvist, Lars, 281, 284
Rathmann, George, 178
Real estate investment trusts (REITs), 9, 226–41
Reality Station, 22
Reich, Robert, 147–48
REITs. *See* Real estate investment trusts
Rhode Gear brand, 48
Roberts, Bert, Jr., 278–81
Ros, Carl Wilhelm, 282, 284

Salomon Brothers Fund, 298–99
Salquist, Roger, 174, 175
Saudi Arabia, 58
Schering-Plough Corp., 139
Schwab, Charles, 71–74
Schwartz, Samuel, 151
Scudder Horizon Plan, 123–24
Scudder International Fund, 36
Scudder New Asia, 302
Security Capital Pacific Trust, 226, 228, 234–35, 237
Security guards, 202–4
Selected American Shares, 264–65
Semiconductors, 106, 109, 247–48
Silicon Graphics Inc., 7, 13–24
Singapore, 34

Six Sigma initiative, 112
South Africa, 35
Southern New England
    Telephone, 58
Spain, 35
Sprint, 245
St. Joe Paper, 262
Steere, William, Jr., 135–36
Stentor, 278
SunAmerica, 262
Sundry, Arthur, 111
Switzerland, 35

T. Rowe Price Associates Inc.,
    78–80, 85
T. Rowe Price International Stock
    Fund, 36, 42
Taiwan, 148
Taligent, 221
Tax Reform Act of 1986, 118, 230
Telecommunicacoes Brasileiras
    (Telebras), 30, 39
Telecommunications, 5–7, 276–86,
    295
Tele-Communications Inc., 215–16
Templeton China World Fund,
    300–301
Templeton Developing Markets
    Trust, 28–33, 40
Tenidap, 134
Texas Instruments Inc., 7–8,
    243–49, 254
Thermedics Inc., 251–52
Thermo Cardiosystems Inc., 252
Thermo Electron Corp., 244–45,
    249–53, 256
Thermo Fibertek Inc., 253
Thermo Instrument Systems Inc.,
    252
Thermo Process Systems Inc., 252
Thermo Remediation Inc., 253
Thermo Voltek Corp., 252
ThermoLase Corp., 253
ThermoTrex Corp., 252–53
Third Avenue Value Fund,
    260–63, 268
Time Warner Cable, 15
Time Warner Inc., 7

Tooker, Gary, 7, 105, 109
Toshiba, 284
Toys "R" Us, 156–66
Trauscht, Donald, 200–202, 204
Tri-Continental Corp., 299
Trippi, Robert, 190–91
Tully, Daniel, 75–78
Turkey, 35

Ultra64, 16
United Dominion Realty Trust,
    229, 235–36, 241
United Kingdom, 35, 50

Value funds, 258–67
Vanguard Variable Annuity Plan,
    123–24
Vanguard Windsor II Fund, 260,
    266–67, 274
Variable annuities, 117–28
Veri-Care Inc., 93
Video jukeboxes, 21
Videophone, 57–59
Vidjet Pro, 213, 215
VistaLite, 48
VoiceNow, 108

Walker, Mike, 90, 92
Walt Disney Co., 293
Walt Disney Studios, 217
Wanger, Ralph, 28–30, 32, 33
Warner-Lambert Co., 139–40
Weingarten Realty Investors,
    228–29, 235, 239
Weisshappel, Robert, 109–10
Wells Fargo, 199, 201–3, 205
West, Thomas, 122
Whitman, Martin, 260–63
Wieman, Clark, 151
Wilson, Pete, 44
Wo Kee Hong, 32
WordWorx video conferencing
    service, 59

Xerox Corp., 61

Zithromax, 133
Zoloft, 133